UCLA VS. USC

UCLA vs. USC

75 YEARS OF THE GREATEST RIVALRY IN SPORTS

LONNIE WHITE ■ **THE LOS ANGELES TIMES**

Los Angeles Times
BOOKS

For Helen and Elwood White
and my wife, Kimberly

Los Angeles Times
BOOKS

Editors: Mike James, Carla Lazzareschi
Design: Mike Diehl
Copy Editors: Bobbi Olson, Gary Rubin
Photo Research: Eric Lynxwiler
Image Retouching: Ron Lachance
Print Coordinator: Allan Martinet/BAM Graphics

ISBN 1-883792-27-4

© 2004 Los Angeles Times

Los Angeles Times
202 West First Street
Los Angeles, CA 90012

Every effort has been made to insure that the information
contained in this book is accurate. Any errors are
inadvertent, and we apologize for them in advance.
Corrections will be published in any future editions.

First Printing August 2004
Printed in the U.S.A.

Los Angeles Times
Publisher: John P. Puerner
Editor: John S. Carroll
Book Development General Manager: Carla Lazzareschi

TABLE OF CONTENTS

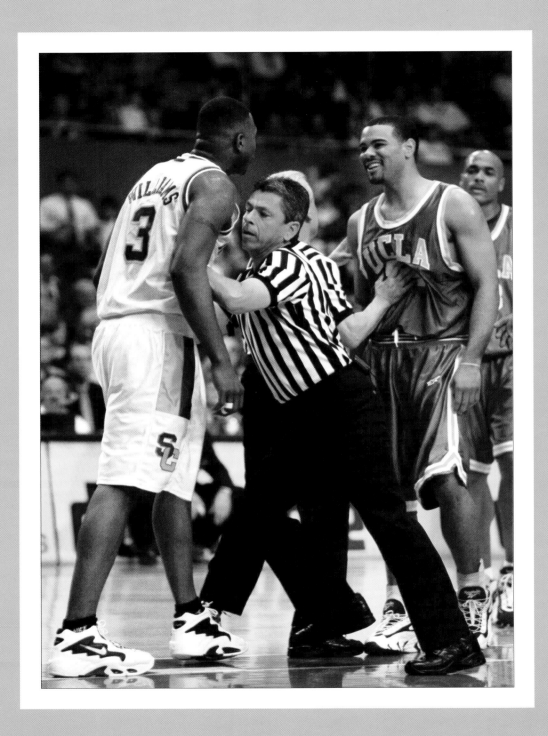

There are many great college sports rivalries across the country, but none matches the overall magnitude of USC–UCLA.

Alabama–Auburn, Michigan–Ohio State, Cal–Stanford are storied football rivalries. But when it comes to across-the-board competition in every sport, USC–UCLA stands alone.

It's the only football rivalry between two major universities in the same city. With campuses less than 12 miles apart, it's often friend against friend, brother against brother and family against family.

And what makes the rivalry in every sport even more intense is the level of competition.

Between them, the two schools have combined to win 219 team national championships, more than the entire Atlantic Coast Conference. They have also produced 732 Olympians (392 from UCLA and 340 from USC) who have won a total of 412 medals, more than Canada and Mexico combined.

As former UCLA football coach Red Sanders said, playing USC is not a matter of life or death, "it's more important than that."

I got my first glimpse of the rivalry over the Thanksgiving holiday in 1972. I was 8, and I became mesmerized while watching tel-evision in my New Jersey home.

USC was playing UCLA in a football game at the Memorial Coliseum. Outside my house, it was dark, rainy and cold, a miserable, drab East Coast night.

But on television, the sun shone brightly before the early-evening game in L.A., fans in vibrant colors filled the stadium. Cardinal and gold on one side. Blue and gold on the other. I felt as though I were sitting inside the Coliseum that night.

I got chills every time USC's Anthony Davis touched the ball. But I also liked the wishbone offense UCLA Coach Pepper Rodgers ran with Mark Harmon at quarterback. Plus, I thought the Bruins' white cleats were really cool.

In the end, I found myself rooting for Coach John McKay's Trojans, who won, 24–7, to clinch a Rose Bowl berth. The reason? The horse, of course.

I was sold after watching Traveler gallop around the Coliseum field after every USC touchdown. That night, I announced to my mother that I was going to college at USC.

■ Opposite: Officials push apart **USC's Gary Williams,** left, and **UCLA's Kris Johnson** following a heated moment in the 1997 game at the Sports Arena.

9

That feeling lasted about four months.

In March, I was captivated by a basketball game on television. The championship game of the 1973 NCAA tournament featured UCLA, going for its seventh consecutive national title, against Memphis State.

Earlier in the day, I had gotten into a debate with a couple of my recreational basketball teammates. They liked Memphis State because of Larry Finch and Larry Kenon. I rooted for UCLA because of Coach John Wooden and Bill Walton.

That night, Walton was unstoppable. He set NCAA championship game records by making 21 of 22 field goals and scoring 44 points to lead UCLA to an 87–66 victory.

My teammates were silent the next day at practice. That night, I told my mother I had a new plan. I was going to UCLA.

Four years later, I met the rivalry in person.

My older brother, Timmy, was a multi-sport high school athlete who was recruited by nearly every college football powerhouse in the country, including USC and UCLA.

On one winter day in 1977, coaches from USC and UCLA were in our neighborhood looking to talk to my brother. For me, it was a great experience to meet John Robinson and Terry Donahue.

After taking two recruiting trips to visit the campuses of both schools, my brother decided to attend USC the next year. I eventually followed in his footsteps and played football at USC from 1982 to 1986. As an alumnus, my loyalties have been with the Trojans. But I have always had a genuine respect for UCLA and consider the rivalry a wonderful part of my life, because these are two excellent schools with storied programs often competing at the highest levels possible. And it's a rivalry that has been growing

for nearly nine decades.

Its roots date to 1919, when UCLA was established as the University of California, Southern Branch, with its a campus on Vermont Avenue.

At that time, USC, founded in 1880, played against such schools as Occidental, Pomona and occasionally UC Berkeley. Though some were concerned about competition from a new rival in Los Angeles, USC welcomed Southern Branch at least in the beginning.

The two schools met for the first time in a major sport in the spring of 1920 when the Southern Branch Cubs knocked off the Trojans' highly regarded baseball squad, 7–6, in a spirited game at Exposition Park.

USC swept two baseball games from the Southern Branch, 9–7 and 4–2, the next year. But the Southern Branch tennis team handed the Trojans a 5–2 defeat in a postseason match.

Then, before any rivalry could take hold, USC put an end to it. Eager to retain its sports dominance in Los Angeles, USC partisans realized that playing a new school in L.A. was a no-win situation for USC. According to this calculus, the Trojans would gain nothing from beating the Southern Branch, because these victories would be expected, and any losses would only enhance the upstart school's reputation at the expense of the Trojans. So USC's faculty members decided to ban all competition in major sports against the Southern Branch.

For the next seven years, the Trojans and Southern Branch athletic teams went their separate ways until USC was essentially forced into changing its position to accommodate the fast-growing state school.

In 1927, the Southern Branch began

building its campus in Westwood and changed its name to the University of California at Los Angeles. After several strong seasons winning a variety of titles in the Southern

■ **Lonnie White, 1985**

Conference, UCLA was invited to join the more prestigious Pacific Coast Conference, forerunner of the current Pacific-10, creating a rivalry with USC whether the Trojans wanted one or not.

During the time USC refused to play UCLA, the Trojans grew into national powers in track and field under Coach Dean Cromwell and football under Coach Howard Jones. That's why the Trojans felt that they were more than ready when UCLA officially became a conference rival in January 1928.

The following month, the first of a three-game basketball series at the Olympic Auditorium officially became the first competition between the schools as they are now known. USC was the heavy favorite going into the game and won 45–35 in front of a record-setting crowd of about 9,000. But five days later, UCLA came roaring back with a 34–27 win, and two days after that, the Bruins took the third game of the series

It's been a battle like that ever since.

—**Lonnie White**

Forewords

■ ■ ■ ■ ■ ■ ■ ■ ■ ■

BILL WALTON
UCLA

Three-time All-American Bill Walton led UCLA to two NCAA basketball titles in his three seasons playing for John Wooden, from 1972 to 1974. His teams won their first 73 games, part of the school's NCAA-record 88 consecutive victories.

During his college career, Walton turned rebounding into an art form. He ranks first in UCLA history with 1,370 rebounds, holds the school record of 605 rebounds in a single season and twice had an astounding 27 rebounds in just one game.

He was also an incredibly accurate shooter, making 65.1% of his shots, second only to Jelani McCoy (1996–98) in UCLA history.

Selected first overall by the Portland Trail Blazers in the 1974 draft, Walton led the franchise to its only NBA championship in 1977. Walton won his second title in 1986 with the Boston Celtics.

Walton, inducted in 1993 into the Basketball Hall of Fame, now works as a television basketball commentator and has a reputation for never mincing his words.

I remember my first varsity game against USC. I was playing center against Ron Riley. The game was just getting going when Riley caught me with one of his elbows right in the mouth. I was spitting out teeth and blood all game. That was my introduction to the UCLA–SC rivalry.

John Wooden gave us the tools to overcome obstacles and adversity. We never worried about what our opponents were going to do, especially USC. We learned how to practice against an imaginary, ideal opponent so as to not waste time and effort.

At UCLA, you got the opportunity to train your mind, make decisions and compete. I don't know what they did over at USC.

I love the UCLA–SC rivalry; there's no other one like it. Football, basketball, baseball, volleyball, track and field. The battles are always epic, and it doesn't matter what the records are going in.

When I was at UCLA, USC had some good teams with good players. But to me, the Trojans represented the devil. Whenever UCLA defeated USC, that meant everything was right in the universe. I'm proud to say that we never lost to USC when I attended UCLA. We had one close game my senior year, but all the rest were easy victories for the Bruins....

I will always be a UCLA Bruin.

UCLA

UCLA 32

BILL WALTON

ROD DEDEAUX
USC

Rod Dedeaux, one of the nation's most successful college baseball coaches, led USC to 11 national championships and 28 conference titles over a span of an incredible 45 seasons. He had an overall record of 1,332–571–11, and when he retired in 1986, he had won more games than any coach in college baseball history. As a student at USC, Dedeaux was a three-year letterman as the Trojans' starting shortstop from 1933 to 1935.

For me the rivalry goes back to my baseball playing days. Obviously, UCLA was a big rival, and as I developed as a player, one of the most thrilling ballgames in my career came against the Bruins.

We were playing for the 1935 CIBA (California Intercollegiate Baseball Association) championship, and I was captain of the USC team. We had a great sophomore pitcher named Joe Gonzales, and we got down to the bottom of the ninth inning with a one-run lead, the bases loaded and their No. 4 hitter was up.

Everything was at stake. The batter had a full count, and we knew that a walk would tie the game and a hit would win it for them. That batter fouled off 11 straight pitches.

Gonzales, who would end up playing briefly in the major leagues, had all the pressure on him, and he was really putting something on every pitch. Then finally, Gonzales struck him out.

I've always said that nothing could have been more intense than that moment. You had great drama in a great rivalry. Gonzales was throwing heat but still mixing up his pitches for strikes. That was one of the greatest exhibitions of pitching that I've ever seen, at any level. That was when the rivalry really took hold with me.

Throughout my career, every game against UCLA was intense. That our guys and their guys had either gone to high school or played semipro ball together amplified it that much more. We drew very good crowds. Always a packed house.

We may have dominated in baseball over the years, but times were different then. There were so many great schools in the West, but only one team could go to the College World Series.

Many times, UCLA was better than some of the other teams from around the country that ended up going to the series, but because we had the edge, we represented the division. In 1963, we were playing UCLA in the game that would decide the winner of the conference. Our leadoff hitter hit the first pitch for a home run; that held up for a 1–0 victory, and we went on to win the national championship. All of the guys on the club that season felt that UCLA was the best team we faced. Who knows what would have happened if the rules of today were in place then, when so many more teams have the chance to qualify. UCLA would have been able to get to the regionals, and once you get there, anything can happen.

I've always felt that, as intense and competitive as the rivalry is between USC and UCLA, it's always been wholesome. It's great for both universities and great for sports. There's no other place that has two major universities in the same city that compete at such a high level academically and athletically. To have a city so divided into two sides. It's brother against brother. That's the way it has always been.

■ ■ ■ ■ ■ ■ ■ ■ ■ ■ ■ ■

CHERYL MILLER

USC

Cheryl Miller, the woman many contend is simply the greatest female basketball player ever, finished her USC career as the school record holder in points, scoring average, rebounds, steals, field goals and free throws. She was named NCAA tournament MVP twice, made three Final Four appearances with the Trojans (winning two of them) and three times won the Naismith Award as the premier player in women's basketball.

As a Trojan, Miller scored 3,018 points, averaging more than 20 points a game each of her four seasons, and was a four-time All-American from 1983 to 1986. The Trojans were an astonishing 112–20 with Miller on the team and 6–2 against their cross-town rivals.

Miller returned to coach the Trojans for two seasons, leading them to a 26–4 record in 1993–94 and 18–10 in 1994–95. She is now a respected television commentator on basketball.

Not surprisingly, Miller has special memories of her years at USC and playing UCLA, where her younger brother Reggie, a future NBA All-Star, played in college.

When I was being recruited out of high school, it came down to UCLA and USC. I made my decision when the twins [USC All-Americans Pam and Paula McGee] told me that you can either play two years with us or two years against us. After I thought about that for a second, I knew I was going to USC.

It also did not help that on my trip to UCLA, [Coach] Billie Moore pressured me to make a verbal commitment. That turned me off. Then

after I announced that I was going to USC, UCLA made a big deal that I had turned them down. They called me a flake and that I was unreliable. They also said that I was overrated as a player. This all added to the rivalry for me. That's when it became personal.

The most unfortunate thing for me was that I never played well at Pauley Pavilion. I had a lot of friends that played for UCLA, but every time we played them, the games were nasty. Elbows were being thrown all over the place. In one game, I got knocked unconscious when I tried to avoid a screen and got clocked.

Reggie was pretty much set that he was going to go to USC. But I didn't really want him to, because we had grown up in each other's shadows so much. I just thought that if he wanted to get to the next level, he should go to UCLA. At that time, USC men's program was not cranking out players to the NBA, and UCLA was a perfect fit for him.

So after he decided to become a Bruin, we made a pact not to root against each other. Once he started playing for UCLA, one of the toughest things was watching him play at the Sports Arena. USC fans would boo him and call him names and everything else. I know one time, I couldn't take it and stood up and said something to someone who was really being rude. People would tell me, "Come on, Cheryl, you're a Trojan!" and I would always tell them, "Yes, but that's my brother!" It was the same way for Reggie at UCLA when I played there. I always tell him he's the only cool Bruin I know.

RAFER JOHNSON
UCLA

Rafer Johnson enrolled at UCLA in 1955, a 6-foot-3, 200-pounder on a football scholarship. But Johnson was first and foremost a track and field athlete, in an age when the sport was far more popular nationally than it is today.

Johnson, who also played basketball for the Bruins, won the gold medal in the decathlon in the 1960 Olympics, establishing an Olympic record in the event. UCLA has always played a major role in his life. His brother, Jim, was a defensive back for the Bruins; his daughter, Jenny, played volleyball at UCLA for four years in the 1990s; and son Josh captained the Bruins' track team in 1998.

My first competition against USC came on the basketball court when I was a freshman. At that point it was just another basketball game to me. But I soon understood the magnitude of the rivalry.

The track and field dual meet was an incredible challenge. I was very motivated to try to beat USC because UCLA had never defeated the Trojans in a dual meet. They had won many national championships, and I really wanted to be on a UCLA team that would finally turn the tables.

Early in my career at UCLA, I would listen to the older guys on the team talk about how one day the Bruins would beat SC in a dual meet. Much to my dismay, we never did.

Whenever we went up against USC, I would typically compete in three, four and sometimes five events. We came very close to beating them my junior year, but SC beat us in the mile relay, which gave them the victory. That was the closest we came to beating them in a dual meet.

To this day, if I had one thing in my athletic career to do over, I'd run a leg on that mile relay team. I remember that I was pretty tired. I had probably scored 15 or 20 points in that meet already before the relay. Coach Ducky Drake didn't ask me to run, but I still wish that I had.

It's funny, but in looking at the UCLA–USC rivalry, it was more intense for me when my brother, Jimmy, played against the Trojans in football. I felt the pressure then. It was always such a big event.

Then my daughter Jenny comes along. Whenever her teams played USC in volleyball, the intensity was just unbelievable. They would meet twice a year, and the atmosphere was so powerful.

And it doesn't change. My son, Josh, was captain of the track team in 1998 and the intensity there was even more overwhelming.

It's one thing to go through the rivalry yourself as an athlete, but it's totally different when you have a brother or child involved.

■ ■ ■ ■ ■ ■ ■ ■ ■ ■ ■

MIKE GARRETT
USC

Mike Garrett was USC's first Heisman Trophy winner. As a senior tailback in 1965, he rushed for 1,440 yards to cap off a versatile three-year college career. From 1963 to 1965, he accumulated 4,876 total yards: 3,221 rushing, 48 passing, 399 receiving, 498 on punt returns and 710 on kickoff returns.

Garrett also started at cornerback for the Trojans and was an all-league outfielder on the baseball team in 1965. He was drafted by the Pittsburgh Pirates and Los Angeles Dodgers, but football was his passion.

He went on to play eight seasons in the National Football League and won a Super Bowl championship playing with the Kansas City Chiefs in 1970. He was inducted into the National Football Foundation's College Football Hall of Fame in 1985.

Garrett, a charter member of USC's Athletic Hall of Fame, became the Trojans' athletic director in 1993.

———

When I was growing up in East Los Angeles, everyone in my neighborhood was a UCLA fan because of Jackie Robinson and Kenny Washington. Then in the 1950s, when the Bruins had Sam Brown and Ronnie Knox, I knew all their players. I loved how they looked, from going out of the huddle to the color of their uniforms. So I always pictured myself playing in a single wing for the Bruins. That's all I knew.

When I watched UCLA play, I could see a lot of guys like myself, from Doug Peters, Sam Brown and Rommie Loudd. They were all UCLA people, and I identified with that. At that time, athletes of color were more inclined to go to UCLA. I knew all of the athletes of color at UCLA in every sport.

UCLA and Coach Bill Barnes had been recruiting me, and in my senior year, USC started to come after me. I remember going to the SC–UCLA game that year and watching it for the first time from a neutral position. Then UCLA started acting hesitant; one moment they were interested in me, then the next they wanted me to go to a junior college, which I didn't want to do.

I wasn't a great student, but I knew I could go to any school. Colleges from all over were recruiting me, then in the eleventh hour, USC told me Coach John McKay wanted me. That's all it took.

I always knew there was a great rivalry between USC and UCLA, but I had always seen it from the Bruins' viewpoint. It did not take long for that to change. In no time, I knew I really wanted to beat the Bruins. After planning to go to UCLA for so long, things were different now. No one is more committed than a convert.

We beat UCLA my sophomore and junior years, but they beat us my senior year. I remember my sophomore game the most because that's the first year that I started, and I scored a touchdown. For a little Boyle Heights kid, to score in the USC–UCLA game is a pretty big accomplishment.

JOHN WOODEN
UCLA

John Wooden was hired as the basketball coach at UCLA in 1948 and coached the Bruins for 27 seasons before retiring in 1975 as the most successful collegiate basketball coach ever, a distinction he still holds. During his tenure at UCLA, he won 10 national championships and had a 620–147 record, including a 62–20 mark against USC.

Basketball has been the major force in Wooden's life since childhood. He was an all-state high school player and college player of the year in 1932, when he led Purdue University to a national championship. He played semi-pro basketball for seven years before beginning his career as a coach.

Under Wooden, Bruin teams enjoyed four perfect 30–0 seasons, 88 consecutive victories, 38 straight NCAA tournament victories, 20 conference championships and 10 national championships, including seven in a row. His top players included All-Americans Walt Hazzard, Gail Goodrich, Lew Alcindor, Lucius Allen, Mike Warren, Sidney Wicks, Curtis Rowe, Henry Bibby, Bill Walton, Keith Wilkes, Richard Washington and Dave Meyers.

A six-time coach of the year, Wooden is one of only three men (the others are Lenny Wilkins and USC alumnus Bill Sharman) elected to the Basketball Hall of Fame as both a player and a coach.

———————

When I was hired by UCLA, I really didn't know much about the intensity of the rivalry.... It really surprised me how people hated the other. I never felt that way, but I also had never been in a situation with two major universities in the same city before.

UCLA wasn't an old established university like SC, and [the Trojans] had won nearly 75% of the games in the rivalry before I started coaching in Westwood. But after I arrived, we turned it around.

I always felt that it was more important to win the conference, which made every conference game take on the same meaning. But it did not take long for me to notice how intense it was when we played USC....

Although we won most times, our games were always competitive and hard fought. SC never conceded anything to us, even when I had my stronger teams in the 1960s and '70s. We held an edge, but we knew USC would play us tough.

In the days when only the team that won the conference championship got into the [NCAA] tournament, there were plenty of games that took on more emphasis when we played SC.

[In 1969], they beat us once when we had Alcindor, and [in 1971] they really had an outstanding team. The only two games they lost that season came against us, and they didn't get to play in the tournament....

You had to feel bad for them because they were better than a lot of teams that played in the tournament that season, but that's the way the rules were back then. ∎

THE Early Years:

Trojans Rule!

In the days of leather helmets on the football field, canvas sneakers on the basketball court and cinders on the quarter-mile track, USC dominated the new school across town.

■ Trojan fans brought their signature card stunt to the inaugural game in 1929.

■ Opposite: The 1929 game at the Coliseum was a 76-0 Trojan blowout.

could only manage an occasional victory over the Trojans. But their games were heated from the start.

In track and field, it was more of the same. In 1935, USC began a string of nine national championships with a program filled with Olympic standouts, while UCLA struggled to maintain a high-caliber program.

Nevertheless, despite often one-sided competition, games and meets between these two schools generated front-page interest from Day One. Consider that the 1936 football game between these two schools that had played only twice before drew 90,000 to the

The Trojans had an established football program by the time UCLA finally got a game scheduled against them, and the first meetings were as lopsided as anyone could imagine. The underdog Bruins did manage a couple of ties on the football field, games that in many ways were considered defeats by USC and victories by UCLA.

In basketball, there was little in those early years to presage John Wooden's dynasty at UCLA. In fact, for many years the Bruins

Coliseum and it's clear that this rivalry has long struck a chord in Southern California.

■ ■ ■ ■ ■ ■ ■

FOOTBALL

The football rivalry between UCLA and USC began in earnest in 1936. Yes, the schools had played twice before that, in 1929 and 1930, but there was no question who was going to win those two games. The only real question was whether the players in UCLA's fledgling program would walk off the field after losing or be carried off on stretchers.

The Trojans routed the Bruins, 76–0 and 52–0, in those first two mismatches. But in 1936, the game was an entirely different story.

In front of 90,000 in the Coliseum, the Trojans learned firsthand that the school across town had grown up. The Bruins dominated the first half and held a 7–0 lead at intermission on Billy Bob Williams' two-yard touchdown run in the second quarter. USC tied the score in the third quarter when Jimmy Jones scored on a four-yard run to cap a 13-play, 52-yard drive. That's the way the game ended, in a 7–7 tie. That represented a huge moral victory for UCLA. It was a result that only a few years earlier would have been unfathomable.

Indeed, when these schools first met at the Coliseum in 1929, USC Coach Howard Jones was the undisputed king of college football on the West Coast. His Trojans were defending national champions, and his book, *Football for the Fan*, was one of California's top sellers. Furthermore, USC had a roster filled with standout players returning from its "Thundering Herd" championship team, including captain Nate Barragar, quarterback Russ Saunders and

**GAMES WON
1920s & 1930s
FOOTBALL
USC 4 ▪ UCLA 0
2 TIES**

■ **USC football coach Howard Jones, left, joins his UCLA counterpart and good friend, Bill Spaulding, for a round of golf in 1936.**

backs Jess Mortensen and Harry Edelson. Meanwhile, the Bruins were just in their second year as part of the Pacific Coast Conference, having failed to win a single conference game in their debut season.

Leading up to the game, the *Los Angeles Times* reported on the matchup with an eye toward its place in the future. "Opening the season for the first time in local history with a Pacific Coast Conference game, the Trojans of Southern California and the Bruins of U.C.L.A. clash in the Coliseum this afternoon. In years to come, this game will probably be one of the football spectacles of the West."

No one expected a close game. The biggest debate in the weeks leading up to the game was whether Jones would run up the score.

Bill Spaulding, who had taken over the Bruins' program in 1925, was hoping to improve on UCLA's miserable 1928 season in the PCC, when they lost all their conference matchups and were outscored, 129–19.

The 1929 USC team was one of Jones' best. The Trojans had five sets of backs and designated two first teams, depending on the style of attack. They never passed and, despite their predictability, dominated teams with hard-nosed play.

USC's school newspaper, the *Daily Trojan*, had this scouting report on the first football game of the rivalry: "If Spaulding sees that his Bruins haven't a chance to hold the Trojans, he will probably pull his first string out before they are injured."

UCLA never had a chance. On Sept. 28, 1929, in front of a crowd that has been estimated at 35,000 to 50,000, the Trojans ran all over the Bruins, en route to the 76–0 victory. Running behind All-American guard Barragar

■ UCLA's football field in 1930, above, and Howard Jones giving a few pointers to the Trojans during a Coliseum practice.

and blocking back Erny Pinckert, USC rushed for an incredible 753 yards and collected 26 first downs. Saunders ran 50 yards for the first score and finished with three touchdowns. Jess Hill, Gaius Shaver and Pinckert each scored twice for the Trojans, who limited UCLA to 124 yards and four first downs.

UCLA did not take the defeat lightly. In the 1930 Southern Campus yearbook, the Bruins warned that "the siege of Troy has begun."

Unfortunately for the Bruins, the siege didn't exactly get rolling when UCLA opened the 1930 season against the Trojans for the second time in as many years.

USC totaled 28 first downs and 550 yards from scrimmage in the 52–0 victory. Marshall

Howard Jones USC

He never lost to UCLA

Howard Harding Jones may have never gotten the chance to become one of the most legendary coaches in USC football history if it hadn't been for Elmer "Gloomy Gus" Henderson and Knute Rockne.

Henderson had made the Trojans' program respectable in the 1920s but could never beat California. In his six seasons, from 1919 through 1924, his Trojans had a 45–7 record and twice won 10 games in a season, including a Rose Bowl victory in 1923. But Henderson was 0–5 against Cal.

Rockne didn't help matters when, just after his Notre Dame team had defeated Stanford in the 1925 Rose Bowl, he told reporters, "I'll have to come out and coach USC to show them how to beat a team from the North." Henderson was soon out, and USC set its sights on acquiring Rockne.

Well, it turned out that Rockne was only joking. So the Trojans turned to their second choice, Jones, who had earned a solid reputation as a no-nonsense coach in the Midwest and East.

Jones had coached an undermanned Duke team to a 4–5 record in 1924 before he got the call from USC. He proved to be a perfect fit in L.A., and under his guidance, the Trojans grew into a national power.

Before Jones' arrival, the program had never produced an All-American or won a national championship. But in 16 years as coach, Jones developed 19 All-Americans, won national championships in 1928, 1931, 1932 and 1939, and had undefeated seasons in 1928, 1932 and 1939.

USC also won eight Pacific Coast Conference titles and was undefeated in five Rose Bowl appearances under Jones, whose overall record at USC was 121–36–13, a remarkable .750 winning percentage.

At Yale, Jones had played end, most of the time in the shadow of his brother Tad, who went on to coaching fame at their alma mater. After graduating in 1908, Howard Jones coached Syracuse to a 6–3–1 record before returning to Yale for just one season, producing a 9–0 team that did not give up a point in 1909. The next season, Jones coached Ohio State to a 6–1–3 mark.

For most of the next six years, Jones tried his hand at a business career and returned to Yale to coach for another season (1913). Then in 1916, Jones committed to coaching full time, at Iowa.

In his eight years there, the Hawkeyes won 42 games and lost 17, scoring a staggering 1,082 points. Jones led Iowa to undefeated seasons in 1921 and 1922, and his 1921 team ended Notre Dame's 21–game unbeaten streak with a 10–7 victory.

When Jones took over at USC in 1925, his priorities were to defeat Cal and Stanford every year; they were the powers. (He held an 8–6–1 mark against Cal, 8–7–1 against Stanford.) Jones' teams didn't even play the Bruins until 1929, and from then on, he held a 5–0–2 advantage over what was then the "other school" in L.A.

Jackie Robinson

■ Trojan students Margaret MacDonald left, and Louise Castella clean Tommy Trojan after the statue was spattered with paint before a 1938 football game.

exposure. And when it came to exposure, USC wanted all it could get for itself.

After the Trojans' 16–14 victory over Notre Dame in 1931, USC players were greeted like conquering heroes in Los Angeles when a crowd of 300,000 attended a parade in their honor.

The Times' Braven Dyer did the narration for a full-length feature movie of the Trojans' victory over Notre Dame, and the film was a hit throughout Los Angeles.

USC won 30 of 33 games in the early 1930s and national championships in 1931 and 1932. Featuring a run-dominated offense, Jones' teams not only ruled the West Coast but also the entire college football world.

USC's 1932 national championship team yielded only 13 points all season. In

Duffield accounted for three touchdowns and Orv Mohler added two more for the Trojans in front of 40,000 at the Coliseum.

The Bruins went on to win three of their final seven games that season, but their efforts did not impress USC enough to keep the series going. Looking for stronger competition and unable to agree with UCLA on whether to play a game early or late in the season, the Trojans dropped UCLA from their schedule and replaced the Bruins with St. Mary's.

Many at USC saw no advantage in continuing to play UCLA at that time; all the continued series could do would be to increase UCLA's

10 games, the Trojans blanked Utah, Washington State, Oregon State, Loyola, Stanford, Oregon, Notre Dame and Pittsburgh in the Rose Bowl.

From 1931 to 1933, USC was loaded with All-Americans. Johnny Baker, Stan Williamson, Shaver and Pinckert were named to the 1931 team; Raymond "Tay" Brown, Aaron Rosenberg and Ernie Smith in 1932; and Larry Stevens, Irvine "Cotton" Warburton and Rosenberg in 1933.

As far as the Trojans were concerned, UCLA was little more than an afterthought at that time. But Spaulding was slowly building a

Ralph Bunche UCLA and Brice Taylor USC

African American pioneers

UCLA and USC long ago welcomed talented students of all backgrounds. Two of those pioneers are Ralph Bunche and Brice Taylor, men whose abilities carried them far beyond the fields of sport. Although they did not compete against each other's school, their contributions helped to establish the character of their institutions and shape the nature of one of college sports' great rivalries.

Ralph Bunche, who attended UCLA when it was known as the Southern Branch, is the school's first high-profile African American athlete and represents the very roots of its long tradition of individual athletic achievement.

Bunche, a member of one of the last classes to graduate in 1927 from the Vermont Avenue campus, was a starting guard on the school's Southern Conference championship basketball teams for three years and a member of its football and baseball teams. In addition, he wrote a column for the campus newspaper, served as a student body leader and was valedictorian of his graduating class.

■ Ralph Bunche

After earning his master's and doctorate from Harvard, Bunche researched the conditions of blacks in America for years with Swedish sociologist Gunnar Myrdal and later helped draft the charter of the United Nations.

In 1948, Bunche risked his life on a United Nations peacekeeping mission. When Count Folke Bernadotte, the mediator he had been assisting, was assassinated on Sept. 17, 1948, Bunche took over negotiating the armistice agreements among Israel and Egypt, Jordan, Lebanon and Syria. For this, Bunche was awarded the Nobel Peace Prize in 1950, becoming the first person of color to be so honored. Until his death in 1971, he spent his life teaching, working with the U.N. and fighting for civil rights.

UCLA recognized its internationally renowned alumnus in 1969 by naming Bunche Hall in his honor.

On Sept. 26, 1925, the day Howard Jones made his debut as USC's head football coach, the Trojans played a doubleheader and crushed Whittier, 74–0, and Caltech, 32–0.

USC's offensive leader was quarterback Morton Kaer, but its heart was guard Brice Taylor. Despite being born without a left hand, Taylor was a force on both sides of the ball and became USC's first All-American in 1925.

As one of the original players of Jones' fabled "Thundering Herd" teams, those undersized squads that dominated with speed rather than size, Taylor stood out, but not for his size. The Thundering Herd, which averaged less than 175 pounds and 5 feet, 10 inches, relied on the 5-foot-9, 185-pound Taylor to set the pace. And the Seattle native was up to the task.

Under Jones, USC rarely passed and seldom tried to fool opponents with trick plays. The Trojans defeated teams with toughness, and Taylor helped dominate opposing lines.

Taylor, one of USC's many African American football players in its early years and a descendant of the Shawnee Chief Tecumseh, also competed for the Trojans' track team and was a member of a world-record-setting mile-relay team in 1925.

He was inducted into the USC Athletic Hall of Fame in 1995.

■ Brice Taylor

Kenny Washington UCLA

First Bruin football star

Near the end of the 1937 season, UCLA Coach Bill Spaulding was in desperate need of help. His Bruins were wrapping up a dismal 2–6–1 campaign, including defeats in five of their final six games.

But in the Bruins' season finale, a 19–13 loss to USC, a player finally emerged to give Spaulding some hope for the future. His name was Kenny Washington, a versatile African American sophomore halfback who was to become UCLA's first consensus All-American in football and the first Bruin to lead the NCAA in total offense.

The Bruins trailed USC, 19–0, entering the fourth quarter; then Washington, who played in an era when halfbacks did more passing than quarterbacks, simply took over the game.

He led UCLA on a long touchdown drive, and then the Trojans elected to kick off instead of receive. Washington made them regret it. With the ball on the UCLA 27-yard line, he dodged would-be tacklers and launched the football 62 yards for a 73-yard touchdown pass play to cut the Trojan lead to six points.

On UCLA's final drive, Washington led the Bruins to the end zone again, only to have the play nullified by a penalty. In the closing seconds, UCLA was a few yards from pay dirt but could not score. Still, Washington's late heroics threw the Coliseum into a frenzy and offered a preview of Bruin fortunes for the next two seasons.

Invariably, it was against USC that Washington had his biggest successes.

Even USC's 1938 yearbook, El Rodeo, made special note of the performance, saying Washington "saved the Westwooders from a complete rout.... Outside of Washington's sensational slinging, the Bruins were badly beaten...."

Although USC's powerful Rose Bowl–bound team defeated UCLA again in 1938, 42–7, Washington was again the Bruins' bright spot. His 10-yard touchdown pass to Woody Strode accounted for UCLA's only score.

But in 1939, UCLA got at least a measure of revenge. Both schools entered the game undefeated. In front of 103,000 passionate fans at the Coliseum, the teams battled to a scoreless tie, with Washington treated to a hero's cheer by the capacity crowd when he walked off the field.

In his memoirs of the 1939 game, Strode wrote: "Kenny Washington didn't play sixty minutes that day. He only went fifty-nine minutes and forty-five seconds. [Coach] Babe Horrell took him out with fifteen seconds left so the fans would have a chance to give him a hand."

Washington played an incredible 580 of 600 possible minutes during the 1939 season and became a first-team All-American. But even though he had led the nation in total offense, he could not play in the East-West Shrine game for the nation's top seniors, a game that had never included an African American player.

And because the National Football League of that era still had an unwritten rule preventing blacks from competing, Washington played locally on semipro teams.

But Washington, along with Strode, finally got the chance to play in the NFL when Dan Reeves moved the Cleveland Rams to Los Angeles and the Coliseum commissioners stipulated as part of the agreement that the team be integrated. As a result, Reeves signed Washington and Strode and broke the modern color line in the NFL in 1946.

respectable program at UCLA. From 1931 to 1933, UCLA went 15–12–2 and had impressive victories over Montana, Stanford and Washington State.

Talk of renewing the rivalry began to heat up again in 1934, when the Trojans struggled to a 4–6–1 season while the Bruins finished 7–3. The 1935 season passed without the two teams meeting, but for the second consecutive year, UCLA had a more successful team than USC. The Trojans finished a disappointing 5–7, while the Bruins ended up 8–2 overall and tied for the PCC championship with Stanford and California, with a 4–1 mark.

USC could no longer ignore UCLA, which had become the nation's fastest growing university.

The Bruins' Westwood campus was under constant construction, adding new administration buildings, an open-air theater and other facilities. The school's reputation attracted students from all over the world. In 1934, UC Berkeley was the state's largest educational center, with 11,731 students, but in just 15 years of existence, UCLA had built an enrollment of 6,784.

Jones, who arrived at USC from Iowa, and Spaulding, who left Minnesota to take over at UCLA, had both arrived on the West Coast from the Big 10 Conference at about the same time; 1925 was their first season as head coaches at the L.A. schools. They were good

▪ **Los Angeles' most fashionable department store urged Trojan and Bruin fans alike to dress up for the first game in 1929.**

friends who often played golf and bridge together. And each felt that reviving the cross-town matchup was important, especially since the much-improved Bruins had become a force that could no longer be ignored.

The Times' Braven Dyer noted the Bruins' improvement on Nov. 19, 1935: "Since the Bruins last played the Trojans, under the able coaching of Bill Spaulding, the Bruins have improved so steadily that the present season found them in the running for the Pacific Coast Conference title."

In late November 1935, UCLA and USC agreed to renew their rivalry the following year. But there was a sticking point. USC wanted the game to be played early in the season. UCLA preferred the game to be played near the end of the season to give the Bruins time to mature for the city battle. After several meetings between UCLA Provost Ernest Moore and Spaulding, and USC President Rufus B. von KleinSmid and Jones, an arrangement was reached to create a traditional game like Cal–Stanford.

The Pacific Coast Conference also had a role in getting the rivalry going again. Starting in 1936, the conference ruled that UCLA, USC, Oregon, Oregon State, Washington, Washington State, Stanford and California would play each other in football every year. Although Mon-

■ Right: Before becoming known as the Bruins, the Southern Branch's good luck charm was a mutt named Raggs.

■ Below: The Trojans' canine talisman, George Tirebiter.

■ Opposite: Top: USC's Morley Drury was captain of the football team and a standout on the water polo and ice hockey teams. Bottom: Jess Hill was a star in football, baseball and track for USC.

tana and Idaho still belonged to the conference, the schools were excluded from football because of weak programs.

UCLA needed the USC football game. The Bruins' entrance into the Pacific Coast Conference was eating up school funds because of added travel expenses, and a high-profile game every year against USC would be a boost to the UCLA program financially. UCLA had taken out a $50,000 loan from the University of California Regents in 1933 to help balance its budget. This game, which would draw huge crowds, could help pay it off.

Once USC was set on the UCLA schedule, the Bruins certainly treated it as something special. They held pep rallies and bonfires during the week leading up to the game and covered USC's Tommy Trojan statue with blue and gold paint. USC responded by burning the letters "SC" on the Westwood campus lawn.

Jones knew that the pressure was on USC to beat UCLA, and he wasn't happy that the Trojans headed into their first Turkey Day showdown against the Bruins with a two-game losing streak and a 4–2–1 record.

The day of the 1936 game, *The Times* wrote: "Six years ago, Southern California slaughtered U.C.L.A., 52–0, in what was just another football game.... Today the Trojans and Bruins clash on even footing."

After the teams played to the 7–7 tie, a scramble for the ball nearly created an all-out brawl. It took both coaches, Jones and Spaulding, along with the game's referee, to prevent it. School officials later decided to have the ball bronzed and made into a trophy to be awarded each year to the winning team.

The next day, *The Times* reported on the real birth of what was about to become one of the country's premier football rivalries: "To those fuddy-duddies who point to the half century of tradition behind the Yale and Harvard game, we, like the chap who said his railroad was not as long as some but just as wide, wish to state that while the Trojan-Bruin rivalry may not be as old as some, it certainly is just as hot."

In 1937, both teams entered the game with losing records. The Bruins were 2–5–1, while the Trojans were 3–4–2. Behind Grenny Lansdell's two touchdowns, USC completely owned the Bruins for the first three quarters and held a 19–0 lead. But over a 26-second span in the fourth quarter, UCLA's Kenny Washington passed for two touchdowns to cut the score to 19–13. Minutes later, Washington nearly passed for a

third, but the Trojans held on for a 19–13 victory.

Still, Washington's second of two touchdown passes to Hal Hirshon was the talk of the town the next day. It was a 62-yard heave and, according to *The Times* account that day, "the longest authenticated throw in college football."

From Braven Dyer's account: "You'd have to be a bit goofy to think anybody could throw a football that far.... During the hectic nine minutes, Washington completed six of nine passes for 144 yards—certainly one of the great passing performances of all time. After the game, Bill Spaulding, jocular Bruin coach, knocked on the door of the Trojan dressing room and joshed, "Come on out, Howard, it's safe; we've stopped throwing passes.'"

Despite their victory, the Trojans' once prestigious program was clearly deteriorating. Slumping attendance figures at the Coliseum paralleled USC's decline on the field. From 1934 to 1937, the Trojans were 17–19–6, and their attendance had dropped from 615,000 fans for the 1933 season to 490,000 in 1937.

The Times' Paul Zimmerman analyzed Jones' problem before the 1938 season: "Howard had a lot of fine stars who spent three years on the bench when they could have played at some of the other schools.

"The high school players figured that out for themselves, and many decided to go elsewhere. Of course, alumni and coaches at other schools were stepping up their recruiting. By the same token the Jones staff and alumni naturally got to riding on their oars, assuming every great prep star would want to be a part of 'The Thundering Herd.'"

Nevertheless, 1938 brought more of the same for the Bruins in the big game. USC spotted UCLA a touchdown before running away with a 42–7 victory in front of 65,000. UCLA outplayed USC in the first quarter and trailed by only six points, 13–7, at halftime. But in the second half, the Trojans outgained the Bruins, 287 yards to 64, and scored 29 unanswered points.

The 1939 game took the Los Angeles rivalry to a new level. With the Bruins needing a victory to earn their first Rose Bowl berth and USC needing at least a tie, the game ended in a scoreless tie at the Coliseum.

Behind the brilliant running of Jackie Robinson and Kenny Washington, UCLA drove 76 yards to the USC four-yard line and had first down and goal to go in the game's final minutes. The Bruins needed only a field goal to secure a Rose Bowl berth and had one of the best kickers in the PCC in Robinson, but first-year coach Babe Horrell's team failed to score after three running plays

and a batted-down pass.

Before the fourth-down play, UCLA quarterback Ned Matthews conducted a vote in the huddle on what to call. The deciding vote was left for Matthews, and he called for a pass from Washington to speedy end Don MacPherson.

Unfortunately for the Bruins, USC defensive back Bobby Robertson knocked down Washington's pass in the end zone.

Los Angeles Times sportswriter Shav Glick covered the 1939 game for a Pasadena newspaper as a teenager: "That was one of the most frustrating games that I've ever seen,"

■ While preparing a pregame bonfire in Leimert Park in 1934, USC students captured some UCLA and UC Berkeley students attempting a raid and held them in cages.

Glick said. "They had four downs to score late in the game and they didn't make it, even though they had Kenny Washington and Jackie Robinson. Knowing that a tie sent SC to the Rose Bowl, I still don't understand why UCLA didn't kick a field goal.

"Jackie averaged about seven yards every time he touched the ball, and they didn't give it to him once. There's no way that game should have ended in a tie."

Thanks to UCLA's questionable decision to go for a touchdown, USC went on to the Rose Bowl, where the Trojans defeated Tennessee, 14–0, and took home nearly $120,000 for playing in the game.

■ A few members of USC's marching band of 1935.

Paul Zimmerman of *The Times* wrote this on Dec. 10, 1939: "Instead of trying for a place kick for three golden points, or perhaps a sweep with Jackie Robinson or Kenny Washington running the ends, these Bruins went after a pass into the end zone on fourth down. It was like throwing away three of a kind and drawing to a royal flush, this gamble that the Uclans took, and they didn't make it.

"Picture for yourself this wild scene, with 103,000 persons sitting on the edges of their seats almost too weak from excitement to move after that great drive of 76 yards that had given Coach Babe Horrell's boys the ball

on Troy's 4-yard line with four downs in which to cross the goal.

"It was one of the cleanest, yet most bitter struggles in Coliseum history, with only one rule infraction penalty called during the afternoon…. In the dressing rooms, Bruins and Trojans were mingling after the contest to congratulate each other on fine play. Which is the finest display of sportsmanship anyone could ask of this torrid cross-town rivalry.

"In the final analysis, there was nothing wrong with this ball game—but the final score."

BASKETBALL

UCLA hasn't always had a winning basketball program, but the Bruins did start off having success on the hardwood in their first season as the Southern Branch Cubs in 1919–20.

Captain Silas Gibbs led the Cubs, coached by Fred Cozens, to a 12–2 record and second place in the Southern Conference. The Southern Branch went on to win at least a share of five consecutive conference titles from 1921 to 1927 under Cozens and then Caddy Works.

During this time, USC watched the Southern Branch's accomplishments from a distance. The Trojans were considered a budding national football power, but their basketball program was up and down. Until former USC football standout Leo Calland took over as coach before the 1927–28 season, the Trojans tossed around the school's basketball head coaching position like a hot potato. USC had 15 coaching changes from 1907 to 1927; even legendary track coach Dean Cromwell and the school's football coach, Elmer Henderson, spent time on the Trojans' basketball bench.

So the Bruins had reason to have high

hopes when the schools were finally scheduled to meet for the first time in a three-game series late in the 1927–28 Pacific Coast Conference season, officially the first match-ups between the two schools as they are now known.

Yet, in front of what was then a record-breaking crowd at the Olympic Auditorium, the Trojans rode the strong inside play of Jess Mortensen to a 45–35 victory on Feb. 18, 1928. A standout halfback on the football team, Mortensen was the Trojans' top scorer, with a 10.8–point average, and he nearly defeated the Bruins by himself, controlling the game down the stretch with a series of off-balance shots and scoring 12 of his game-high 18 points in the second half.

The Bruins, however, swept back-to-back games the next week in front of sellout crowds at the Olympic. Captain Jack Ketchum led UCLA to a 34–27 victory in a fight-filled Thursday night game. To combat USC's size advantage, UCLA Coach Caddy Works used the Bruins' speed and marksmanship to their advantage. By turning the offense over to quick guards Sammy Balter and Bob Baker, UCLA was able to open the court, and that left Ketchum open for easy shots. The Bruins were able to hold off a late USC rally to set up the rubber match, played two nights later at the Olympic. In front of another record-breaking crowd of 9,000, Works called on a tight-smothering defense early to counter the Tro-jans' size. With UCLA's student body excited about the chance to win the series against USC, the Bruins rode the crowd's energy and outran the Trojans in the second half to win easily, 47–37, and take the first season series, 2–1.

USC returned the favor in the first of three games in 1929. At the Olympic Auditorium, backup forward Frank Smith made a key basket to seal a 28–23 victory for the Trojans. Thanks to stellar play from Lloyd Thomas, the Trojans had an easier time with the Bruins in the second game, winning 39–31. Thomas was unstoppable, and the Trojans limited UCLA to five points over the first 16 minutes of the second half to break the game open.

Pre-1930 USC Olympic Medalists

TRACK AND FIELD			
Emil Breitkreutz	1904	800m	Bronze
Fred Kelly	1912	110m Hurdles	Gold
Alma Richards	1912	High Jump	Gold
Earl Thomson	1920	110m Hurdles	Gold
Lee Barnes	1924	Pole Vault	Gold
Charles Borah	1928	400m Relay	Gold
Lillian Copeland	1928	Discus	Silver
James Corson	1928	Discus	Bronze
Clarence 'Bud' Houser	1924	Discus	Gold
		Shot Put	Gold
	1928	Discus	Gold
Charles Paddock	1920	100 meters	Gold
		200 meters	Silver
		4x100m Relay	Gold
	1924	200 meters	Silver
Frank Wykoff	1928	4x100m Relay	Gold
DIVING			
Michael Galitzen	1928	Springboard	Silver
		Platform	Bronze
SWIMMING			
Clarence 'Buster' Crabbe	1928	1500m Freestyle	Bronze

UCLA ended its third season in the PCC on a positive note when sophomore Dick Linthicum led the Bruins to a 44–33 victory in front of another sellout Olympic crowd. Captain Sammy Balter led an aggressive Bruin defense that shut down the Trojans in the second half. Linthicum had 12 first-half points, but UCLA had lost the season series, 2–1. Even UCLA's yearbook, Southern Campus, had flattering words about the Trojans' play that season: "In three of the most thrilling combats ever witnessed at the Olympic Auditorium, the Cardinal and Gold emerged triumphant; the Trojans for at least a year were to hold the upper hand in the intense rivalry which has been growing between the two universities."

Before the start of the 1929–30 season, USC named Sam Barry head basketball coach, and he slowly began upgrading the Trojans' program. Barry's deliberate coaching style helped increase the intensity of the rivalry over the next three seasons. From 1930 to 1932, USC and UCLA played nine times, the Trojans winning five.

Things really got heated in the first game of the 1932 three-game set at the Olympic. After the Trojans jumped out to a 5–2 lead, Barry ordered his players to hold the ball in a "stationary offense," an attempt to break up the Bruins' zone defense. But Works was ready for this tactic and issued strict instructions to UCLA's players not to break out of their defense. The game remained at a standstill while the crowd, according to the USC 1932 yearbook, El Rodeo, "amused themselves by throwing peanuts, pennies, papers and profane language at the Trojans. The game was stopped several times, while the managers of both schools cleaned the floor."

At the time, rules did not require a team to bring the ball across the center line, and USC captain and guard Cliff Capp simply stood holding the ball in the Trojans' end. Occasionally, Capp would toss the ball to fellow USC guard

1930s USC Olympic Medalists

TRACK AND FIELD

Ed Ablowich	1932	1600m Relay	Gold
Kenneth Carpenter	1936	Discus	Gold
Lillian Copeland	1932	Discus	Gold
Foy Draper	1936	400m Relay	Gold
Al Fitch	1936	1600m Relay	Silver
Duncan McNaughton	1932	High Jump	Gold
Earle Meadows	1936	Pole Vault	Gold
Delos Thurber	1936	High Jump	Bronze
Simeon Toribio (Philippines)	1932	High Jump	Bronze
Robert Van Osdel	1932	High Jump	Silver
Frank Wykoff	1932	4x100m Relay	Gold
	1936	4x100m Relay	Gold

GYMNASTICS

George Roth	1932	Club Swinging	Gold

DIVING

Michael Galitzen	1932	Springboard	Gold
		Platform	Silver
Frank Kurtz	1932	Platform	Bronze
Velma Dunn Ploessel	1932	Platform	Silver
	1936	Platform	Silver

SWIMMING

Clarence 'Buster' Crabbe	1932	400m Freestyle	Gold
Paul Wolf	1936	800m Freestyle Relay	Silver

Julie Bescos, but that was it. At one point, USC's leading scorer, Jerry Nemer, and the Bruins' top player, Don Piper, read the newspaper comics together while waiting for something to happen. Nothing did, and the half ended with USC ahead, 5–2.

At the opening of the second half, USC extended its lead to 8–2, but the Bruins rallied when the Trojans began to open up their offense. USC held on to a 17–15 lead with three minutes remaining following a basket from Nemer when things broke down for the Trojans. UCLA's Piper tied the score at 17–17 with a tip-in with a little over a minute to play, and the Bruins ended up winning the game, 19–17, on a midcourt shot by center Bud Rose at the buzzer.

1930s UCLA Olympic Medalists

BASKETBALL			
Sam Balter	1936		Gold
Carl Knowles	1936		Gold
Frank Lubin	1936		Gold
Don Piper	1936		Gold
Carl Shy	1936		Gold
GYMNASTICS			
Ray Bass	1932	Rope Climb	Gold
Dallas Bixler	1932	High Bar	Gold
Edward Carmichael	1932	Vaulting Horse	Bronze
Thomas Connelly	1932	Rope Climb	Bronze
Phillip Erenberg	1932	Club Swinging	Silver
TRACK AND FIELD			
George Jefferson	1932	Pole Vault	Bronze
Jimmy LuValle	1936	400m Dash	Bronze
Bob Young	1936	4x400m Relay	Silver
YACHTING			
John Biby Jr.	1932	8-meter Class	Gold
William Cooper	1932	8-meter Class	Gold
Richard Moore	1932	8-meter Class	Gold

In the second meeting, USC again tried to slow the game down and again fell short. UCLA's Linthicum scored the winning basket in a physical, 26–24, victory. After the game, UCLA supporters complained about the Trojans' old-fashioned attack, and Barry apparently must have taken the criticism seriously. He set his aim at UCLA, and the Trojans would not lose another basketball game to the Bruins until 1943.

With a new starting line-up featuring muscle-bound Bob Erskine at center, Barry's Trojans took it to the Bruins with a 35–31 victory in the third game of the 1932 series. Knowing that they had already clinched the city series for the second consecutive season, the Bruins were ready for the Trojans' rough play. Although they lost the game, the Bruins threw as many blows as they took. UCLA led for most of the game, but USC rallied late in the second half behind the hot shooting of Nemer and Erskine. It was the first of 42 consecutive victories in the rivalry for the Trojans.

By 1936, Barry's program was in full swing. The Trojans were known as a physical team, and that season Barry rarely played more

GAMES WON
1920s & 1930s
BASKETBALL
USC 35 - UCLA 7

than six players in a game. The Trojan defense dominated in their four-game sweep over the Bruins. With Eddie Oram and Bob Muth spearheading Barry's aggressive defense, the Bruins averaged less than 28 points against the Trojans in the series. In the final game, USC rode Jerry Gracin's 16 points and limited UCLA to nine field goals in a 55–28 walk-away victory.

Things got worse for the Bruins in 1938, when the rivalry was so lopsided that the Trojans outscored the Bruins by 68 points in sweeping a four-game series. USC's yearbook, El Rodeo, described the Trojans' first victory over UCLA this way: "The Southern Californians' first conference game was with their favorite stooges—the Bruins of U.C.L.A., who had tried unsuccessfully since 1932 to defeat a Barry five."

Behind sophomore Ralph Vaughn's game-high 19 points, USC defeated UCLA, 48–31, in the first meeting. After crushing the Bruins, 40–30, in the second game, Barry toyed with his lineup for the third matchup. The Trojan coach moved Gail Goodrich from forward to guard, and the result was a 52–33 USC victory at the Pan-Pacific Auditorium.

UCLA's yearbook, Southern Campus, broke down the Bruins' final game against USC this way: "Resting on the bottom rung of the conference ladder, the Bruins were determined to salvage something out of a poor season and break S.C.'s luck. But old man jinx was as strong as ever and the luckless Bruin again went down in defeat."

Senior guard Hal Dornsife did most of the damage for the Trojans, who again won easily, 57–35.

**MEETS WON
1920s & 1930s
TRACK & FIELD
USC 6 - UCLA 0**

TRACK AND FIELD

The first collegiate program to gain national attention in Los Angeles was track and field under USC Coach Dean Cromwell in the late 1920s. Cromwell first took over the Trojans in 1909 from Harvey Holmes and immediately made track and field a priority on campus.

Cromwell, who briefly left the program in 1914 and 1915, provided the structure for a dominant program by attracting world-class athletes. In 1926, the Trojans won the school's first NCAA championship behind thrower Clarence "Bud" Houser.

By the time UCLA was ready to take on the Trojans, Cromwell's program had grown into a national powerhouse loaded with future Olympic champions. Unfortunately for the Bruins, their undermanned track program suffered through years of growing pains.

Dale Stoddard captained the first track team at the Southern Branch in 1920, finishing third in the 100- and 220-yard sprints in the Southern Conference championship meet. But for the most part, track and field was not a successful sport at UCLA for years.

When USC faced the Bruins in the first dual meet between the schools in the spring of 1934, the Trojans already had won three NCAA team titles and 13 individual national championships. So it wasn't too much of a shock when USC ran away to an 87–44 victory at the Coliseum. That was the first victory of a streak in dual meets involving the schools that would last the next 32 years.

USC's Kenneth Carpenter would later win the discus at the 1936 Berlin Olympics.

George Jefferson UCLA

Olympian effort rewarded

In the summer of 1932, UCLA pole vaulter George Jefferson picked the perfect time to have a career day.

No one expected much from the young Bruin track athlete at the Los Angeles Summer Olympic Games at the Coliseum. If any medals were going to be won by a Southern California collegiate athlete, they were going to be won by someone from USC.

A year earlier, Jefferson had stepped on a piece of glass, severing a tendon in his foot. The injury proved only to be added motivation for Jefferson, who decided to make one final effort at becoming a world-class pole vaulter.

Across town, USC's Bill Graber held the world record at 14 feet, 4.5 inches and was considered the king of the pole-vaulting world.

Jefferson worked hard on his comeback and qualified for the Olympic team with a personal best 13 feet, 6 inches. In 12 months, he had gone from an injured hopeful to the Bruins' first U.S. Olympic track and field team member.

On the day of the competition, the favorites to medal were Japan's Shuhei Nishida, a consistent 13-10 vaulter, Stanford's Bill Miller, who had a best mark of 14 feet, and Graber.

Jefferson knew things were going well for him when he matched his personal best on his first attempt. His confidence grew when he cleared 13-8. But then he knocked the bar down on his initial try at 13-10.

Jefferson began to worry when Miller and Nishida made the height, but he kept hope when his USC rival, Graber, also failed. Then on his second attempt, Jefferson sailed over the bar with room to spare.

At 13-11, Jefferson was attempting a leap five inches higher than he had ever cleared. He made it on his first try, putting the pressure on Graber.

The USC world-record holder could not keep pace, and Jefferson wound up with a bronze medal, the first UCLA athlete to win an Olympic track and field medal.

The 1932 Los Angeles Games were also where UCLA athletes won their first Olympic gold medals. John E. Biby Jr., Richard F. Moore and William H Cooper were three of the 12 crew members of the U.S. gold-medal winning eight-meter yacht team; and gymnasts Ray Bass and Dallas Bixler won gold, Bass in the rope climb and Bixler in the high bar.

The Bruins have had at least one competitor in every Olympics since 1928 and have won gold medals in every

Olympics attended by the U.S. since 1932. Overall, UCLA has won 195 medals (98 gold, 51 silver and 46 bronze).

Competing athletes were given small potted oak trees as souvenirs of the Games, and Carpenter and Foy Draper brought their trees back to USC, where they stand today in the center of the campus.

Although UCLA was no match for the Trojans as a team in the 1930s, the Bruins did have some outstanding athletes. James LuValle won the NCAA 440-yard title in 1935 and won a bronze medal in the 400-meter dash for the U.S. in the 1936 Olympics. Like many other African American athletes recruited by UCLA in the late 1930s, Lu Valle also excelled off the playing field. After graduation, he became a noted chemist and worked at

■ USC runner Lou Zamperini, the nation's greatest collegiate miler in the late 1930s, trains with Coach Dean Cromwell.

Dean Cromwell USC

The champion maker

Dean Cromwell was the head track and field coach at USC for 38 years. His teams won eight Pacific Coast Conference titles in 11 years of PCC competition and 12 national titles in 19 attempts. His teams finished second in NCAA competition five times.

From 1935 to 1943, his Trojans won nine consecutive NCAA titles, and during his tenure, USC athletes won 33 national collegiate titles and set 17 individual and relay world records.

Little wonder he was nicknamed "Maker of Champions."

Cromwell was hired by USC as football and track coach in 1909 and spent most of his energy the first few years on the gridiron. But he turned his attention to track when the school replaced the football program with rugby from 1911 through 1913. The attention paid off. The Trojans started producing some of the nation's top track and field athletes, with three competing in the 1912 Olympic Games in Stockholm.

Cromwell left in 1914 to seek other opportunities, then returned in 1916. After three years coaching both football and track, he left the gridiron for good and concentrated on track.

From 1912 to 1948, USC track and field athletes won 24 gold, five silver and three bronze medals in Olympic competition.

At the 1936 Berlin Olympics, USC track athletes scored enough points, 37, to have finished among the top five countries in the world. Cromwell, who coached the 1936 and 1948 U.S. Olympic teams, tutored champions in every Olympic Games from 1912 to 1948.

Some of the world-class athletes Cromwell coached: sprinters Charles Paddock, Frank Wykoff and Mel Patton; jumpers Al Olson and John Wilson; throwers Bud Houser, Jess Mortensen and Kenneth Carpenter; vaulter Bill Graber; and miler Lou Zamperini.

the Office of Scientific Research and Development, which aided in the effort to develop the first atomic bomb.

Tom Bradley, the late five-term mayor of Los Angeles, also competed on the Bruins' track team in the late 1930s. A three-year letterman for the Bruins and one of their toughest competitors, Bradley competed in the 440- and 880-yard runs and on UCLA's top relay teams.

But even though UCLA began recruiting better athletes in the late 1930s, the Bruins still could not keep up with Cromwell's Trojans. USC won nine consecutive national track and field championships, starting in 1935. Led by athletes such as Lou Zamperini, a two-time NCAA champion in the mile in 1938–39; Clifford Bourland, who enrolled at USC in 1939 and became a two-time NCAA champion in the 440; Erwin Miller, who won the national quarter-mile title in 1939; and Johnny Wilson, who won at least a share of the NCAA high jump titles in 1939–40, the Trojans owned the track and field world.

Zamperini broke the national collegiate mile record with a time of 4:08.3, a mark that stood for 15 years. At the 1936 Olympics, Zamperini competed in the 5,000-meter race and finished eighth. After college, Zamperini served as an Army Air Corps captain during World War II. His plane crashed in the Pacific and he drifted on a small rubber raft without food for 47 days before being captured by the Japanese. He was held captive and tortured for two years before being released in 1945, an event that made the front pages of the *Los Angeles Times* and *New York Times*.

After graduating from USC in 1943, Bourland enlisted in the Navy and served during the remainder of World War II. Returning to USC for graduate studies in 1947, Bourland

won a gold medal as a member of the U.S. 4x400-meter relay team at the 1948 London Olympic Games. Bourland also placed fifth in the 200 meters at the Games.

Although women's athletics were played only at the intramural level at that time, USC did have a championship weight thrower in Lillian Copeland. She won nine national AAU championships in three events—shot put, discus and javelin—from 1925 to 1931 and set world records in the javelin in 1926, 1927 and 1928. Copeland won an Olympic silver medal in the discus in 1928 and four years later took the Olympic gold medal in the event.

■ Jess Mortensen, a football, basketball and track letterman for the Trojans, won the NCAA javelin title in 1929.

BASEBALL

On Nov. 23, 1889, USC played its first baseball game and lost to a club team named Bonny Brae, 13–10. And it didn't get any better very soon. For the next 19 years, the Trojans' baseball program barely stayed alive with one part-time coach after another. It wasn't until 1908 that USC named its first full-time coach, Harvey Holmes, who also coached the football team. Holmes led the Trojans to a 17–2 record on the diamond.

The Trojans' program, however, was foundering when the Southern Branch was established in 1919. In 1913, the program was abolished to encourage the school's best athletes to concentrate on track and field. From 1914 to 1917, USC's law school team represented USC on the baseball field, and in 1918–19, the teams were loosely organized by students, including one unit that lost to the Southern Branch, 7–6, in 1919.

In 1920, Elmer "Gloomy Gus" Henderson became the Trojans' baseball coach, and he brought some measure of organization to the program. Henderson, who also coached USC's football team for six seasons and basketball team for one, led the Trojans to a 9–4–1 record, including a 4–1–1 mark against college teams.

While baseball was still finding a home at USC in the 1920s, the sport was setting roots across town. Even before the school had moved to Westwood and changed its name to UCLA, the Bruins had become somewhat of a baseball power. They had won the Southern Conference title in 1924 and in 1925 defeated USC, 5–3. To close out the 1928 season, the Bruins took two of three games from the Trojans to win the first city series.

USC tried to discredit UCLA's series victory because the Trojans were looking ahead to a two-week trip to play games in Japan. USC's baseball team left for the Far East two days after playing its final game against the Bruins. The next season, the Trojans again lost the first game of the three-game series. But USC responded to win the final two games, including a 10-inning, 5–4 effort in the third game.

Over the 1930 and 1931 seasons, the Trojans, coached by Sam Barry, won six in a row over the Bruins and outscored them, 59–23. Just as he had done with the basketball program, Barry turned things around in his first baseball season, despite having only two seniors on the roster. The Trojans' 1930 team won the school's first conference title behind the pitching of George Sutherlen and hitting of Garrett Arbelbide.

With Arbelbide getting three hits, including a home run, and stealing four bases, USC crushed UCLA, 12–1, at Westwood on May 5. Two days later, the Trojans followed their first victory with a 12–2 win at home and then completed the sweep at Westwood on May 10 with a 11–9 victory in 1931.

USC won the city championship in 1932 with back-to-back victories over UCLA at Los Angeles' Wrigley Field. The first game was a pitchers' duel between USC's George Buchanan, who struck out 12 and gave up only two hits, and UCLA's Bill Winter. The Tro-

**GAMES WON
1920s & 1930s
BASEBALL
USC 26 • UCLA 7**

■ Trojan baseball coach Elmer "Gloomy Gus" Henderson

jans won, 3–1, with two runs in the 10th inning on a UCLA error. In the second game, Buchanan was not as sharp, but he pitched well enough to pick up the victory in a wild 10–9, USC victory.

UCLA didn't play USC in 1933, but the schools resumed their rivalry in 1934 with the Trojans winning the season series, 2–1. Thanks to two home runs from Julie Bescos, USC pitcher Jim Appleby won both of his starts

Bill Ackerman UCLA

"Mr. A" was an ace

Any history of UCLA's tennis program starts with William C. "Bill" Ackerman, who began playing for the Southern Branch Cubs in 1920 as a freshman.

By his sophomore year, Ackerman had taken over the fledgling program as the team's tennis instructor. He couldn't be given the title of coach while still a student, but that didn't stop him from leading the team to five consecutive Southern Conference tennis championships.

Ackerman got his first victory over USC in 1922, when the Southern Branch defeated the Trojans, 5–2, in a postseason match. By the time UCLA joined the Pacific Coast Conference in 1928, Ackerman had the program in full swing—and was its official coach.

UCLA's 1928 yearbook, Southern Campus, had this to say:

"Unknown to the many who watch a team from the stands, there is usually some outstanding personality working quietly behind the scenes to bring out in a team its best qualities of fighting spirit as well as of mechanical performance.

"The man responsible for the rejuve-

nation of the 1928 tennis squad was Coach William Ackerman. The success of the team is a tribute to his ability as a coach and his personality as a man."

In 1932, Ackerman led the Bruins to their first PCC team tennis title. He would end up winning 10 at UCLA before retiring after the 1950 season.

Ackerman, affectionately nicknamed

"Mr. A," coached many great players at UCLA, including Jack Tidball, who in 1933 became UCLA's first NCAA singles champion.

In 1950, Herb Flam helped lead Ackerman's club to his only NCAA team title, winning the singles title and the doubles championship with partner Gene Garrett.

Ackerman, who died in 1988, was inducted into the Collegiate Tennis Hall of Fame at the 100th NCAA tennis championships in 1984. But on campus, he cannot be forgotten; UCLA's student union was named in his honor.

against the Bruins by scores of 9–1 and 6–2.

USC continued to roll out one solid team after another under Barry, who led the Trojans to at least a share of five conference titles in the 1930s. Barry's most complete team may have been the 1935 Trojans. Behind talented captain Rod Dedeaux, who would become one of college baseball's most well-known coaches, and sophomore pitcher Joe Gonzales, the Trojans won with defense and pitching and finished tied with California for first place in the conference. USC swept UCLA in three games, with Gonzales earning the victory in each game.

The following year, the Trojans shared the conference title with St. Mary's and handily beat the Bruins in both their encounters.

The Bruins led the first game, 2–1, heading into the eighth inning when they fell apart, with an epidemic of errors over the last two innings, and lost, 9–2. In the second meeting a week later, UCLA again held a lead late in the game only to lose, 11–10, on a rally by the Trojans in the bottom of the ninth. Finally, after playing USC close for two games, UCLA was no match in the season finale for both teams, with the Trojans winning, 16–1.

■ ■ ■ ■ ■ ■

TENNIS

The earliest championship meeting between USC and the Southern Branch was in a postseason tennis match in 1922 when Bill Ackerman coached the Southern Branch Cubs to a 6–2 victory over USC. The Cubs won five consecutive Southern Conference titles under Ackerman, who developed one of the nation's top programs.

**MATCHES WON
1920s & 1930s**

TENNIS

UCLA 7 ■ USC 5

In 1928, UCLA and USC met for the first time in a Pacific Coast Conference match, and the Bruins blanked their city rivals, 7–0. Ackerman's squad embarrassed the Trojans with Fred Houser, Bob Laird and Bob Struble leading the sweep.

In 1929, senior Frank Westsmith finished a three-year career with two victories to lead UCLA to a 5–2 win over USC. For the next couple of years, UCLA won most matches between the schools.

That led to a change in strategy by the Trojans for their second match against the Bruins in 1932. Instead of playing their stronger players in the top singles matches, the Trojans called on their three weakest men. But the tactic backfired when UCLA's "weaker" players still defeated USC's ace players.

As Ackerman's tennis program grew into the dominant force on the West Coast, with the Bruins winning their first PCC title behind tennis legend Jack Tidball in 1934, the Trojans slowly improved. USC had strong teams in 1934 and 1935, but the Trojans did not taste true success until 1938, when they walked through the conference behind smooth-stroking Joe Hunt. For three years, USC took command of the rivalry with UCLA until the Bruins ended a seven-match losing streak in 1939. With Kristo Sugich and captain Bradley Kendis winning a decisive doubles match, UCLA defeated the Trojans, 5–4.

■ ■ ■ ■ ■ ■ ■ ■

ICE HOCKEY

Other than football, hockey might have been the most popular competition between UCLA and USC in the late 1920s. USC first

■ Opposite: Legendary UCLA tennis player and coach, Bill Ackerman, in 1984.

Fred Cady USC

Always poolside

In the mid-1920s, Southern California became known for its collection of great swimmers and divers, and the man responsible for coaching many of them was USC's Fred Cady.

By the winter of 1928, Cady had completely turned around a foundering program and led the Trojans to their first Minor Sports Carnival championship. Behind senior Jimmy Smith, USC won the final relay race to outscore second-place UCLA by two points.

Over the next 33 years, Cady consistently produced winners at USC. He coached 39 Olympians, including swimmers Clarence "Buster" Crabbe, James Gilhula and Wallace Wolf, and diver Michael Galitzen (also known as Mickey Riley).

Crabbe, who had transferred to USC from the University of Hawaii in 1930, became the Trojans' first All-American swimmer the next year. In 1932, he set an Olympic record in the 400-meter freestyle at the Los Angeles Games.

Cady also coached swimmers and divers at the Los Angeles Athletic Club, where he worked with such greats as Esther Williams, Georgia Coleman and Harold "Dutch" Smith. He was diving coach to the U.S. Olympic teams in four consecutive Olympics: 1928, 1932, 1936 and 1948.

From the mid-1920s until he retired in 1956, Cady also ran the Trojans' water polo program, producing a dozen Olympians along the way.

One of Cady's top athletes was Wolf, who not only swam for the U.S. in the 1948 and 1952 Olympics but also played water polo in the 1956 and 1960 Games.

Wolf, a three-time All-American swimmer, won a gold medal in swimming at the 1948 London Games and a silver medal as a member of the U.S. water polo team at the 1955 Pan American Games.

Cady, who had been a circus performer known for diving into a pool of flames, was famous for his wit and waxed, pointed mustache. He was also a sculptor and painter, whose works are now considered valuable possessions.

He painted wharf scenes, desert nocturnes and cityscapes as well as horse portraits.

He was inducted into the International Swimming Hall of Fame in 1969. The American Diving Coaches Association annually awards the Fred A. Cady Memorial Award to the nation's outstanding diving coach.

---

fielded a team in the winter of 1924, and the sport took off. The Southern Branch's first team hit the ice in 1925, and the Grizzlies, as they were then called, finished their debut season undefeated.

In 1926, the Southern California Ice Hockey League was formed with USC, Occidental, Southwestern University and the Southern Branch. But because of a USC faculty ruling that prevented any athletic competition against the Southern Branch, the Trojans didn't face the Bruins on ice for two years. UCLA went undefeated and won the first league title in 1927, with the Trojans finishing second with one defeat. That set the stage for a long-awaited two-game showdown in 1928.

A sellout crowd of nearly 1,500 filled the Palais de Glace to watch the competition. With football captain Morley Drury providing rugged

**GAMES WON
1920s & 1930s**

ICE HOCKEY

USC 38 - UCLA 2

1 TIE

Opposite:
Fred Cady,
center, with Paul
Wolf, left, and
Wally Wolf (no
relation), right,
in 1950.

defense and Roland Bienvenue and Jack Cohen taking care of the offense, the Trojans blanked the Bruins, 2—0. A month later, USC defeated UCLA again with a come-from-behind 4—3 victory. The Bruins held the lead until USC scored two goals in the final two minutes, with Richard Belliveau scoring the game-winner.

In 1929, Arnold Eddy took over as coach at USC and invigorated the Trojans' hockey program. In the early 1930s, Doc Hartley became co-coach with Eddy, and USC won 36 games in a row, dominating the newly formed Pacific Coast League. Featuring Canadians Al Chatton and Paul Weisbrod, USC controlled the Bruins along with the rest of the teams on the West Coast, winning three consecutive league titles in the early 1930s.

USC's four-year winning streak ended with an overtime loss to Loyola in 1933, and the next season, the Bruins ended their own losing streak to the Trojans. UCLA's co-coaches, Havey Taafe, who led the Bruins to back-to-back undefeated seasons in 1927—28, and Dr. Walter Mosauer, put together a solid team that not only beat USC but also won the Hoover Cup at Yosemite National Park in 1934.

UCLA's success over the Trojans, however, didn't last. USC had a lineup filled with Canadians, a fact that UCLA followers were only too eager to point out.

■ ■ ■ ■ ■ ■ ■ ■ ■ ■

WATER POLO

Behind captain Jimmy Smith, USC crushed UCLA, 11—0, in the first round of the Pacific Coast Minor Sports Carnival on March 31, 1928. With football player and hockey specialist Morley Drury providing the same type of physical play he displayed on the gridiron and hockey rink, the Trojans manhandled their competition in taking home the overall championship in 1927—28.

Drury was known as "the noblest Trojan of them all" for his all-around career at USC. He was one of USC football coach Howard Jones' favorite players because of his aggressiveness, agility, stamina and durability. Drury was often the most versatile player on the football field. He ran, passed, blocked, tackled, kicked and punted. But he also displayed this type of versatility playing other sports at USC, including water polo. Without Drury in the lineup, USC's team struggled in early-season games in October and November. But after Drury began to play full time in February 1928, the Trojans' play improved dramatically.

Lining up at the left guard position, Drury dominated play all over the pool. Although he didn't score many goals, Drury brought life to the USC program. The next year, the Trojans kept their edge over UCLA with two difficult victories during the regular season and finished ahead of them at the Minor Sports Carnival in 1929.

Throughout the 1930s, the stronger USC's swimming and diving program became, the more the Trojans' water polo program grew. Coach Fred Cady's first water polo player to make the U.S. Olympic team was Kenneth Beck, in 1936 and 1948. Beck was inducted into the U.S. Water Polo Hall of Fame in 1976. ■

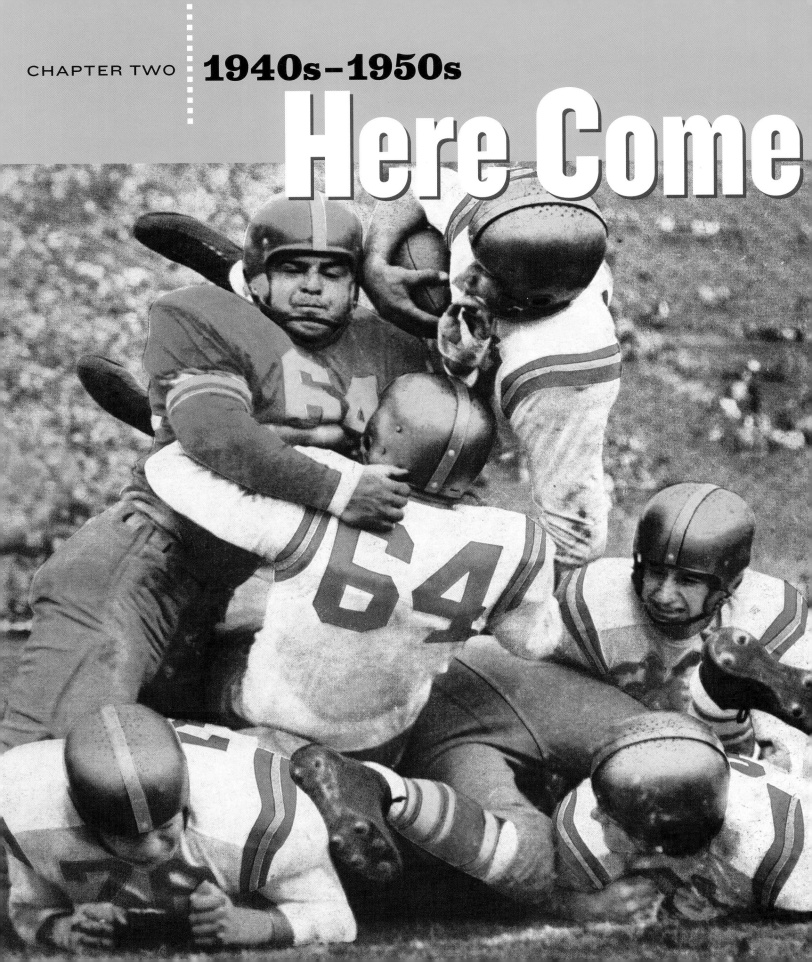

CHAPTER TWO

1940s–1950s

Here Come

the Bruins!

After more than a decade of some sound beatings by the Trojans in most major sports, the Bruins began to turn the tables in the 1940s.

Opposite: Bob Davenport dives for a one-yard touchdown in UCLA's 13-0 victory over USC in 1953.

In 1942, the Bruins' football team surprised everyone in the Pacific Coast Conference, going 6–1 in league play, including a 14–7 victory over USC, and earning the school's first trip to the Rose Bowl, where it lost to Georgia, 9–0.

In 1947, Elvin "Ducky" Drake took over as UCLA's track and field coach and led the Bruins to an NCAA and Pacific-8 Conference title.

And in 1948, John Wooden was hired as basketball coach. Not only did Wooden quickly march the Bruins to PCC titles in his first four seasons, but he also ultimately led them to heights never before or since achieved by a college basketball program.

Meanwhile, across town, USC was still having the kind of success that helped stoke the fires of the rivalry between the two schools. The Trojans played in a couple of Rose Bowl games in the '40s and '50s, and the basketball program won four conference titles.

In track and field, Dean Cromwell, Jess Hill and Jess Mortensen coached the Trojans to 12 NCAA titles during that period, and in baseball Sam Barry and Rod Dedeaux led USC to its first two national championships. Finally, during that time, the two schools dominated all of college tennis. From 1946 to 1959, UCLA won five national titles and USC won four.

FOOTBALL

For UCLA Coach Edwin "Babe" Horrell, the 1940 season was a nightmare from start to finish. Horrell had taken over for Bill Spaulding after the 1938 season and led the Bruins to a 6–0–4 record during his rookie coaching season the following year. But in 1940, things fell apart.

Their opening game, a tough 9–6 loss at home to Southern Methodist, offered an unfortunate preview of what lay ahead: an 0–7 start to the season. UCLA didn't want for good players, but they simply didn't have enough of them on offense to pull out the many close games they encountered. The Bruins finished 1–9 that season, with six of the defeats by seven points or fewer.

After five losses, rumors began to spread around Los Angeles that Horrell's job was in jeopardy because of dissention within the team. Horrell would have probably taken more heat if not for USC's troubles across town.

It was becoming clear that longtime USC Coach Howard Jones was getting close to stepping down. After the Trojans defeated Tennessee, 14–0, in the Rose Bowl to finish the 1939 season 8–0–2, Jones knew that his team was going to have plenty of holes to fill the next season.

He was right. In 1940, the Trojans won only three games, lost four, and tied two. It was the worst record of any USC team under Jones; it was also the last squad he coached. But even with his most dismal team ever, Jones still beat the Bruins, 28–12, on Nov. 30 at the Coliseum.

UCLA was crushed by the Trojans, who did a great defensive job on Jackie Robinson while racking up 407 total yards to the Bruins' 143. Even without completing a pass, USC amassed 22 first downs to UCLA's seven. USC's Bob Robertson, who had knocked down Kenny Washington's last-ditch pass when the Trojans played the Bruins to a 0–0 tie in 1939, rushed for 170 yards and a touchdown. Jones retired after the season and died of a heart attack in July of the following year.

The next season, under one-year Coach Sam Barry, the Trojans struggled to a 2–6–1 record. The tie came against UCLA, which finished with a 5–5–1 mark under Horrell.

The Trojans' dominance over UCLA would come to an end in 1942 under Jeff Cravath, who had replaced Barry after the bumbling 1941 season.

UCLA lost its first two games in 1942, but the Bruins then went on a tear, winning six of seven heading into their Dec. 12 showdown with the Trojans. With Horrell's tricky T-formation attack and junior quarterback Bob Waterfield, the Bruins had one of the nation's most explosive offenses.

UCLA's campus buzzed with excitement

■ UCLA's quarterback Bob Waterfield in 1949.

■ Opposite: Top: A UCLA touchdown in the 1943 game was nullified by a penalty, and the Trojans went on to win, 20–0. Bottom: In 1954, UCLA blanked USC, 34–0, on its way to the school's first national football championship.

the week of the game. Comedian Joe E. Brown, the school's highest-profile rooter at the time, and radio pioneer Rudy Vallee performed shows around the campus, and a UCLA war bond drive heading into the game raised nearly $2 million. Knowing that a victory would put the Bruins in position for their first Rose Bowl invitation, Horrell had his team ready to play.

Led by captain Charles Fears, who had attended high school within walking distance of USC at Manual Arts, UCLA defeated the Trojans, 14–7, at the Coliseum. A touchdown run by Ken Snelling and a 42-yard pass from Waterfield to Burr Baldwin got the Bruins to a 14–0 lead. Mickey McCardle's fourth-quarter touchdown wasn't enough to bring the Trojans back, and UCLA celebrated its first football victory in nine tries against the Trojans.

The game went almost exactly as the *Los Angeles Times*' Al Wolf predicted. In his column before the game, Wolf had written: "This is the day when [Al] Solari explodes. That's one UCLA touchdown. Waterfield will throw for another. The Bruins can't bottle McCardle all afternoon, so call it, 14–7." Wolf not only called the winner and exact score but also two of the three touchdowns.

UCLA made it to the Rose Bowl but lost, 9–0, to Georgia.

Before the start of the 1943 season, with the world at war, the Pacific Coast Conference adopted a wartime emergency schedule that included two games between USC and UCLA that year: the season opener and regular-season finale for both teams.

Behind All-American end Ralph Heywood, T-formation quarterback Jim Hardy and line-

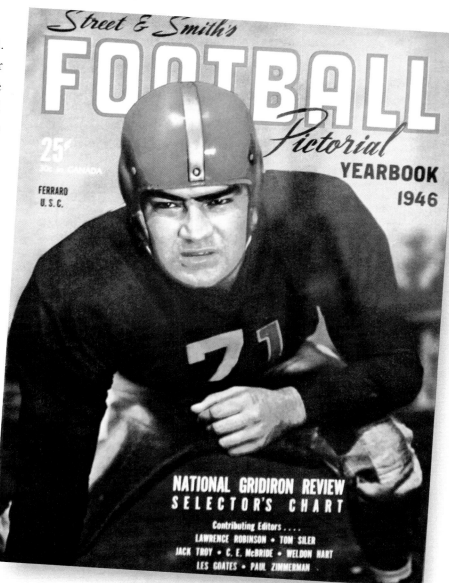

man John Ferraro, future president of the Los Angeles City Council, USC swept UCLA, 20–0, in the season opener and 26–13 in the finale, a win that sent the Trojans to the Rose Bowl, where they beat Washington, 29–0.

In 1944, the Bruins and Trojans again played each other at the start and end of the regular season. The first meeting, Sept. 23, endures as a classic.

With two minutes remaining and USC leading, 13–0, UCLA made a furious comeback. Halfback Johnny Roesch gained 34 yards in four carries and scored to cut the Tro-

■ The late Los Angeles City Councilman John Ferraro, pictured here, kept this magazine cover hanging in his City Hall office.

jans' lead to 13–6. Then on the final play of the game, Roesch electrified the crowd with an 80-yard punt return for a touchdown. Waterfield, who had missed his first conversion attempt, tied the score with a kick that hit the crossbar, wobbled along it for several feet, then bounced over.

The second game fell far short of the first; USC trounced UCLA, 40–13, and earned its second straight trip to the Rose Bowl, where it got its second straight shutout victory in the Jan. 1 game, a 25–0 win over Tennessee.

Just weeks after his last loss to USC, Horrell resigned from UCLA, having gone 4–5–1 that season and 0–3–1 against the Trojans since leading the Bruins to their first victory in the rivalry. Nearly four months later, UCLA turned to a former Bruin player to turn the program around. Bert LaBrucherie had played halfback under Bill Spaulding from 1926 to 1928 and was a cele-

brated coach at Los Angeles High for 16 years.

LaBrucherie's Bruin coaching debut was against USC in the Coliseum on Sept. 21, 1945. UCLA got off to a strong start when All-American lineman Al Sparlis helped lead the Bruins on their first scoring drive, capped by Gene Rowland's 10-yard touchdown run in the second quarter. But UCLA couldn't hold its early lead. The Trojans rallied with a 65-yard scoring drive before halftime and Ted Tannehill added a fourth-quarter score to give USC a 13–6 victory.

In the Dec. 1 rematch, the Trojans took a 19–0 first-half lead with Joe Bowman throwing scoring strikes to Tannehill, Harry Adelman and Roy Cole. USC's defense controlled the second half of a 26–15 victory that gave the Trojans their third consecutive Rose Bowl berth under Cravath. UCLA actually held an edge in statistics, accounting for 275 total

■ **Action from the 1942 game**

Red Sanders UCLA

Gave Bruin football needed kick

Henry R. "Red" Sanders coached UCLA's football program for nine seasons, from 1949 through '57, and he's often remembered as the man who led the Bruins to their only national championship season, in 1954.

But he also deserves credit for turning the UCLA–USC rivalry in the Bruins' favor. In nine games against the Trojans, Sanders' teams were 6–3. Before his arrival, USC held a 10–2–3 edge in the series.

The Times' Dick Hyland wrote this about Sanders' Bruins after they crushed USC, 34–0, in 1954: "There is no doubt in my mind, and there has not been since the season started, that the Trojans are a better collection of athletes than the Bruins. The training and team play of Sanders' Bruins make them more effective."

Sanders, who got his nickname as a youngster, although his hair was not red, lived in the South before accepting the UCLA job, growing up in Nashville, Tenn., and enrolling at Vanderbilt University there in 1923.

Sanders lettered four years in baseball, football and basketball at Vanderbilt and was captain of the baseball team as a senior. In 1927, he began his coaching career as a backfield aide at Clemson and for the next 12 years worked various jobs, from playing professional baseball to coaching at a military academy in Tennessee.

In 1940, Sanders took over as head coach at Vanderbilt, and during his six seasons there (1940–42 and 1946–48, interrupted by military service) he consistently upset superior Southeastern Conference teams. He was SEC coach of the year in 1941 and runner-up in 1946 and 1947.

But that still did not make him a popular choice when UCLA Athletic Director Wilbur Johns named him as the successor to Bert LaBrucherie. Although Sanders was recommended to Johns by the likes of Army's Red Blaik, Michigan's Fritz Crisler and sportswriter Grantland Rice, he was not exactly greeted with open arms by the Los Angeles media.

"A male, Caucasian, 43, last night was named U.C.L.A.'s new football coach," one local sportswriter wrote. "He was the survivor after 43 names had been culled and rigged over. Just why he was the survivor is not yet known. One school of thought is that his name stuck in the hatband."

Sanders proved his early Southern California critics wrong. His Bruins were 66–19–1 in nine seasons, and nine of his players were first-team All-Americans.

A coach always open to change, Sanders altered the Bruins' uniforms from dark blue to powder blue, and he switched the color of the numerals on the jerseys from yellow to white.

On the field, Sanders was also a pioneer. He changed the Bruins' offense from a T-formation attack to an old-fashioned single-wing. He installed a 4–4 set on defense, using four down linemen and four linebackers, and the Bruins grew into one of the toughest defensive teams in the nation.

Sanders also perfected the squib kick, a weak blooper of a kick that rolled down just shy of the goal line; the Omaha Rush, an all-hands effort to hurry and harass a quarterback; and the spread punt formation.

Sanders died of a heart attack on Aug. 14, 1958, but his legacy will always live on with UCLA football.

yards to USC's 261 and getting 11 first downs to the Trojans' eight. After the game, LaBrucherie told *The Times*: "I guess it wasn't my turn for the Rose Bowl yet."

LaBrucherie and the Bruins had to wait only a year for their number to come up. In 1946, the war was over and UCLA's roster was

■ **UCLA Coach Red Sanders, right, congratulates USC Coach Jess Hill on the Trojans' 14–12 victory in 1952.**

loaded with talent. With veterans flooding back to campus and the school's athletic program growing in popularity, the Bruins had about 200 lettermen, freshmen, armed service stars and transfers show up for the first day of football practice at Spaulding Field in September. It was the largest turnout for a UCLA team in any sport in school history. And LaBrucherie took full advantage. He coached the Bruins to a perfect regular season that

began with a 50–7 victory over Oregon State.

UCLA was primed to end its six-game winless streak against USC when the schools met Nov. 23. UCLA, 8–0 at the time, was ranked fourth in the nation; USC was 5–2 and had won four games in a row. In the rain and mud, LaBrucherie decided on an ultra-conservative game plan and punted five times on first down, four more on second down and eight times on third down. LaBrucherie figured that the Bruins' defense would control the game after UCLA had taken a 6–0 lead in the first quarter when Don Malmberg returned a blocked kick 16 yards for a touchdown.

USC tied the score late in the second quarter on a four-yard run by Don Doll, which capped a 43-yard drive, but ultimately LaBrucherie's cautious game plan paid off. On the last play of the third quarter, UCLA's Ernie Case punted from the USC 45-yard line to the Trojans' Mickey McCardle, who caught the ball at the five. McCardle fumbled when hit by UCLA's Al Hoisch, and West Matthews recovered for the Bruins. Three plays later, Case scored and then added the conversion kick in UCLA's 13–6 victory. The victory gave UCLA its first unbeaten, untied regular season and an invitation to the Rose Bowl, where they lost to Illinois 45–14.

At USC, losing to UCLA and not going to the Rose Bowl did not go over well, and Cravath began feeling some pressure in the 1947 season. He and the Trojans responded, heading into their annual showdown on Nov. 22 with a 7–0–1 record.

USC's defense, which had given up only 27 points all season, proved to be the difference in the Trojans' 6–0 victory in front of a standing-room-only crowd of 102,050 at the Coliseum. Although the game was short on scores, it was long on thrills. After Jim Powers completed a 33-yard second-quarter touchdown pass to Jack Kirby to give USC a 6–0 lead, the Trojans' defense did the rest, including a great goal-line stand that ended with Gordon Gray's fourth-down interception.

The victory was the last high point of the season for USC, which lost to Notre Dame the next week, 38–7, and to Michigan in the Rose Bowl, 49–0.

For UCLA, the loss to USC ended a 5–4 season that included three shutout losses. Just like Horrell before him, LaBrucherie was feeling pressure from alumni because of the Bruins' inconsistency and his inability to beat USC.

In 1948, things did not get any better for the Bruins. UCLA dropped to eighth place in the PCC with a 3–7 record, which included a 20–13 loss to the Trojans.

USC, which finished with a 6–3–1 record in 1948, took control of the game shortly before halftime. Quarterback Dean Dill completed a 60-yard scoring pass to Jack Kirby with two seconds remaining in the half to give the Trojans a 14–6 lead at intermission.

■ Two Trojan stars who had big careers in the NFL.

After the 1948 season, UCLA replaced LaBrucherie with Red Sanders. It turned out to be the perfect hire. In his first season, Sanders led an underdog Bruin team to a 6–3 record that included big road victories at Iowa and Stanford.

But the 1949 UCLA team's season ended on a sour note with a 21–7 loss to USC. Behind sophomore quarterback Dean Schneider, who had never taken a snap in a varsity college game, the Trojans did just enough to win.

USC's final score with two seconds remaining in the game, however, did not go over well with the Bruins. Nor did they care for the game's officials, who ejected standout tackle George Pastre in the second quarter and called questionable pass interference and unsportsmanlike conduct penalties against the Bruins at key points of the game.

But the Bruins had to wait a year to get even.

USC headed into its game against UCLA in 1950 with a dismal 1–4–2 record, and things were made worse by injuries to standouts Bill Bowers, Frank Gifford and Schneider that put them on the sideline. But UCLA was also missing key players because of injuries: Joe Marvin, Johnny Florence, Dave Williams and Bob Moore.

In one of the most satisfying victories recorded by UCLA in the cross-town rivalry, the Bruins crushed USC, 39–0. In two years, Sanders made good on a promise to beat USC, and his team did it in grand style. Just one week after losing, 35–0, at California, the Bruins dominated the Trojans behind sophomore running back Ted Narleski, who rushed for 138 yards, completed two of three passes and scored three touchdowns.

The Times' Dick Hyland wrote about the game on Nov. 26, 1950: "Outthought, outfought, outclassed. In three words, that tells the tale of the football classic at the Coliseum yesterday where the Bruins of UCLA belted the Trojans of SC all over the lot."

The victory was really special for UCLA halfback Howard Hansen. Three days before the game, Hansen's wife, LaVon, died

after a long illness. Sanders wanted Hansen to sit the game out, but the senior refused. UCLA's yearbook, Southern Campus, described Hansen's play against the

Trojans in 1950: "Coming up with a superlative game, the best of his career, red-headed Howie completely bamboozled Trojan defenders with his dazzling reverses. It was the third time in Uclan history that the Westwooders toppled the boys from south of the county jail."

After losing to UCLA, Cravath's job was in serious jeopardy. USC's alumni and faculty wanted him out, but Cravath had the support of the student body. This impasse did not last long. On Dec. 12, 1950, *The Times'* Braven Dyer wrote: "Jeff Cravath is through as Trojan football coach. He will be asked to 'resign' within a few days. *The Times* learned last night that powerful alumni interests have persuaded the administration to get rid of the man who has been head coach for the last nine years....

"Most of the high-ranking officials within the administration were 100% behind the grid coach, but so much pressure was brought to bear by outside 'advisers' that these executives finally decided, for the good of the over-all football picture at SC, to ask for Jeff's resignation."

Cravath had only one losing season at USC, and he led the Trojans to four Rose Bowl appearances, but he never could overcome being the person who coached USC to its first two Rose Bowl losses and the coach who lost to UCLA for the first time. His career record against the Bruins was 8–3–1, respectable by today's standards, not so

■ **Bill Kilmer passed and ran for the Bruins in the late 1950s.**

respectable at that time.

With UCLA the new top dog in town, thanks to the arrival of Sanders, the Trojans didn't look far for Cravath's replacement. USC President Fred D. Fagg Jr. named Jess Hill, a three-sport standout for the Trojans in the late 1920s. Hill, who played in the first USC–UCLA football game in 1929, was an intense coach who enlivened the Trojan program. He led USC to a 7–1 record heading into his first game against UCLA in 1951.

The Bruins were having somewhat of a down season under Sanders, taking the Coliseum field with a 4–3–1 record on Nov. 24. Led by sophomore running back Paul Cameron, who needed only 41 yards of total offense to break Kenny Washington's single-season school record of 1,394, the Bruins knew that they would make their season with an upset victory over the Trojans.

The game wasn't even close. With Cameron accounting for 128 yards to break Washington's mark, the Bruins defeated the Trojans, 21–7, winning back-to-back games in the rivalry for the first time. The play that broke the Trojans was a UCLA double-reverse in the third quarter. Ike Jones made his first carry of the game count with a 20-yard touchdown.

The next day, *The Times'*

Braven Dyer wrote: "If things like this keep up it won't be long before Sanders and his lads have won all four legs on the Trojan Horse."

Losing to UCLA and then Notre Dame the following week gave USC three consecutive losses to close the 1951 season after a 7–0 start. It was a very disappointing end to what had begun as a storybook season for Hill. But the next season would be the Trojans' year for payback.

For the second time (1939 was the other), everything was on the line when UCLA and USC faced each other in 1952: The outcome of the game would determine the PCC title and a Rose Bowl berth.

Both teams entered the contest with perfect records. USC was 8–0, the Bruins 8–0. The Trojans were ranked third in the nation and had outscored their opponents, 233–26. The Bruins were ranked third and had given up more than one touchdown in only one game. The Bruins, under Sanders, were going for their unprecedented third consecutive victory over the Trojans. This game was more than just another edition of a great Southern California rivalry; it attracted attention around the country.

Before a Coliseum crowd and a national television audience on Nov. 22, USC took a

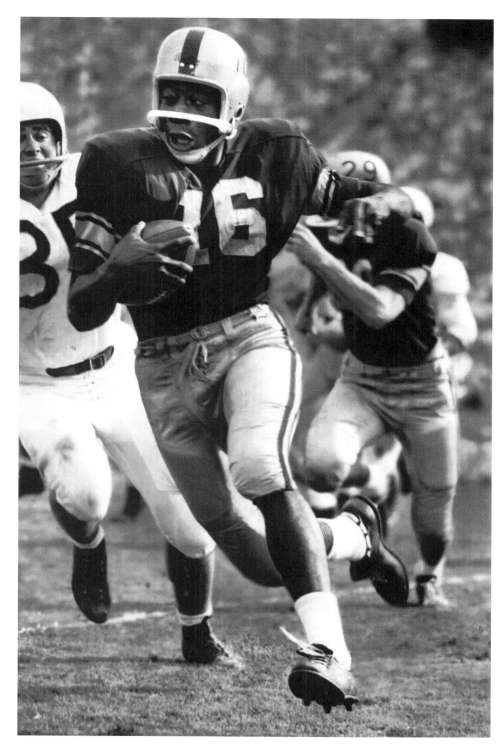

7–3 lead in the second quarter when Al Carmichael and Jim Sears combined on a 70-yard touchdown run. On the play, Carmichael was about to be tackled after a six-yard gain when he somehow pitched the ball to Sears, who ran untouched for a score.

UCLA rallied with a safety and a one-yard

■ Trojan quarterback Willie Wood eludes his would-be tacklers in 1957.

touchdown run by Bill Stits to take a 12–7 lead at halftime. To start the second half, the Bruins took the kickoff and marched to the USC 18-yard line when a mistake turned the game. While rolling out to his left, Cameron was hit as he released the ball, and USC's Elmer Willhoite intercepted the pass and returned it 72 yards to the UCLA six.

A few plays later, Sears completed a fourth-down pass to Carmichael in the flat to give USC a 14–12 lead that held up the rest of the way thanks to the Trojans' dominating defense as USC beat UCLA for the first time since 1949.

The Times' Jack Geyer described USC's win like this the next day: "The play separated the men from the boys and the heads from the shoulders."

In 1953, UCLA was ranked fifth heading into the big game, USC was ninth, but the Bruins were establishing themselves as the West Coast's premier program. With Cameron running for a touchdown and setting the UCLA single-season scoring record, the Bruins completely frustrated USC in a 13–0 victory. The Trojans were limited to 38 passing yards by the Bruins, who later lost to Michigan State, 28–20, in the Rose Bowl.

The following year, UCLA finally put everything together and won the school's first national championship in football. Thanks to Sanders' 4–4 defensive set, the Bruins gave up only 40 points all season, and their single-wing offense was in good hands with tailback Primo Villanueva and his backfield mates: Jim Decker, Terry Debay and Bob Davenport. The key to the Bruins' success was their strong line play with tackle Jack Ellena and guard Sam Boghosian. UCLA had outscored its opponents, 333–40, and entered the game with USC undefeated at 8–0.

Because of the no-repeat rule, which was in effect for part of the 1950s, PCC and Big 10 teams were not allowed to play in consecutive Rose Bowls, and that opened the door for the Trojans. USC, which entered the UCLA game with an 8–1 record, needed a victory to secure the Trojans' second trip to Pasadena in three years.

For the Bruins, the game against the Trojans was their Rose Bowl.

A capacity crowd of 102,548 showed up on Nov. 20, despite temperatures of more

■ Four trumpeters from the USC Marching Band model their new uniforms in 1950. From left: Ray Moran, Dan Eshoff, Bob Taylor and Howard Talkington.

than 100 degrees at the sun-baked Coliseum; 51 spectators were treated for heat prostration; two suffered heart attacks. And the two teams locked themselves into a tight, intense matchup.

The Bruins held a precarious 7–0 lead in the third quarter, but the Trojans appeared to be on the way to tying the score until Decker intercepted a pass by USC's Jim Contratto.

That ignited the Bruins. UCLA scored 27 points in the fourth quarter and sped away

A Place to Play
Finding just the right home takes decades

In the early days, USC and UCLA scrambled to find available, adequate places to compete against each other, though for football and track and field, the Los Angeles Memorial Coliseum was a first-class venue.

The Coliseum opened in 1923, and USC has called the historic site home ever since. The Trojans played there for the first time on Oct. 6, defeating Pomona College, 23–7, in front of a crowd of 12,863.

In 1927, the Bruins also began playing their football games at the Coliseum. But because USC is within walking distance of the stadium, the Bruins never truly felt comfortable calling the Coliseum home.

In the early 1950s, UCLA began exploring the possibility of building an on-campus stadium. The idea gained steam in 1954 when the Bruins finished the season unbeaten and ranked No. 1 in the nation. But the movement couldn't generate the kind of financial support such a massive undertaking would require, and the idea fizzled shortly after Coach Red Sanders died in 1958.

After Coach Tommy Prothro's winning season in 1965 and the Bruins' victory over Michigan State in that season's Rose Bowl, the idea resurfaced. But again, the school could not justify spending $6 million to $7 million on a new stadium when the 96,000–seat Coliseum seemed perfectly adequate for the Bruins' needs.

After the Oakland Raiders had moved to Los Angeles in 1982 and began playing games at the Coliseum, UCLA decided that it was time to move to Pasadena. The Bruins have been there ever since.

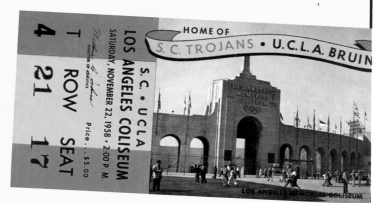

Basketball games between the two schools were held in several arenas during the rivalry's infancy. The old Pan Pacific Auditorium in West Los Angeles and the Olympic Auditorium near downtown in the 1930s and 1940s were a far cry from the large, comfortable arenas of today, but they were the locations of many heated contests between the schools.

And then there was the Men's Gymnasium on the Westwood campus. In 1948, John Wooden took over as UCLA's basketball coach. The Bruins didn't have a lot of talent when he arrived, but they did have one advantage: their home court.

Playing in the cramped men's gym, the Bruins always held a psychological edge over their opponents because the fans were essentially right on the court. Opposing players sometimes found it almost too loud to think.

Of course, the gym did not have air conditioning, and air circulated inside about as well as it does in a Swedish sauna. Hot muggy days had a way of creating a pungent smell. That's how the men's gym earned the not-so-affectionate nickname of the B.O. Barn.

Athletic Scandal 1950s Style

Pacific Conference folds in its wake

In 1915, the Pacific Coast Conference was created with California, Oregon, Oregon State and Washington as the league's original schools. The next year, Stanford and Washington State joined. Then, in 1922, USC came aboard with Idaho.

By the time UCLA was admitted in 1927, Montana State was already in the league. But once USC and UCLA's football programs began to grow, it didn't take long before the PCC was down to eight schools with Idaho and Montana State no longer in the mix.

The conference prospered in the 1940s as the PCC gained respect around the nation for its strong athletic programs. However, things began to change in 1956, when the PCC began to punish programs that paid athletes under-the-table money from school-associated booster clubs.

USC and UCLA were hit hard by the ruling. The PCC charged that both Southern California universities had booster groups in charge of giving athletes $40 more than the $75 a month that the conference allowed them to earn.

The Trojans and Bruins each lost five seniors for five football games that season and eventually were put on probation. UCLA, which had been warned three times of laxity in its athletic employment program, was put on three years' probation and fined $15,000. USC received a two-year probation and was fined $10,000. California and Washington were also punished.

After weeks of investigations, the PCC discovered a long history of illicit payments, phony-job rackets and illegal raffles within the programs. The scandal not only hurt the four schools involved but also created bitterness among the universities in the PCC. In December 1957, UCLA and USC, along with Cal, announced their intentions to withdraw from the PCC, and in 1959, the conference folded.

At that point, USC, UCLA, California and Washington formed a new league: the Athletic Association of Western Universities.

By the time the AAWU began play in 1959, Stanford had joined, and in 1962, Washington State was added. In 1964, Oregon and Oregon State joined, and in 1968, the name of the league was changed to the Pacific-8 Conference. The current Pac-10 lineup was completed when Arizona and Arizona State joined before the 1978 season.

---

with a 34–0 victory to secure its perfect season and a share of the national championship.

UCLA ended up No. 1 in the United Press International poll; the Bruins finished second to Ohio State in the Associated Press poll.

USC, which lost to Notre Dame the next week, finished as runner-up to the Bruins in the PCC and lost to Ohio State, 20–7, in the Rose Bowl to complete the 1954 season 8–4 with losses in its final three games.

The Bruins couldn't duplicate their success in 1955, but they still continued to dominate on the West Coast. Behind versatile tailback Ronnie Knox, UCLA won eight of nine games heading into the USC game, but it would have to go into that matchup without Knox, who had suffered a broken leg against Washington a week earlier.

Jon Arnett and Contratto led the Trojans, but USC needed more than those two against the fired-up Bruins, who won, 17–7. Arnett provided the Trojans' main highlight when he ran the opening kickoff back 97 yards for an apparent touchdown. It was called back because of a penalty, and that was pretty much it for USC. Backup Bruin tailback Sam Brown had a career game with 150 yards and a touchdown in 27 carries.

The Victory Bell

Its tale is told

The winner of each UCLA–USC football game is awarded the Victory Bell to keep until the next season. It's a tradition that dates back to 1941, and the story behind it is as rich as the crosstown rivalry itself.

The 295-pound bell originally clanged from atop a Southern Pacific freight locomotive. It was given to UCLA in

1939 as a gift from the UCLA Alumni Association. For two seasons, cheerleaders rang the bell after each UCLA score.

At the opening game of UCLA's 1941 football season against Washington State,

six members of USC's Sigma Phi Epsilon fraternity worked their way into the UCLA rooting section. The Bruins defeated the Cougars, 7–6, in a thrilling game, and afterward the USC fraternity brothers easily blended in, helping students load the bell onto a waiting truck bound for Westwood.

The scheming Trojans then stole the key to the truck and, while the Bruins went to get a replacement, the USC students drove off with the bell.

The bell was hidden for more than a year, first in the fraternity's basement, then in hide-outs in the Hollywood Hills, Santa Ana and other locations. Once it was even concealed beneath a haystack.

The controversy died down for a while, until a picture of the bell was printed in the Wampus, a USC student magazine. The rivalry was sparked to new heights.

Several Bruins threatened to kidnap

USC student body president Bob McKay if the Trojans failed to return the bell. UCLA students painted USC's Tommy Trojan statue; Trojan students burned USC initials on UCLA campus lawns. Police were called several times. The conflict escalated to the point that USC President Rufus B. von KleinSmid threatened to cancel the 1942 USC–UCLA game if the students didn't stop acting like, well, college students.

On Nov. 12, 1942, the bell was wheeled in front of Tommy Trojan, and the student body presidents of both schools (USC's McKay and UCLA's Bill Farrer) signed an agreement stating that thereafter the winner of the Trojan-Bruin football game would keep the bell for the following year. In the case of a tie, the school that had won the previous year's game would retain the bell. The USC Alumni Association later repaid the UCLA Alumni Association for half the cost of the bell.

At the time, the arrangement might have seemed like a bad deal for the Bruins, since they had yet to defeat USC. But that first year, 1942, UCLA beat the Trojans, 14–7.

Although the Victory Bell is one of college football's most famous trophies, it is one of the least visible, remaining in a warehouse or vault virtually all year. The universities display the bell only during the first three quarters of the game and on the Monday after the game, when it is delivered to the winning school's campus. Sometimes blue (after a Bruin win) and other times cardinal (after a Trojan win), the Victory Bell now remains under lock and key.

Football Fun and Folly
High jinks on the field and off

For three-quarters of a century, UCLA and USC have had more than their share of practical jokes and school spirit-inspired events. Some have worked; some, well, have been slightly less effective.

Beat SC Week and Beat the Bruins Week are part of a rivalry that didn't take long to gain steam. Legend has it that USC students unloaded a cart of manure on the Westwood campus before the Southern Branch officially opened as UCLA in 1929.

A look at a few of the early high jinks:

The Great Water Hoax

In 1946, UCLA was positioning itself to finally take over college football in Los Angeles. Heading into their Nov. 23 game against the Trojans, the Bruins had won all eight of their games while their crosstown rivals were a disappointing 5–2.

The Bruins were loaded with speed. Coach Bert LaBrucherie, who had played halfback at UCLA for Bill Spaulding in the 1920s, featured an explosive team that averaged more than 400 yards a game in offense. The Trojans, on the other hand, relied mostly on defense to win.

Worried that USC could lose to UCLA for the first time since 1942, a couple of USC supporters called Los Angeles newspapers late the night before the game and said Trojan students had used fire hoses to flood the Coliseum field.

The callers told the newspapers that students figured that the only way the Trojans could win was if the field was muddy enough to slow UCLA's collection of quick runners. A "bloody brawl" supposedly had ensued between USC and UCLA students on the field.

Wire services picked up the story, and the next morning the report was in newspapers all over the country.

The story was a hoax.

The two schools and Los Angeles police later denied that such an incident had occurred, and the newspapers printed apologies.

With a field to its liking, UCLA defeated USC, 13–6. The following week the Bruins beat Nebraska and advanced to the Rose Bowl, where they lost to Illinois, 45–14.

The Dognap Caper

The water hoax call might have been motivated by a prank by UCLA earlier that week.

George Tirebiter was an unofficial USC mascot, a homeless dog that walked around the USC campus and had become associated with the football program early in the season when students began to take him to games.

Days before the 1947 game, UCLA students kidnapped Tirebiter and re-

turned him with the letters "UCLA" shaved on his back.

Trojan Goofs

On Dec. 1, 1937, three days before the USC and UCLA football teams were to play for the fourth time, a small group of USC Kappa Alpha fraternity members burned USC initials into a lawn on the Westwood campus.

Campus police caught the students in the act. In trying to escape, the students crashed their car into a curb, then broke a bulletin board at the main entrance as they tried to swerve around the Bruins' Founders Rock.

Perhaps the worst of the pranksters' punishment was that they were forced to sit on the ground for nearly two hours as UCLA students berated them.

The excitement that traditionally accompanied the big game was muted in 1956, when both USC and UCLA were among PCC schools that had been put on probation and penalized by the conference because athletes had been paid under the table by booster clubs. Both teams had lost starting players to suspension.

When the schools met on Nov. 24, neither was in the hunt for the Rose Bowl, the first time that had happened since 1951. Only 63,709 showed up to see the Trojans end a three-game losing streak to UCLA. Jim Conroy, who began the season as the fourth-string quarterback, led USC to a 10–7 victory, with Ellsworth Kissinger kicking the winning field goal.

After that season, Hill retired as head coach to become USC's athletic director and was replaced by his former line coach, Don Clark.

Clark, who had played guard at USC in 1942 and from 1946 to 1947, inherited a football program short on experience and depth; only 14 lettermen returned for the 1957 season. USC lost its first five games and was outscored, 81–32. By the time the Trojans played the Bruins, they were 1–7 and had fumbled the ball 37 times.

It was a very different story across town. Sanders' Bruins were 7–2 and riding a three-game winning streak. UCLA defeated USC, 20–9, behind junior tailback Don Long, who threw two touchdown passes, scored a touchdown and intercepted a key pass when the game was still undecided. Long completed nine of 13 passes for 181 yards.

That would be the final game Red Sanders would coach. On Aug. 14, 1958, Sanders, 53, died of a heart attack. George Dickerson, a former player and a 12-year assistant with the Bruins, was named as Sanders' replacement. However, it was an ill-fated appointment.

Dickerson suffered from manic depression and lasted only three games before Bill Barnes replaced him. Despite having Bill Kilmer, a future All-American and NFL star quarterback, leading their offense, the Bruins could not overcome the turmoil of such unexpected change. They were 3–6 heading into the USC game.

USC wasn't having a terrific season either, only 4–4, but the Trojans still had a longshot chance at a Rose Bowl bid under second-year coach Don Clark.

In front of only 58,507 in the Coliseum, USC was hampered by injuries to starters Willie Wood, Al Prukop, Monte Clark and George Van Vliet and trailed, 15–7, early in the fourth quarter. They tied the score, 15–15, on a 74-yard kickoff return by Luther Hayes and a two-point conversion run by quarterback Tom Maudlin. The Trojans had a chance to win the game in the final seconds but ran out of time on the UCLA 19-yard line, resulting in the fifth tie between the schools and the first since 1944.

By the start of the 1959 season, both UCLA and USC had left the PCC and joined the newly formed Athletic Association of Western Universities, with Washington, California and Stanford. The Trojans won their first eight games, with wins over the three other conference schools, and were ranked fourth in the nation heading into the UCLA game. The Bruins were struggling at 3–3–1 and were the decided underdogs, but as so often is the case in this rivalry, emotion can mean more than pure talent.

UCLA, refusing to fold against a far better team, benefited from a controversial pass-interference penalty called on USC's Jerry Traynham and used a late touchdown run by Ray Smith to defeat the Trojans, 10–3.

BASKETBALL

The Trojans were the class of the basketball court under Coach Sam Barry in the early 1940s. They hadn't lost to the Bruins

UCLA ★ 1949

since 1932 and began the 1939–40 season as defending Pacific Coast Conference champions.

Behind All-American forward Ralph Vaughn, the Trojans won their second consecutive Southern Division league championship with a 20–3 record, defeating the Bruins in all four of their meetings that season.

In the first meeting at the Shrine Auditorium, USC won, 50–32, with big man Dale Sears its key player. Sears scored 17 points to take the spotlight away from an expected scor-

ing duel between Vaughn and the Bruins' Jackie Robinson. Robinson led the PCC in scoring with a 12.4–point average in league games; Vaughn was second at 11.5. But both players were shut down effectively while Sears dominated the game in leading the undefeated Trojans to their 10th victory of the season.

Three weeks later, USC had an easier time in a 60–26 victory at the Shrine, with Vaughn scoring a game-high 14 points. When the teams faced each other in back-to-back games in Westwood in the final month of the regular season, the Bruins came close to ending the Trojans' winning streak.

With Robinson setting the pace, UCLA made a furious second-half rally only to have USC respond with reserve forward Keith Lambert, who had been on the injured list most of the season. Lambert scored four consecutive baskets in the closing minutes to lift the Trojans to a 32–26 victory. The next day, USC clinched the league title with a 47–35 win over UCLA.

The Bruins finished the 1939–40 season 8–17 under first-year coach Wilbur Johns, who had replaced Caddy Works. It was the ninth sub-.500 season in a row for UCLA's basketball program, but at least Johns coached the Bruins to three conference victories. UCLA had not won a PCC game since 1937.

Things got no better for UCLA in 1940–41, a season in which they would lose co-captain Lloyd Anderson to a broken arm and then, two weeks later, fellow captain Bob Null to a concussion. Robinson again led the team in scoring at 11.1 points a game, but he wasn't enough to take the team to respectability.

UCLA was 3–9 heading into its first game against USC, which had won five games in a row. USC ran all over the Bruins, 56–35, at the UCLA campus gym. USC captain Jack Lippert finished with a game-high 18 points; Robin-

■ Alex Hanum, right. Bill Sharman, below left, practices with teammate Stan Christie.

■ Opposite: UCLA Coach John Wooden gives a few shooting tips in his first season in Westwood.

son led the Bruins with 12.

In the second matchup, UCLA at least gave the Trojans a scare. If not for a couple of key defensive plays made by center Joe Reising and Lippert's clutch shooting down the stretch, USC would not have been able to escape with a 43–41 victory.

UCLA came even closer in the third meeting. Behind Robinson's open-court play and relentless scoring, the Bruins built a double-digit first-half lead in front of a stunned crowd at the Shrine. In the second half, USC rallied behind Lippert's scoring and Jack Barron's defense to send the game into overtime. In the extra period, USC's depth wore down Robinson and the Bruins, who lost their 35th consecutive game to the Trojans, 53–47. The next night, USC made sure it wasn't close, defeating UCLA, 52–37.

UCLA's 1941 yearbook described the Bruins' 6–20 season like this: "As usual, the conflicts with the Trojans drew the largest crowds, all wondering if the old jinx still held good, which it did despite the close scores and Bruin optimism."

In 1941–42, UCLA continued its practice of getting close without getting over the top.

Sam Barry had left the team for Navy duty, and for the first time since Barry had taken over in 1930, USC had a new coach, Julie Bescos. The Trojans nearly let him down in his first game against UCLA.

The Bruins made a late surge to take a

Bruin star
Don Barksdale

49–48 lead, but the Trojans went on an 11–2 run in the final two minutes to win. When the schools met for the second time that season, Feb. 13, 1942, the Bruins made a big deal about the date: It was the 10th anniversary of the last time UCLA had defeated USC in basketball.

The Trojan players had no interest in letting UCLA repeat the results of 10 years earlier. USC's Johnny Luber limited UCLA's high-scoring Ernie Handelsman to one basket, and USC won, 42–30. Bescos had a mediocre experience in his only season as the Trojans' coach, finishing with a 12–8 record and second in the PCC Southern Division. But Bescos kept the streak alive with two more victories over the Bruins to close the season as USC outscored UCLA by 33 combined points.

Ernie Holbrook took over the Trojan program in 1942–43 and inherited a well-balanced team. USC won 13 of its first 14 games behind forward Alex Hannum and captain Ted Gossard. Hannum would later play in the NBA and coach the 1958 St. Louis Hawks and the 1967 Philadelphia 76ers to NBA titles.

The Trojans had one of the West Coast's top teams and rolled over UCLA, 60–49 and 51–39, in their first two meetings.

But the streak finally came to an end the third time the teams met. In front of a packed UCLA campus gym on March 5, 1943, center

Don Barksdale led the Bruins to a 42–37 overtime victory that ended USC's winning streak at 42 games. Barksdale was the game's leading scorer with 18 points, and Mickey Panovich made several key defensive plays for the Bruins, who outhustled the Trojans down the stretch.

The Bruins nearly made it two in a row in the final game between the two that season, but the Trojans pulled away after Barksdale and guard Ainslie Bell fouled out. USC won, 53–46. UCLA's final record was 14–7, its best in 15 years, but the defining moment was the streak-ending triumph over USC.

The next season, UCLA built on that success and defeated USC in three of four games.

In the first game, the Bruins held USC to its lowest conference score in 12 years with a 33–19 victory. Captain Dick West directed an efficient UCLA attack that was led by Bill Rankin's game-high 15 points. The Trojans won the second game, 48–41, at the Shrine, but that would be the last time they would beat their cross-town rivals that season.

In front of a packed house in Westwood, the Bruins squeezed out a 32–30 victory on a layup by West in the third meeting. Then in the season finale for UCLA, West scored a game-high 17 points in a 40–32 victory. For the first time since 1932, UCLA had won a

Jackie Robinson UCLA

The beginning of a legend

It could be argued that Jackie Robinson, the man who broke the color barrier in major league baseball, is the most significant athlete in American sports history. His success on and off the field helped pave the way for blacks in professional sports and changed forever the sporting landscape in this country.

But before Jack Roosevelt Robinson became a household name with the Brooklyn Dodgers, he was one of the country's most versatile and talented collegiate athletes.

As UCLA's first four-sport letterman, Robinson was a standout for the Bruins for two football seasons (1939 and 1940), two basketball seasons (1940 and 1941) and one each in baseball and track and field (1940).

The Times' Shav Glick began covering Robinson when the future Baseball Hall of Famer attended Pasadena City College from 1937 to 1938. Robinson did not play baseball or compete in track his senior year at UCLA. Instead, at 21, he joined the National Youth Administration, playing baseball to entertain campers and working with disadvantaged children.

At UCLA, Robinson excelled at football, basketball and track, and offered little hint of the Hall of Fame baseball career that lay ahead. Although in his first baseball game as a Bruin Robinson had four stolen bases and four hits, including a home run, he ended his only season on the diamond with a batting average of .097.

But he was an All-Pacific Coast Conference player in football, was the PCC player of the year in basketball and set a school long-jump record that stood for more than 20 years.

Considered nearly unstoppable on the football field, Robinson led the nation in punt-return average in 1939 (16.5 yards) and 1940 (21.0). His career average of 18.8 yards per return ranks fourth in NCAA history.

As a senior, he led the Bruins in rushing (383 yards), passing (444 yards), total offense (827 yards), scoring (36 points) and punt returns. In his two seasons, he rushed for 954 yards (5.9-yard average) and passed for 449 yards.

In basketball, all Robinson did was lead the Southern Division of the PCC in scoring in 1940 (12.4–point average in 12 league games) and 1941 (11.1).

One of his most remarkable achievements was near the end of the 1940 track and field season. Because he was playing baseball, he had missed most of UCLA's track competitions. Nevertheless, he won the PCC championship in the broad jump with a leap of 25 feet, then two weeks later became the NCAA champion in the event when he jumped 24 feet, 10 inches.

UCLA

JACKIE ROBINSON

season series over the Trojans in basketball.

The 1944–45 season was marked by the physical play between the Bruins and Trojans on the hardwood. In the first game, USC used a strong second-half run to win easily, 53–25, at the Shrine. But things got heated in the second contest.

With UCLA playing its best game of the season, the Bruins defeated the Trojans, 41–36, at Westwood, and in separate incidents during the final minutes of the game, Bob Arnold and Stick Rankin were knocked cold by the Trojans, who initiated several rough plays in the second half. The stakes were high for the third matchup with the teams tied for the Southern Division lead. UCLA used a stingy defense to take a 14–3 lead in the first half and closed the deal in the second half as Rankin took over. The Bruins won, 34–28, and grabbed the Southern Division title.

The Trojan program got a boost before the start of the 1945–46 season when Barry returned from military duty to coach the team. He was regarded as the Bruin killer among UCLA supporters for his win streak against the Westwood team dating back to 1932.

Although the Bruins struggled to an 8–16 record, they took special pride in beating a Barry-coached USC team. In the third meeting between the schools at the Shrine, UCLA defeated USC, 45–35.

The next season, benefiting from the influx of veterans returning from the war, Johns' Bruins won the PCC Southern Division, finished 18–7 and, perhaps most significant, swept all four games from the Trojans for the first time in school history.

Barksdale, who had helped the Bruins end an 11-year losing streak to the Trojans in 1943, was too much for the Trojans to handle. Even such quality Trojan players as Fred Bertram and Hannum couldn't handle UCLA.

In the third meeting between the schools, Barksdale scored a season-high 30 points.

In the 1947–48 season, the Trojans bounced back to take three of four games from the Bruins. In the first contest, Bill Sharman, Joe White and Hannum got hot for the Trojans and USC won going away, 56–42. After the Bruins won a sloppy, turnover-filled second game, 51–50, USC closed out the season with back-to-back victories over UCLA at the Olympic Auditorium to finish second in the PCC Southern Division.

After the season, UCLA decided to make a coaching change. Out went Wilbur Johns; in came a new era, not only for UCLA but also for college basketball as a whole. John Wooden took over the program in 1948 and began a Bruin career that would become the most dominant in NCAA basketball history.

It did not take long for Wooden to make his mark. In his first season, Wooden turned the Bruins into an up-tempo, fast-breaking machine. UCLA sailed to a 22–7 regular-season record and the PCC Southern Division title, defeating USC in three of four games.

The Bruins defeated the Trojans in overtime, 74–68, at Westwood the first time the teams met. In the second game, USC played better defense and won, 59–52, at the Olympic.

That set the stage for a crucial third game at the Olympic. Wooden gave a hint of what was to come when he coached an undermanned UCLA team, which was missing several first-string players, to a 51–50 victory over the favored Trojans. The next night, the Bruins won a little easier, 63–55.

UCLA's 1949 yearbook had this to say about Wooden: "Taking over only an average group of boys, Jovial John proceeded to bamboozle the world of sports by producing the scrappiest aggregation of Lanky Lems ever to set foot on a Bruin hardboard patch. To Coach Wooden, a top flight leader in the know-how department and a sterling personality if ever there was one, UCLA has already doffed its hat. Hail the conquering hero, and watch for things to come!"

USC opened the 1949–50 season on a tear. Behind high-scoring Bill Sharman, who averaged 19 points in the PCC, the Trojans won 10 of their first 12 games heading into their first showdown against the Bruins. Barry's Trojans then played their best game of the season in front of a capacity crowd at the Pan-Pacific and crushed the Bruins, 58–45. The 13-point defeat matched the worst Wooden had suffered since taking over at UCLA.

The loss woke up the Bruins, who went on to win their second PCC Southern Division title in as many years under Wooden. UCLA and USC ended the season split at 2–2, but because the Bruins lost only to the Trojans in conference play, they won the league title and earned the school's first NCAA tournament appearance.

Despite his success those first two years, Indiana-native Wooden thought about leaving in 1950. Purdue, his alma mater, wanted him to return to take over the Boilermakers' basketball program, and Wooden was seriously considering going home because he was not comfortable living in Los Angeles. Purdue made what Wooden called "a tremendous offer," a deal that would have given him a perpetual five-year contract with built-in increases, a family membership in country clubs, a new automobile every year, a home on campus and a large insurance policy.

But Johns, UCLA's athletic director, and Bill Ackerman, the graduate manager of the

GAMES WON 1940s — 1950s
BASKETBALL
UCLA 37 - USC 36

Associated Students, refused to let Wooden out of his three-year contract with the Bruins. So Wooden remained in Los Angeles.

In 1950–51, the Bruins claimed the unofficial title of having the best football and basketball programs in Los Angeles. UCLA's football team had embarrassed the Trojans, 39–0, in the fall, and then Wooden led his team to three wins in five games against USC in basketball.

With Jerry Norman creating plays and Dick Ridgway providing an inside force, UCLA won the fifth and deciding game, 49–41, to forge a first-place tie in the PCC Southern Division with USC. The Trojans were coached by first-year Coach Forrest Twogood, who had taken over at the start of the season after the death of his longtime friend Barry.

In 1951–52, the Bruins thoroughly dominated the Trojans, sweeping all four games behind the play of freshman John Moore. The closest game of the four was the final matchup, which the Bruins' won, 63–57, to take home their fourth PCC Southern Division championship in as many seasons under Wooden.

For the next two seasons, USC got the better of Wooden. The Trojans won six of eight games, and Twogood's team took home the PCC Southern Division title in 1953–54 by sweeping back-to-back games over UCLA late in the season.

Twogood's team jelled at the right time after the Trojans had opened the season 5–5. Behind center Roy Irvin's 13.8 points a game, USC headed into a two-game weekend set against UCLA in late February needing to win both in order to clinch the league championship.

Because of the Bruins' recent dominance at home under Wooden, not too many people

Sam Barry USC

A coach for all sports

In USC's athletic history, no one showed more versatility as a mentor than Justin McCarthy "Sam" Barry, a real coach-of-all-trades. No matter the season, Barry could be found on the sidelines, teaching young athletes how to win.

For 17 seasons, Barry coached the Trojans' basketball team to a 260–138 record that included Pacific Coast Conference championships in 1930, 1935 and 1940, and a third-place finish in the 1940 NCAA tournament.

Barry also coached the baseball team from 1930 to 1950. With Barry on the bench, the Trojans had a 219–89–3 record, including a 133–54–2 mark against college opponents. Along with co-coach Rod Dedeaux, Barry led the Trojans to an NCAA championship in 1948.

And to make sure that he wasn't slacking off in the fall, Barry was a football assistant for 12 years under Howard Jones and stepped in as head coach for one season after the legendary coach died in 1941.

After graduating from Lawrence College in Appleton, Wis., Barry coached high school basketball in 1917, then went to Knox College in Illinois and to the University of Iowa upon Jones' recommendation.

Barry coached at Iowa for seven sea- sons and led them to the 1923 Big 10 Conference championship and a share of the title in 1926. He also worked as a football assistant coach under Jones at USC.

As a basketball coach, Barry was regarded as one of the game's best teachers. Three of his players—Alex Hannum, Bill Sharman and Fred "Tex" Winter—all went on to become exceptional coaches.

And he is responsible for one of the most significant rule changes in the game.

In the early days of basketball, a center jump was held at midcourt after every basket. Teams often had one tall player whose sole job was to win the tip so his team could retain possession. Barry launched a campaign to eliminate that rule in 1928, before he arrived at USC. Once on the West Coast, Barry eventually persuaded other coaches to support his view, and the National Basketball Committee eliminated the rule in 1937.

One of the lasting memories of Barry, though, is of his role in a game against UCLA in 1932. After the Trojans took a 5–2 lead in the opening minutes, Barry called on his "stationary offense." In a day when there was no shot clock, it was simply a stall.

Barry had his guards, Cliff Capp and Julie Bescos, pass the ball to each other while UCLA remained in a halfcourt zone defense. The rest of the first half was played like this while a capacity crowd at the Olympic Auditorium littered the court with peanuts, coins and newspapers.

In the end, the tactic didn't work. The Bruins won, 19–17, on a last-minute basket by Bud Rose.

PCC championship and then advanced to the Final Four of the NCAA tournament, only to lose to Bradley in the semifinals.

Unfortunately for the Trojans, Wooden made sure that they returned to earth in 1954–55. With seniors Johnny Moore and Don Bragg taking the role of team leaders, the Bruins swept four games from the Trojans and won a share of their fifth PCC Southern Division title under Wooden. A key player on the Bruins' 1955 team was rugged senior Ron Bane, a three-year starter under Wooden.

In 1955–56, the Bruins played the Trojans only twice and won both games. UCLA outscored USC by a combined 28 points in the back-to-back games played at Venice High and Loyola University. UCLA, which was led by All-American center Willie Naulls, finished the season undefeated in PCC play but was knocked out of the NCAA regional semifinals by Bill Russell and the eventual national champions from the University of San Francisco.

From the account in UCLA's 1956 yearbook:

gave the Trojans a chance. But USC played team basketball and won, 79–68. The next night, the Trojans won again, but they needed a big break to do so.

The Times' Jack Geyer wrote on Feb. 28: "Coach Forrest Twogood's rough, ready and rallying Trojans won their first undisputed Southern Division basketball championship since 1943 by squeezing past the UCLA Bruins, 69–67, last night in an insane asylum called Men's Gymnasium at Westwood.

"Victory came to the Trojans a split-second before the game ended when SC's Chet Carr, a 6-foot, 4-inch forward, uncorked the most important shot of his career. Carr was off to the side of the bucket and about 10 feet away, eyeing the basket the way a mongoose stares at a cobra. He let the ball go and in it went. The gun sounded almost simultaneously."

USC went on to defeat Oregon State in the

"The pre-season feelings were that Johnny Wooden's cage squad would have just an average PCC season, but the Bruins rolled through their 1956 league season with the taking of the PCC championship after their winning streak of sixteen straight league games…. Coach Wooden produced a team which will long stand out in Bruin basketball history."

In 1957, the Bruins had a 22–2 record when they faced the Trojans for the first time. But USC, which would finish the season with a 16–12 record, stunned UCLA, 84–80, behind a strong game from center Jim Pugh. UCLA, which finished second in the PCC Southern Division, won the second meeting, 65–55, played two weeks later.

The Bruins failed to win any share of the PCC Southern Division title the next two years, but UCLA beat USC four consecutive times in the 1958 and 1959 seasons.

In the first meeting between the schools in 1958, USC looked as if it had pulled off an upset when the Trojans held a one-point lead with only seconds to play. But UCLA guard Walt Torrence stole the ball and scored the winning basket at the buzzer to give the Bruins a 52–51 victory. The next night, after UCLA and USC played to a regulation tie, Torrence and captain Ben Rogers stepped up for Wooden in an 80–75 overtime victory.

In two games played at the Pan-Pacific in 1959, the Bruins managed to gain narrow vic-

■ As a student Rafer Johnson, the Olympic Decathlon medalist, stood out on the Bruins' basketball team, opposite above, as well as on their track and field squad, opposite and below.

tories in back-to-back nights in January. Despite strong shooting games from USC's Jim Hanna and Johnny Werhas, UCLA rode Torrence's 25 points to win 57–53. In the second game, Rafer Johnson's quickness and Torrence's scoring led the Bruins to a 65–63 victory.

TRACK AND FIELD

USC, coached by Dean Cromwell, was the dominant force in college track and field in the early 1940s, coming into the decade having won five consecutive national championships. And with Johnny Wilson repeating as high-jump champion and Kenny Dills winning the pole vault, USC squeezed out yet another national title in 1940.

The meet against UCLA that year was no contest, a 98–38 Trojan blowout led by middle distance runner Lou Zamperini, a two-time NCAA champion at 1,500 meters, and sprinter Mickey Anderson, a three-time NCAA 100-meter finalist. UCLA's only bright spot was Jackie Robinson, who would go on to win the NCAA broad jump title.

In 1941, the Trojans dominated the Bruins again, then won another NCAA championship, with quarter-miler Hubie Kerns the team's only NCAA champion. And the next year, it was still more of the same, with USC

routing UCLA, 108–23, on the way to its eighth consecutive national championship.

In 1943, Cromwell enjoyed his last NCAA championship season behind great efforts from sprinters Cliff Bourland and Jack Trout, shot putter Wilbur Thompson and long jumper Edsel Curry.

But the Trojans had a close call against UCLA in the rivalry's annual dual meet. With Cromwell experimenting with his lineup, USC still won, for the 10th time in a row, over the Bruins, but the 71–60 score was far closer than the Trojans had been used to.

Although USC's NCAA championship streak came to an end after the 1943 season, it continued to attract world-class track and field athletes, including sprinter Mel Patton. Enrolling in 1946, Patton became the world's top sprinter as a sophomore and set a world record in the 100-yard dash with a time of 9.4 seconds at the Fresno Relays in 1948.

He won gold medals at the 1948 Olympics in the 200-meter dash and the 400-meter relay. In 1949, Patton returned to USC for his senior year and broke Jesse

Owens' world record in the 220 with a time of 20.2. Patton also anchored USC's world-record-breaking 880-yard relay team.

Meanwhile, the Bruins' track and field program continued to struggle. In 1947, the school hired Ducky Drake as coach, and he gradually improved the program.

After the 1948 season, Cromwell retired from USC and was replaced by Jess Hill. USC hadn't won a national title in five years, and Hill promptly changed that. He made the most of the two seasons he would be track and field coach by winning a couple of national championships.

■ Left: Track Coach Jess Mortensen, center, with shot putter Parry O'Brien, left, and hurdler Jack Davis. Below: Trojan star athlete-turned-coach Jess Hill featured on 1950 program.

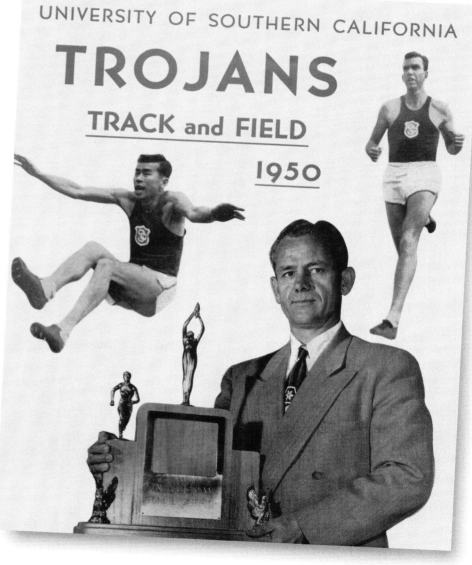

UNIVERSITY OF SOUTHERN CALIFORNIA

TROJANS

TRACK and FIELD

1950

1957 UCLA TRACK & FIELD

RETURNING STARS FROM UCLA's 1956 NCAA AND PCC CHAMPIONSHIP TEAMS . . . AND FRIENDS
Head Coach Ducky Drake and Assistant Coach Craig Dixon gather with the six returning point-winners from last year's first national collegiate championship track team in UCLA's history. Kneeling, from left: Don Vick, second in discus throw and fourth in shot put; Rafer Johnson, second in broad jump and second in high hurdles; and Bob Seaman, fourth in 1500-meter run. Standing, from left: Coach Drake; Dick Knaub, sixth in broad jump; Russ Ellis, fourth in 400-meter dash; Nick Dyer, tied for first in high jump; and Coach Dixon.

■ **Bruin Track and Field program in 1957 featuring coach Ducky Drake and team.**

In the first of those, UCLA actually made some noise. Behind Craig Dixon, who won the high and low hurdles at the 1949 NCAA meet, the Bruins finished second to the Trojans.

But things hit an all-time low for UCLA's track program in 1950 when the Trojans ran away with a 120–11 victory at the Coliseum on their way to their 14th NCAA track championship.

Despite the success of broad jumper George Brown, who won the NCAA title in the event in 1951 and 1952, the Bruins continued to come up short against the Trojans in dual meets. But they finally seemed to be gaining ground.

Before the start of the 1951 season, Jess Mortensen, a former Trojan three-sport standout, replaced Hill as coach. But the Trojans did not skip a beat, winning their third consecutive NCAA title and extending their unbeaten dual-meet streak over UCLA to 18 years.

At the 1952 Helsinki Olympics, USC's track program was again well represented with high-hurdle champion Jack Davis, discus champion Sim Iness and shot put champion Parry O'Brien.

Mortensen and the Trojans added NCAA titles in 1953 and 1954. Quarter-miler Jim Lea, who won national titles those two years, and high jumper Ernie Shelton helped the Trojans extend their championship streak to seven years.

Although Drake was recruiting better athletes and the Bruins had success against other West Coast universities, they still couldn't beat the Trojans, losing dual meets in 1953 and 1954 by a combined total of 79 points.

UCLA's prospects improved in the fall of 1954 when Rafer Johnson enrolled as a freshman in Westwood. As a freshman, Johnson wasn't eligible to compete in the 1955 dual meet, and UCLA still lost to USC, 79–52. But the Bruins stepped up at the NCAA championship meet and finished second behind the Trojans.

In 1956, the Trojans stretched their dual-meet winning streak over UCLA to 24, but the Bruins put an end to USC's national dominance.

UCLA upset the Trojans at the Pacific Coast Conference meet and then two weeks later ended USC's national title run at seven with an inspired showing at the NCAA championships.

**MEETS WON
1940s — 1950s
TRACK & FIELD
USC 20 - UCLA 0**

USC, UCLA and Hollywood

A short step from the field to the set

Because both schools are in the heart of the entertainment world, there have been plenty of Bruins and Trojans who have made a smooth transition from sports to show business.

One of the first and most notable was a tackle named Marion "Duke" Morrison on the 1925 and '26 USC football teams. Morrison had an injury-plagued football career and failed even to earn a letter at USC, but he managed to have a slightly more successful career in front of the camera. After changing his name to John Wayne, the Duke became an international film icon.

USC Coach Howard Jones, who often found summer jobs in the movie industry for his players, got Wayne work in 1926 as an assistant prop man on the set of a movie directed by John Ford.

According to legend, Ford spotted Wayne, an imposing 6 feet 4 and 225 pounds, on the set and asked him to demonstrate a football stance. Wayne did, and before he knew it Ford knocked him to the ground. Wayne picked himself up and said in the deep voice that would be his trademark on the silver screen, "Let's try that once again." This time, Wayne sent Ford flying and the two began a lifelong personal and professional relationship.

Wayne eventually worked his way into movie roles. During the Depression he played in B Westerns until Ford got him the role of the Ringo Kid in his classic film "Stagecoach."

Wayne made more than 200 films during a 50-year career and is regarded as one of the greatest figures in the history of film. In 1969, he won an Academy Award as best actor for "True Grit."

One of Wayne's Trojan teammates, center/guard Nate Barragar, took a different path to Hollywood. He had played a key role on USC's first national championship team in 1928 and was named to the All-America team as a senior in 1929.

Barragar played three seasons professionally before getting into show business. Like many of his teammates, Barragar had taken acting jobs as an extra. But once his playing days were over, Barragar returned to Hollywood and began working in the production departments of various studios.

Over the years, Barragar was part of many award-winning movie and television projects, including "The Greatest Story Ever Told," an Academy Award winner in many categories in 1965.

At 6 feet 5, Woody Strode was an outstanding pass-catching end and a world-class athlete on UCLA's track and field teams of the late 1930s.

Strode, along with fellow UCLA All-American Kenny Washington, broke the NFL's unofficial color line in 1946 when they signed with the Los Angeles Rams, but his professional football career didn't last long.

In 1950, Strode turned to acting and began a film career that lasted more than 40 years. He played the King of Ethiopia in "The Ten Commandments" (1956) and starred as a cavalry soldier unjustly charged in John Ford's "Sergeant Rutledge" (1960). He also had a significant role in the 1960 blockbuster "Spartacus" and worked with Wayne in the 1962 Western "The Man Who Shot Liberty Valance." Strode acted until his death in 1994, his final role that of Charlie Moonlight in "The Quick and the Dead," a 1995 release starring Gene Hackman and Sharon Stone.

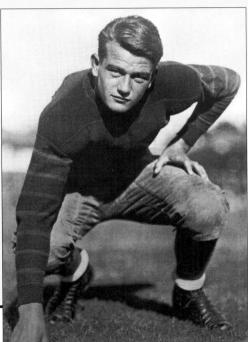

■ Trojan tackle Marion "Duke" Morrison, a.k.a. John Wayne.

Johnson finished second in the broad jump and high hurdles, Ron Drummond won the discus and Nick Dyer tied for first in the high jump to give Drake and the Bruins their first national track and field title.

UCLA could not repeat as champion, however, because the program was put on three years' probation by the NCAA for academic violations in several sports. The penalty prevented the Bruins from competing in the NCAA championships in 1957.

USC, which would win a sixth national title under Mortensen in 1958, beat UCLA in each of the last three years of the 1950s, extending its overall dual-meet winning streak to 80 and their domination during the regular season over the Bruins to 27 years.

BASEBALL

At the start of the 1940s, UCLA still did not have much of a baseball program. The Bruins seemed to get rid of coaches as often as they changed pitchers once Marty Krug left the position in 1939. John Schaeffer, Arthur E. Reichle, Lowell McGinnis and A.J. Sturzenegger each had a turn as UCLA's baseball coach from 1940 to 1943, with the Bruins failing to come close to a .500 record in that span.

Things were very different across town. With Coach Sam Barry, USC's baseball program was the picture of stability. He had taken over in 1930 and, except for a three-year stretch in the Navy, remained coach until he died in 1950. In 1942, Barry made Rod Dedeaux co-coach, and in their six seasons working together, the Trojans won four California Intercollegiate Baseball Association titles and one national championship.

But despite their national success, the Trojans always had to battle when they played the Bruins.

In 1940, UCLA's 4–3, 10-inning victory over USC on April 27 ended the Trojans' hopes of winning the CIBA title. USC responded by pounding the Bruins by a combined score of 19–2 in their final two games, meaningless in terms of the CIBA race but significant measures of revenge.

The next season, USC won all three games against their cross-town rivals on the way to a third-place finish in the CIBA. USC pitchers Ed Vitalich and Bob Foltz each recorded shutouts over the Bruins.

With Dedeaux taking over the

THE UNIVERSITY OF SOUTHERN CALIFORNIA

1947

TROJAN BASEBALL

Trojan team of 1946 · C.I.B.A. Champions

PRESS INFORMATION CIRCULAR

sive UCLA offense that carried the team to a 6–4 conference record. Two of the Bruin league defeats came against Dedeaux's Trojans, who finished conference play undefeated. USC, which also beat UCLA in two nonconference games early in the season, finished 14–2 overall and 10–0 in the CIBA. Ned Haskell led the Trojans' offense with Earl

team when Barry departed for Navy duty, USC's 1942 team returned as CIBA champions with a 12–2 record. One of the Trojans' defeats, however, was to the Bruins, who finished 7–12 under McGinnis. On March 21, UCLA jumped out to an early lead and then coasted behind ace pitcher Rudy Hummes to a 9–6 victory over the highly regarded Trojans.

It was a different story when the teams closed the season with a two-game set. On April 23 at UCLA, the Trojans' Jack Palmer hit a leadoff home run and Vitalich outpitched Hummes in a 2–1 USC victory. Two days later at USC, the Trojans got 27 hits in a 20–1 victory. Bob White led USC in the finale with a triple, double and two singles.

In 1943, Sturzenegger took over at UCLA and the Bruins responded to his coaching with a strong finish in the CIBA Southern California Division. Leadoff man Jack Burgess spearheaded an explo-

Chambers the team's top pitcher.

World War II affected USC's and UCLA's baseball programs in the 1944 and 1945 seasons. Both schools joined California to form a three-team modified CIBA, and the Bruins won

the league title with a 5–3 conference record in 1944, swept a late-season double-header from the Trojans at Westwood on May 27 and finished with a 16–12 overall mark.

In 1945, neither USC nor UCLA could keep pace with Cal, which won the CIBA title. But in their city series battle, the Trojans won three of four games from the Bruins.

After the war, Barry rejoined Dedeaux as co-coach and USC ran away with the CIBA title in 1946. The Trojans finished 15–2 overall and 11–1 in conference play and beat the Bruins in all four of their matchups.

USC had to work overtime for the first of those victories. Hank Workman's home run in the bottom of the 12th inning gave USC a 2–1 victory and broke up a pitching duel between Doug Essick and the Bruins' Jim Daniel. After giving up a run in the first inning, Essick was perfect for the final 11 innings in blanking the Bruins, who were now being coached again by Reichle.

In 1947, Barry and Dedeaux put together the foundation of an eventual national championship team. Behind the pitching of Wally Hood Jr. and Essick, the Trojans finished tied with Cal in the CIBA with an 11–4 conference record. USC also had an opportunistic offense with Bill Lillie, Gordon Jones and Hank Workman.

For the second season in a row, in 1947, the Trojans swept the Bruins. UCLA committed five errors in the ninth inning, and Hood had a strong outing in the first game, won by USC, 9–2, on April 5 at Westwood's Spaulding Field. USC completed the season sweep with back-to-

1940s USC Olympic Medalists

DIVING			
Sammy Lee	1948	Platform	Gold
		Springboard	Bronze
SWIMMING			
Wally Ris	1948	100m Freestyle	Gold
	1948	800m Free Relay	Gold
Wallace Wolf	1948	800m Free Relay	Gold
TRACK AND FIELD			
Clifford Bourland	1948	1600m Relay	Gold
Roy Cochran	1948	400m Hurdles	Gold
	1948	1600m Relay	Gold
Fortune Gordien	1948	Discus	Bronze
Mel Patton	1948	200 meters	Gold
		4x100m Relay	Gold
Wilbur Thompson	1948	Shot Put	Gold

1940s UCLA Olympic Medalists

BASKETBALL			
Don Barksdale	1948		Gold
TRACK AND FIELD			
Craig Dixon	1948	110m High Hurdles	Bronze
Lloyd La Beach (Panama)	1948	100m Dash	Bronze
		200m Dash	Bronze
George Stanich	1948	High Jump	Bronze

back wins over UCLA on March 30–31.

Everything fell into place for the Trojans in 1948. Jones, Lillie and second baseman Art Mazmanian provided the offense, and Dick Bishop and Tom Kipp added to the Trojans' pitching depth for Dedeaux and Barry. Not only did USC enjoy its first 26–victory season against college competition and its third consecutive CIBA title, but the Trojans also won the school's first national championship, a 9–2 triumph over a Yale team that featured future president George H. W. Bush as its captain and first baseman.

After a challenging non-conference schedule that included games against several professional teams, USC finished 13–2 in the CIBA with one of the Trojans' losses coming against UCLA, which finished near the bottom of the conference with a 5–10 mark under Reichle.

In the first of their meetings, Hood limited UCLA to five hits in a 13–0 USC victory, but the Bruins pulled off the upset of the season on April 27 at Westwood when they blanked the Trojans, 2–0, on four hits. USC won the rubber match, 4–3, in 13 innings behind another strong effort by Hood on May 18 at University Park.

USC came close to repeating as national champions in 1949, but the Trojans were knocked out of the College World Series by Wake Forest. During the regular season, USC won its fourth CIBA title in a row and swept two games over UCLA on April 8–9.

In 1950, the Trojans' CIBA winning streak came to an end, in part because of the improvement in Reichle's Bruins. UCLA rode league batting champion Jim Groh's hitting

1950s USC Olympic Medalists

TRACK AND FIELD

Arthur Barnard	1952	110m Hurdles	Bronze
Jack Davis	1952	110m Hurdles	Silver
	1956	110m Hurdles	Silver
Charles Dumas	1956	High Jump	Gold
	1956	Discus	Silver
Fortune Gordien	1956	110m Hurdles	Silver
Sim Iness	1952	Discus	Gold
Desmond Koch	1956	Discus	Bronze
Parry O'Brien	1952	Shot Put	Gold
	1956	Shot Put	Gold

DIVING

Richard Connor	1956	Platform	Bronze
Sammy Lee	1952	Platform	Gold
Paula-Jean Meyers	1952	Platform	Silver
	1956	Platform	Bronze
Gary Tobian	1956	Platform	Silver

SWIMMING

Jon Henricks (Australia)	1956	100m Freestyle	Gold
		800m Free Relay	Gold
Murray Rose (Australia)	1956	400m Freestyle	Gold
		1500m Freestyle	Silver
		800m Free Relay	Gold
Tsuyoshi Yamanaka (Japan)	1956	400m Freestyle	Silver
		1500m Freestyle	Silver

WATER POLO

Miklos Martin (Hungary)	1952	Water Polo	Gold

ROWING

Conn Findlay	1956	Coxed Pair-Oared	Gold

to a 5–10 CIBA record, which included a 7–6, 12–inning victory over USC at Westwood.

The next season, the Bruins fielded one of their strongest teams in years behind football standout Ted Narleski, who had led UCLA in rushing in the fall. Narleski led the CIBA in batting, and the Bruins finished with a 10–6 record in the conference, second by a game to USC. The Trojans won the league title and reached the College World Series again despite splitting four games with the Bruins.

Dedeaux's 1951 team was solid from top to bottom with the Charnofsky twins, Stan and Hal, leading the Trojans in batting, and right-hander Tom Lovrich, the team's top pitcher.

The next season, USC won its second consecutive CIBA championship behind Lovrich, who had a 23–7 record his final two seasons. The Trojans finished 11–5 in league play, including three wins in four games against UCLA.

In 1953, USC finished tied with Stanford for the CIBA title and won all four games against the Bruins, who finished last in the conference. But the Trojans, who were led by Ed Simpson's .404 batting average and Ed Hookstratten's 10–2 record, had their hands full in two one-run games played at UCLA's Spaulding Field.

From 1954 to 1957, USC won four more CIBA championships to extend the streak to seven. The Trojans featured Tony Santino, who had a .360 career average; Gerry Mason, who totaled 19 home runs in 1954–55; and pitcher Marty Zuanich, who had a 15–7 record in 1954–56.

For a while, Reichle was able to keep the Bruins' program competitive against the Trojans. In 1954, UCLA almost spoiled USC's title run by sweeping an early-season doubleheader at Westwood. But the Trojans responded to take the final game, 7–4, at home on May 18.

After the Bruins split with the Trojans again in 1955, USC began to separate itself from its rival. The Trojans outscored the Bruins, 28–13, in sweeping four games during the 1957 season and beat them worse the next year. With a dominant pitching staff led by Bruce Gardner and Bill Thom, the Trojans treated UCLA like a Little League team in 1958, winning by scores of 3–0, 21–2, 23–1 and 15–1 on the way to the school's second national championship. And in 1959, the Trojans ended the decade with their ninth consecutive CIBA championship and extended their winning streak over the Bruins to 16 games.

SWIMMING

Stanford and California were the dominant swimming and diving teams of the PCC in the 1940s and 1950s, with the USC teams of Fred Cady trying to crack the upper echelon. USC regularly defeated UCLA during that time, though both schools had some standout performers.

1950s UCLA Olympic Medalists

TRACK AND FIELD

Charlie Dumas	1956	High Jump	Gold
Rafer Johnson	1956	Decathlon	Silver
Robert McMillen	1952	1500m Run	Silver
George Roubanis (Greece)	1956	Pole Vault	Bronze
Cy Young	1952	Javelin	Gold

MEETS WON 1940s — 1950s

SWIMMING

USC 19 ▪ UCLA 3

Peter Daland USC

UCLA was never his rival

In 1958, Peter Daland took over USC's swimming and diving program, and in his first season coached the Trojans to a 9–0 record in dual meets. Two seasons later, his athletes won USC's first swimming and diving national championship, the first of nine for the Hall of Fame coach.

During Daland's tenure at USC, from 1958 to 1992, Trojan swimmers and divers won 93 NCAA individual and relay titles. His athletes also won 17 national AAU titles (15 men's at USC and two women's at the L.A. Athletic Club). USC finished first or second in the country 21 times in Daland's 35 years.

At the conference level, Daland's teams truly dominated. USC won 17 league titles and produced 155 conference individual or relay titles. His dual-meet record was an astonishing 318–31–1 in 35 seasons. In 20 of those seasons, the Trojans went undefeated in dual meets.

John Naber, who earned four Olympic gold medals and 10 NCAA titles, heads the list of swimmers who were coached by Daland. Included on that list were American-record holders Dave Wharton and Mike O'Brien, Olympians Roy Saar, Murray Rose, Jeff Float, Joe and Mike Bottom, and Bruce and Steve Furniss.

Daland has always maintained a slightly different opinion about USC's rivalry with UCLA than many others who have experienced it.

"First of all, our rival is Stanford and not UCLA," he said. "UCLA should be looking at Berkeley as its rival. Both are large public places. Our rival is Stanford because we are both private schools. To me, you have to talk about universities that are similar. I've always felt that way.

"I feel that basketball and football have gotten sidetracked in this rivalry with UCLA. They talk about bragging rights and all that, but to me and for our program, it's always been very different. Stanford has always been more of a challenge for us.

"After I took over, for the first 10 years, UCLA did not have a strong team nationally. At that point, we had already won five NCAA championships.

"When UCLA did finally win a national title in 1982, that was a stage when we had become quite weak. Our program had declined, possibly from bad coaching, possibly from not having top athletes and possibly because we did not have a big 50-meter pool—while others did.

"It still bothers me that they no longer have a men's program at UCLA. [The program was discontinued in 1994.] Through the years, UCLA got to be pretty solid. They were a good team when Ron Ballatore left. He had the Bruins in the top 10 for 15 years in a row, and there are not too many UCLA teams in any sport that can say that."

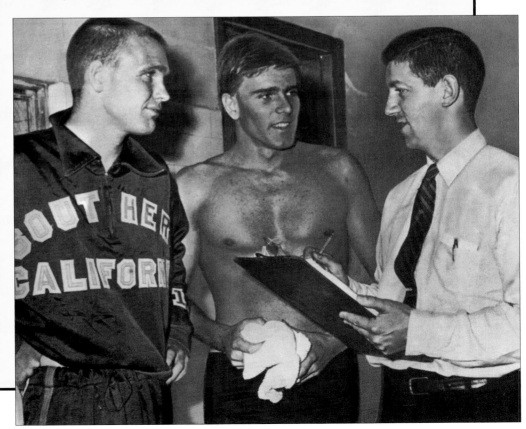

MATCHES WON 1940s — 1950s

WATER POLO

USC 8 — UCLA 5

Before the start of the 1950 season, UCLA hired Brad Cleaveland as swimming coach, but the Bruins still did not win a dual meet. UCLA, which lost to USC twice during the season, did have four-year veteran Don Smith, who established a conference record in the 100-yard freestyle at the PCC championships.

The Trojans had their share of quality swimmers and divers throughout the 1950s, but they failed to win any league titles. Despite having athletes like Wallace Wolf, an eight-time PCC swimming champion from 1948 to 1951, and diver Richard Connor, a four-time league cham-

MATCHES WON 1940s — 1950s

TENNIS

UCLA 8 — USC 2

pion from 1954 to 1956, USC always seemed to fall short against the Northern powers.

WATER POLO

In water polo, USC and UCLA were a little more competitive with each other. The teams split season matches as often as not through the early 1940s until Cady's teams began to improve in the late 1940s.

By 1949, USC had one of the strongest water polo programs in the nation. Dick Kohlhase led the PCC in scoring, and the Trojans finished tied with Stanford for the league title. The Trojans swept UCLA, 11–5 and 13–8, during the season. ■

■ Trojan Yell Kings open the 1958 school year with a bit of spirit. From left: Dick Baldwin, Ernie Stone, Chuck Phillips and Mark Mandala. Opposite: Trojan swimming coach Pete Daland with Jon Henricks, left, and Murray Rose in 1958.

Rise of the Superpowers

Starting with USC's national title in swimming and diving and UCLA's tennis championship in 1960, the cross-town rivals combined for an astounding 34 national titles in the 1960s. The Trojans accounted for 24, with seven in tennis, six in track and field, five in swimming and diving, three in baseball, two in football and one in gymnastics. The Bruins won 10, with Coach John Wooden's basketball teams winning five, Coach J.D. Morgan's tennis teams winning three and Coach Al Scates' volleyball teams winning two.

Lew Alcindor (later Kareem Abdul-Jabbar) soars above his Trojan defenders.

Here are just a few of the highlights from the decade:

■ Under Coach John McKay, USC's football program won two national championships and produced the school's first two Heisman Trophy winners in Mike Garrett and O.J. Simpson. The Trojans defeated the Bruins seven times during the decade and finished ranked in the Associated Press top 10 five times.

■ UCLA basketball began its unparalleled stretch of dominance—10 national championships in 12 seasons. Wooden coached the Bruins to their first title in 1964 and went on to win four more before the end of the decade, generating several All-Americans, from Lew Alcindor, who later changed his name to Kareem Abdul-Jabbar, to Sidney Wicks and Gail Goodrich, the son of the USC star from the late 1930s.

■ In tennis, the national title regularly went to the winner of the USC vs. UCLA matchup. Behind such players as Arthur Ashe and Jack Tidball, the Bruins had a tennis program that was better than any other program outside Los Angeles. Three titles in 10 years would be the envy of just about any athletic director. But, unfortunately for the Bruins, USC had the more successful program in L.A. and won seven championships under Coach George Toley in the decade.

■ Rod Dedeaux coached the Trojans to three national baseball titles with teams that included All-American Tom Seaver.

■ Coach Jess Mortensen led the Trojans to an outdoor track and field national title in 1961, and Vern Wolfe coached the team to four more outdoor titles and one indoor over the rest of the decade. In 1966, the Bruins defeated the Trojans in a dual meet for the first time ever and went on to win a national title under Coach Jim Bush.

■ In swimming and diving, Coach Peter

Daland led USC to five national titles from 1960 to 1966, thanks to such All-American swimmers as Murray Rose, Thomas Winters, Lance Larson and Roy Saari.

■■■■■■■■■

FOOTBALL

It's not hyperbole to say that UCLA and USC have never played a football game quite like the intense, winner-take-all showdown of 1967, a matchup that pitted USC, which had lost only one game that season, against UCLA, then ranked the top team in the nation.

As Paul Zimmerman wrote in *The Times* on Nov. 18, 1967, the day of the game:

"In addition to deciding the city title, Rose Bowl honors and the Pacific Eight crown, this game also may determine the national championship and the Heisman Trophy winner.

"Never in the history of college football have two teams approached the climax of a season with so much at stake."

Sports Illustrated called it simply "Showdown in L.A." and gave the regional matchup a huge national audience by featuring it on the cover of the national magazine.

It's seldom a game can live up to such a buildup. This one did.

When the afternoon was over, a full house of nearly 100,000 at the Coliseum, plus a national television audience of millions, had witnessed a game that arguably is one of the greatest ever in college football history.

The seeds for the game were planted years earlier when both schools sought new coaches to strengthen their football programs. First, in 1959 USC hired John McKay, a little-known assistant coach from the University of Oregon, as an assistant to Coach Don Clark. After being promoted to coach the following year, McKay quickly made his mark, leading the

Trojans to a national title in 1962.

Over in Westwood, the UCLA program endured three straight losing seasons before bringing on Tommy Prothro as coach for the 1965 season. Prothro invigorated the Bruins' program with an innovative and unpredictable offense triggered by quarterback Gary Beban that beat USC in both their 1965 and '66 meetings.

By 1967, McKay's priority was beating Prothro and his pesky Bruins. Not only would a victory in 1967 send the Trojans to the Rose Bowl for the second consecutive

■ Trojan coach John McKay is carried off the field after a win over UCLA in 1962.

year, but McKay felt that it also would answer his critics who believed Prothro had his number and had stolen his thunder among Los Angeles football fans.

So, to put it mildly, there was a lot riding on that Nov. 18 game.

UCLA, led by Beban, now a senior, had

won seven of its eight previous games, amassing in the process 311 points while allowing just 108. The only blemish on a perfect season was a tie against Oregon State.

Meanwhile, USC, paced by O.J. Simpson, the junior college transfer from San Francisco, had won its first eight games in the 1967 season, outscoring its opponents, 223–61, on Simpson's hard running. The Trojans had vaulted to the top of the national rankings until losing, 3–0, to Oregon State the week before the showdown with UCLA.

That loss, in the rain and mud at Corvallis,

■ **Bruin coach Tommy Prothro gets a joy ride after a 1966 victory over USC.**

not only cost the Trojans their No. 1 ranking among the nation's college football teams, but also, to add further insult, their replacements at the top spot were the Bruins.

UCLA's Greg Jones opened the scoring with a 12-yard run in the first quarter. USC tied it at 7–7 when Pat Cashman intercepted a

Beban pass and ran it 55 yards for a touchdown, and the Trojans took a 14–7 lead into halftime on a 13-yard run by Simpson.

On the second play of the second half, Beban hooked up with George Farmer on a 53-yard pass play to tie the score, 14–14. USC's defense took over until Beban put UCLA ahead with a 20-yard touchdown pass to Dave Nuttall early in the fourth quarter. But the Bruins' lead was only six points, 20–14, when Zenon Andrusyshyn's extra-point try was wide.

With Toby Page in at quarterback in place of starter Steve Sogge, Simpson got the ball repeatedly as the Trojans tried to answer Beban's last score. Then on third-and-seven from the USC 36-yard line, Page called a pass play for receiver Ron Drake.

At the line of scrimmage, however, Page noticed that UCLA's linebackers had anticipated a pass, so he audibled to 23–blast, Simpson's favorite play.

Page handed the ball to Simpson and he headed for the left side of the line. Guard Steve Lehmer and tackle Mike Taylor led the way through a huge hole for Simpson. After USC center Dick Allmon knocked down a Bruin linebacker, Simpson ran toward the left sideline and then got a block from Drake, who knocked two UCLA defenders out of the way.

Simpson turned back toward the middle of the field, going right and, escorted by teammate Earl McCullouch, sprinted his way to a game-winning 64-yard touchdown run in a dramatic 21–20 victory.

According to the book "60 Years of USC–UCLA Football," Prothro watched the game-winning play unfold, leaned over to an assistant and, referring to McCullouch, grumbled, "Isn't but one guy can catch Simpson now and he's on the same team."

From *The Times'* Paul Zimmerman:

The 1967 Game

Everything was on the line

The cross-town rivalry was perhaps the least of what mattered in the 1967 matchup between the UCLA and USC football teams. The winner of that November game was assured a spot in the Rose Bowl and a clear shot at the No. 1 national ranking. Also at stake was the Heisman Trophy. USC's candidate was junior halfback O.J. Simpson; UCLA's contender was senior quarterback Gary Beban.

The Trojans won the game, 21–20, on Simpson's electrifying 64-yard cross-field touchdown run in the fourth quarter and went on to the Rose Bowl, where their victory earned them the No. 1 national ranking for the season. Beban, who put together one of the best games of his collegiate career despite playing with badly bruised ribs, passed for 301 yards and two touchdowns and led three drives into USC territory that ended with missed field goals. He won the 1967 Heisman Trophy and remains the only Bruin so honored.

Here's what the two stars of the game remember of that day:

O.J. Simpson:

"I have always said that the 1967 game was easily the highlight of my athletic career. It was far beyond even when I ran on the 4x100 world record team at SC and even more than the 2,000 yards. [In 1973, Simpson became the first NFL player to rush for over 2,000 yards in a season.] I never felt more elated or joy after any athletic event than I did after that game....

"We were coming off a real low point from a week earlier when we lost, 3–0, to Oregon State.... So we were glad to have a chance to redeem ourselves and have a shot at history....

"In 1966, I attended the game as a junior college recruit for USC and saw how intense the rivalry was. I watched UCLA make a fourth-quarter comeback and win. I remember thinking to myself that I would show them the next year.

"[Before the touchdown run] I was tired and had told [USC quarterback] Toby Page to give me a blow. It was third and seven [from the USC 36-yard line], and we had a passing play called. But he switched to a running play at the line of scrimmage. I was so surprised.

"When [Page] did that, UCLA went into a pass-mode on defense.... When I broke outside, I could hear McKay yelling for me to go, and I was trying to zigzag. I was tired and knew that I didn't have that burst.... I was so oblivious to the crowd. I just remember that I almost collapsed

Sports Illustrated

NOVEMBER 20, 1967   40 CENTS

GARY BEBAN

USC vs. UCLA: SHOWDOWN IN L.A.

O. J. SIMPSON

when [teammate] Earl McCullouch hugged me in the end zone.

"The rest of the game was just a blur. I kept waiting for Gary Beban to bring UCLA back to take back the lead, but it never happened."

(Simpson, who now lives in Florida, won the Heisman Trophy in 1968 and went on to a record-breaking 11-year professional career in the NFL. He later became a sports announcer, celebrity pitchman and sometime actor before being accused in the 1994 Los Angeles murder of his ex-wife and her acquaintance. He was acquitted of the criminal charges a year later, but in 1997 he was held liable in civil court for both deaths and ordered to pay millions in restitution to the victims' families.)

Gary Beban:

"We came into the game confident. We were No. 1 in the nation and we had beaten USC for the last two years. We were playing in a game [which would likely settle the national championship] that few college players ever get because of opportunities that we had created for ourselves.

"When we came onto the field we had to cross the track that was filled with TV cables, and we felt the energy of the Coli-

■ **Top: O.J. Simpson races for the winning TD in 1967. Bottom: Quarterback Gary Beban.**

seum immediately. You could tell it was going to be a special day.

"I never saw O.J.'s run because my ribs were always being worked on when I wasn't in the game. But when we came back [after the Simpson touchdown], we still had 10 minutes. We still had time to score and we assumed that we were going to score.

"The seniors hadn't lost a game on California soil in our college careers. We were a relatively undefeated team—just two ties and three losses in three years—and we had always beaten SC in our careers. We didn't have a defeated attitude at all; we just assumed we would score.

"In the end we were disappointed. It was the end of the season and the end of a college career for me. We had gotten so close. But still we had gotten so far. That game was the best of the series. Everything in college sports was on the line: the city championship, the conference title, the Rose Bowl and the national championship. Even the Heisman. There was nothing else you could put on the table. This was the pinnacle of college football.

"What else could you ask for?"

(After leaving UCLA, Beban was drafted by the Los Angeles Rams but was immediately traded to Washington, where he played two seasons with the Redskins before leaving pro football for a career in real estate. Beban is executive managing director for global corporate services in the Chicago office of the real estate firm of CB Richard Ellis. He was elected into the College Football Hall of Fame in 1988.)

"Whether that run earns Simpson the Heisman Trophy and moves coach John McKay's Trojans back as the No. 1 team in the nation remains for the voters to decide later. But the witnesses will remember this game as one of the greatest."

Times columnist Jim Murray wrote afterward: "Whew!

"I'm glad I didn't go to the opera Saturday afternoon, after all. This was the first time in a long time where the advance ballyhoo didn't live up to the game.

"The last time these many cosmic events were settled by one day of battle, they struck off a commemorative stamp and elected the winner President.

"On that commemorative stamp, they can put a double image—one of UCLA's Gary Beban and one of USC's Orenthal James Simpson. They can send that Heisman Trophy out with two straws, please."

Beban did win the 1967 Heisman, becoming the first (and only) Bruin to get the award. But Simpson and the Trojans got the ultimate team prize when USC defeated Indiana in the Rose Bowl and took home the school's sixth national championship, the second under McKay.

Such a finish might have seemed virtually impossible seven years earlier as the new decade started. The Trojans finished 4–6 in the 1960 season, McKay's first at the helm. The team's high point that year was a victory over UCLA that ended a three-year winless streak against the Bruins.

Heading into that showdown at the Coliseum, USC and UCLA were going in opposite directions. The Trojans, who had scored only six points in losing their first three games under McKay, had lost two in a row before facing the Bruins. Under Bill Barnes, in his second full

season coaching UCLA, the Bruins were starting to come together and had won four consecutive games, the last three by shutouts.

McKay started sophomore quarterback Bill Nelsen against a team that had the top offense and defense in the Athletic Association of Western Universities. UCLA's offense was led by versatile halfback Bill Kilmer, who was expected to be too much to handle for the leaky Trojans' defense, which had given up at least 34 points in its two previous games.

The Trojans jumped to a 14–0 lead on two second-quarter touchdowns, a 21-yard pass from Nelsen to end Marlin McKeever and a two-yard run by fullback Hal Tobin. The Trojan defense focused on shutting down Kilmer in the second half, and he was limited to 29 yards rushing and completed only four of 17 passes for 80 yards with three interceptions. USC, which out-gained UCLA 333–171, won 17–6.

In 1961, the Bruins got their revenge.

UCLA had begun the season sluggishly and, struggling on offense, lost two of three games. But the Bruins got on track behind multipurpose back Bobby Smith and running back Mike Haffner and won their next five.

Meanwhile, the Trojans and McKay were suffering through another mediocre season despite the team's switch to an I-formation offense that featured tailback Willie Brown leading a powerful running game. But the ground attack wasn't too strong against the Bruins on a rainy November day at the Coliseum.

With a Rose Bowl bid on the line for the first time in nine years, UCLA used a 31-yard field goal and a six-yard touchdown run by Smith to defeat the Trojans, 10–7, and earn its first trip to the Jan. 1 bowl game since the 1955 season. Although UCLA lost to Minnesota, 21–7, in Pasadena, their 7–4 season

■ Opposite: Trojan stars— and brothers— Marlin and Mike McKeever, along with USC's first Heisman winner, Mike Garrett.

looked a lot better than USC's 4–5–1.

Not a lot was expected from USC in 1962. But with several juniors returning as starters, including quarterback Pete Beathard, end Hal Bedsole and Brown, McKay's program was definitely coming together. Heading into their game against the Bruins, USC was ranked No. 1 in the nation with an 8–0 record.

UCLA had also started the season off well with a 9–7 victory over top-ranked Ohio State and a 35–7 win over Colorado State. But then the Bruin offense lost its way; UCLA scored only 50 points in losing four of its next five games.

With a 3–4 record, the Bruins took the field against USC at the Coliseum, looking to salvage the season with a victory. UCLA took a 3–0 lead into half-time on a 35-yard field goal by Larry Zeno. The Bruins continued to contain USC in the second half until Brown made a high-light-reel catch on fourth down to set up a two-yard touchdown by Beathard.

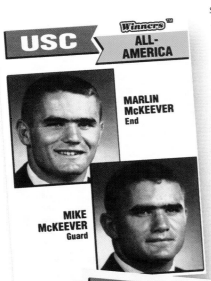

The Trojans scored again in the final minute to defeat UCLA, 14–3. USC then beat Notre Dame the next week and Wisconsin in the Rose Bowl to win the program's fifth national championship.

In 1963, Mike Garrett took over at tailback, and the Trojan offense became even more explosive. Garrett was quick and ran with power, and

McKay had the back he wanted to build an offense around.

But USC quickly fell out of the running for another AAWU title, perhaps making it easier for McKay to give UCLA a heavy dose of Garrett in the season finale. Garrett, a sophomore, ran all over the Bruins, who had limped into the game with a 2–7 record. It wasn't even close as the Trojans won, 26–6. Garrett ran for 119 yards to finish the season with 833 rushing yards.

In 1964, the Bruins improved to 4–6, but their defense was a concern, giving up at least 20 points in eight of the 10 games. USC, which had high expectations at season's start, was a disappointing 5–3 heading into the UCLA game.

Still, the Trojans had an outside chance of returning to the Rose Bowl, but they needed a victory over UCLA and an Oregon State loss. USC did what it could, trouncing the Bruins, 34–13. Oregon State, however, also won and got the Rose Bowl bid.

Garrett rushed for 181 yards, and quarterback Craig Fertig passed for three touchdowns for the Trojans, who won their third in a row over UCLA with their most lopsided victory over the Bruins in 20 years.

The Bruins' struggling finish that season—they lost their last three games—ended the Barnes era. He resigned shortly after the loss to USC.

Enter James Thompson "Tommy" Prothro.

An assistant to Red Sanders at Vanderbilt in the late 1940s and at UCLA in the 1950s, Prothro was head coach at Oregon State before returning to Westwood. Although UCLA was coming off three consecutive losing seasons, Prothro was optimistic the spring before his first season as coach, in part because of a developing sophomore quarter-

■ **Opposite: the play that won the 1965 game. Bruin QB Gary Beban (top) sets up to pass to Kurt Altenberg (bottom), who hauls in it for a touchdown.**

back named Gary Beban.

Prothro spoke of Beban to *The Times'* Al Wolf that May: "He's not great in any department, but he's good in all aspects of quarterbacking and just might develop greatness. I certainly hope so."

Prothro did not have to wait long to see that his prediction about Beban was correct. Taking advantage of Prothro's creative offensive schemes, Beban led the Bruins to a 6–1–1 record and a No. 7 ranking heading into the game against USC.

For USC, the 1965 season had been solid except for a midseason loss at Notre Dame and a season-opening tie against Minnesota.

With both teams unbeaten in conference play, the winner was assured a trip to the Rose Bowl, which raised the stakes for both McKay and Prothro.

The Times' Paul Zimmerman wrote: "If there is anything that hurts coach John McKay more than defeat, it is getting beaten with the long pass. It is for this reason that he has worked his USC defense overtime this week. Gary Beban of UCLA loves to unload the big bomb on opponents."

It turned out that the Bruins did need a trick play to beat the Trojans. They also needed plenty of Beban. Behind two touchdown passes from quarterback Troy Winslow and a field goal by Tim Rossovich, USC held a 16–6 lead with four

minutes remaining in the fourth quarter. Many Trojan supporters were getting their plans together for the Rose Bowl when UCLA rallied.

Following USC's fifth turnover of the game, Beban completed a 34-yard touchdown pass to Dick Witcher and a two-point conversion to Byron Nelson to make the score 16–14. Then Prothro called an onside kick, which UCLA recovered on the Trojans' 48. With 2:39 remaining, Beban sent UCLA to the Rose Bowl when his 48-yard touchdown pass to Kurt Altenberg gave the Bruins' a 20–16 victory at the Coliseum.

Despite being out-gained in yardage, 424–289, including 210 yards rushing from Garrett, UCLA won the AAWU title, and after the game a crowd of 3,000 students held up traffic on Westwood and Wilshire boulevards to clang the Victory Bell. (The Trojans salvaged something from the season the following month when Garrett won the Heisman Trophy, the first ever for USC.)

The Bruins finished their 1965 season with a 14–12 victory over No. 1 Michigan State in the Rose Bowl. The victory was the Bruins' first in six trips to Pasadena, and for Prothro the win capped off a very successful 8–2–1 season.

The Times' Jim Murray wrote about Prothro's impact on UCLA's football program in 1965: "They never call the team the 'Red Tide,' the 'Purple Puddle,' the 'Brown Wave,' the 'Thundering Herd,' or any other ringing alterations selected by other schools. For one reason. Usually, UCLA was more like a 'Pink T,' or the 'Thundering Bird,' The Red Tide was coming from its nose. If the student body rose to chant 'we're No. 1,' they meant in chemistry—or interior decoration...."

"J. Thompson Prothro changed all that.... Coach Prothro took a squad that had lost six of its last seven games and had given up 147 points in five of those games. How he convinced them they could play football has to rank as the greatest snow job since 1888."

Prothro repeated his magic in 1966. With Beban back as the leader of the Bruins and Mel Farr emerging as a dominant back, UCLA won eight of its first nine games. The Bruins' lone loss came against Washington, but they were still ranked No. 8 in the nation heading into their showdown against the Trojans.

Even with Garrett having graduated, USC still had a strong team in 1966. The Trojans had a 7–1 record going into the game and were in position to win the AAWU title.

Things were crazy around Westwood the week leading up to the game. Beban had suffered an ankle injury against Stanford the previous game, and there was some question whether the All-American quarterback could play. Prothro said he wouldn't; the Trojans believed otherwise.

With defensive back Nate Shaw, tackle Ron Yary and flanker Rod Sherman, the Trojans had plenty of talent, and when Norman Dow replaced Beban, no one gave UCLA much of a chance.

But Dow, who was making his first start in his last-ever game as a Bruin, proved to be the difference in the game. He scored the game's first touchdown on a five-yard sweep in the third quarter. After USC tied it on a short run by Dan Scott, Dow took over.

With less than 10 minutes remaining in the fourth quarter, Dow's running sparked a long UCLA drive that was capped by a reverse by Cornell Champion for a touchdown. The Bruins won, 14–7.

Immediately after the game, the debate over which team should go to the Rose Bowl began. USC was the conference champion, but UCLA had won their matchup.

On Monday after the game, nearly 7,000 people attended a campus rally to honor the Bruins' victory. But an hour into a lively celebration, UCLA, with a 3–1 conference record, learned that USC had been selected by the AAWU conference to go to the Rose Bowl. It was at this rally that the lingering nickname of "gutty little Bruins" took shape.

While talking to the crowd, Dow said, "I read all the newspapers and I think they overworked my part in the victory." The crowd responded with a spontaneous, "No!"

Then Dow added: "I'm honored to be on such a gutty team."

An image was born.

USC lost to Notre Dame the next week, then lost to Purdue in the Rose Bowl, 14–13, to finish the season 7–4.

By 1968, with Simpson returning for his senior season, the Trojans were looking for their first repeat as national champions. Over at UCLA, the Bruins were strug-

■ The 1969 Trojan football media guide featured coach John McKay. Opposite: Guards watch over a swaddled Tommy Trojan statue on a rainy night before the 1963 Bruin game.

TROJAN FOOTBALL 1969 University of Southern California

Football Fun and Folly: Part 2

Pranks and blunders, 1950–1970

In the 1950s and 1960s, competition between USC and UCLA continued to produce some very successful and not-so-successful pranks.

In 1957, a Trojan student posing as a Bruin joined the UCLA card stunt team, the group of fans who create large images with placards during football games. Before the big game, he altered the cards to display the USC logo in the corner of the group image when the cards were flashed. By the time his chicanery was discovered, there was no time to undo the damage.

Never had the Bruins' card stunts received such wild cheers from the USC side.

Before the 1958 game, more than 100 USC students were put on guard to protect the school's mascot, Tommy Trojan, which sits in the middle of campus. In previous years, UCLA had somehow managed to get to the mascot with paint, glue and even a blowtorch.

But with so many Trojans acting as security, the Bruins had to take their attack to a new level. They went to the air with a rented helicopter and showered Tommy Trojan with 500 pounds of fertilizer.

In 1966, two USC freshmen were caught putting anti-Bruin posters on UCLA campus trees and buildings. They were taken to separate fraternity houses and kept overnight. The young Trojans had their pants filled with cold mayonnaise and ice cubes, and their clothing was soaked with beer and shaving cream.

Both men also had their heads shaved, and one was painted from head to toe in blue and gold. They were found chained to a fire hydrant on the UCLA campus the next morning.

In 1958, a group of USC students kidnapped the driver for the company that delivered the Daily Bruin to the UCLA campus and substituted his load of newspapers with about 3,000 copies of a satirical replica of the UCLA paper.

On the front page of the SC version of the Daily Bruin were pictures of USC football coach Don Clark and USC President Norman Topping. The banner headline read, "Highly Spirited SC Rates Wide Choice."

The USC students, disguised in UCLA blue sweaters, distributed the phony papers in the Daily Bruin's regular campus circulation boxes.

Perhaps the most outlandish prank never got off the ground. In November 1961, Los Angeles police were tipped off about a couple of USC students who supposedly had planted explosives in the Coliseum field before the game.

Police dug up what were believed to be three half-sticks of dynamite behind the east goal post. Wires leading to the wall in front of the USC cheering section were anchored near an electrical outlet. Police did not announce their finding until after the game and kept the wires under surveillance, but nobody went near them.

Less than a month later, two USC students confessed that they had planted the sticks, which were smoke bombs, not dynamite.

gling to get by without Beban, their 1967 Heisman winner, who had graduated a few months earlier.

With sophomore Jim Nader and junior Bill Bolden stepping in at quarterback for Beban, the Bruins' had to rely heavily on tailback Greg Jones and a stingy defense. The combination led to a 3–6 record heading into USC week.

■ **O.J. Simpson accepts his Heisman Trophy in 1968.**

who scored two touchdowns and had a 68-yard punt return. Trailing, 21–16, in the fourth quarter, the Bruins drove deep into USC territory only to have Nader's fourth-down pass to Gwen Cooper knocked away by linebacker Bob Jensen.

Simpson, who would win the Heisman Trophy in 1968, completed the scoring with a short touchdown run late in the game.

Prothro had the Bruins back among the nation's best teams in 1969. In quarterback Dennis Dummit, a transfer from Long Beach City College, the Bruins had one of the best passers in the nation, and he led UCLA to an 8–0–1 record heading into the USC game.

The Bruins were running opponents off the field. They scored at least 32 points in seven of their nine games before playing the Trojans. Prothro's team finally featured the high-powered offense that he loved.

USC tailback Clarence Davis, a junior college transfer who had taken over for Simpson, led the Pac-8 in rushing, but the Trojans' biggest strength was on defense with the Wild Bunch, a nickname for USC's front line.

With the Rose Bowl on the line, the Bruins struck first with a halfback option touchdown pass from quarterback Dummit to Farmer in the opening quarter. Since a tie wouldn't qualify them for the Rose Bowl, the Bruins went for the two-point conversion and failed.

USC took a 7–6 lead on a 13-yard run by Davis, but the Bruins regained their edge when Dummit completed a seven-yard touchdown pass to Gwen Cooper late in the fourth quarter. But again, UCLA missed a two-point conversion attempt.

With USC trailing, 12–7, and a little

Thanks to Simpson, who led the nation in rushing, USC won its first eight games and took the field against the Bruins undefeated. The Trojans had already won the Pacific-8 Conference title and a berth in their third Rose Bowl in a row.

But despite that record, the Trojans had to fight for their lives against the Bruins on a foggy day at the Coliseum. With Simpson rushing for 205 yards in 40 carries, the Trojans managed a hard-fought 28–16 victory.

The Bruins had a chance to win late thanks to the play of running back Mickey Cureton,

GAMES WON
The 1960s
FOOTBALL
USC 7 ▪ UCLA 3

more than three minutes remaining in the game, Jimmy Jones led the Trojans on a furious final drive. On fourth-and-10, Jones overthrew Sam Dickerson on the sideline. But interference was called on UCLA's Danny Graham, giving USC an automatic first down on the Bruin 32.

On the next play, Jones completed a touchdown pass to Dickerson in the right corner of the end zone to give the Trojans a 14–12 victory and their fourth consecutive trip to the Rose Bowl, where they defeated Michigan to close out the '60s.

For Graham and the Bruins, the loss to the Trojans was difficult to accept. *The Times'* Dwight Chapin wrote on Nov. 23: "It was so quiet you could hear a rose petal fall. The only sound in the UCLA locker room was the occasional slam of a door as the players slowly made their way out of their cubicles and to the showers. The sound of the doors swinging shut would crack and then it would be quiet—very quiet—again.

"Some of them sobbed behind those locker-room doors, unbelieving, waiting in the solitude for the reprieve that wasn't to come. It was Danny Graham, the young man of misfortune, the young man guilty of pass interference that gave USC life—and later the ball game—who was able to articulate the sorrow best.

"'It seems,' he said, 'like my whole life just went down the drain.'"

■ **UCLA students parade the Victory Bell along Westwood Boulevard after the Bruins' 1961 win.**

About Trojans, Bruins and Mascots

Some trials—and a lot of errors

It's hard to imagine USC not being known as the Trojans, but that was the case when the University of Southern California was founded in 1880. The school was referred to as the Methodists or Wesleyans until 1912, when Warren Bovard, USC's director of athletics, asked Los Angeles Times sportswriter Owen Bird to give the university a new nickname.

Bird came up with "Trojans" because he compared USC players of the time to noble Trojan warriors who were facing teams that were bigger and better equipped. Bird loved how USC teams had a fighting spirit and began to refer to them as Trojans in all his articles, starting with a track and field meet between USC and Stanford on Feb. 28, 1912.

UCLA also had to go through more than one nickname before sticking with the Bruins. Regarded as the younger sibling of the University of California Berkeley Bears when founded in 1919, UCLA was known as the Southern Branch Cubs its first four years.

The student body decided on the Grizzlies in 1923, and that was UCLA's nickname until the school began competing in the Pacific Coast Conference in 1928. But the University of Montana, which already was in the PCC, made noise about a new team coming into the conference with the same nickname it had used for 30 years.

The Southern Branch became UCLA, and the next year the nickname was changed to Bruins.

In the early 1930s, UCLA students asked that the school use a live rented bear as a mascot. That lasted for several years until the bears' behavior in front of large Coliseum crowds during football games became problematic. The situation reached a head when the bear escaped from its trainer and clawed a person in a wheelchair.

The Coliseum banned UCLA's "wild" mascot the next year.

The Bruins switched to more manageable bear cubs in the early 1940s, but young bears grow into adults. In the early 1950s, UCLA bought a 6-month-old Himalayan bear from India and named him "Little Joe Bruin." But Little Joe Bruin grew into Big Joe Bruin and became too large to use as a mascot at games.

In 1961, the Bruins' alumni tried again and acquired another bear named Josephine. She was kept in the backyard of UCLA rally committee chairman Russ Serber and lasted a season. But like her mascot predecessors, Josephine eventually grew too large and was moved to a zoo.

By the mid-1960s, UCLA had given up on the live animal mascot and began using costumed students, creating Joe Bruin. In 1967, the first female mascot, Josephine Bruin, joined her male counterpart at games.

Traveler, the white horse with a Trojan warrior astride, made its debut at the Coliseum for a USC football game against Georgia Tech on Sept. 22, 1961.

Bob Jani, then USC's director of special events, and Eddie Tannenbaum, a junior at USC, had observed Richard Saukko riding his white horse, Traveler I, in the 1961 Rose Parade and asked Saukko and Traveler to serve as a mascot during USC games at the Coliseum by galloping around the field after every Trojan touchdown while the school band played "Conquest."

Traveler didn't get a lot of work in that first game, a 27–7 loss, but over the years, he has become one of the most famous college mascots in history.

BASKETBALL

At the start of the 1960s, UCLA had yet to win a national championship under Coach John Wooden, and USC was still considered a serious challenge for the Bruins.

Neither team was in the hunt for the Athletics Association of Western Universities league title in the 1959–60 season, a season in which the Bruins and Trojans played each other five times. Wooden's team lacked a dominant player, but the coach was still able to get enough out of his team to defeat the Trojans three times in a 14–12 season.

USC, however, took the most important game of the season series. With an NCAA District 8 at-large bid at stake, the Trojans defeated UCLA, 91–71. Steve Kemp led the Trojans with 19 points, and All-American center John Rudometkin added 18 for USC, which got the NCAA nod over UCLA because the Trojans had a better overall record.

That made for a heated final game between the schools on March 5, 1960, at the Sports Arena.

With the city series even at 2–2, USC and UCLA played each other evenly, and with 21 seconds remaining, the Bruins held a 68–66 lead. Kemp and UCLA's Bill Hicks got tangled

■ Bruin star Walt Hazzard.

up diving for a loose ball and Kemp managed to gain control, dropping Hicks to the floor.

Hicks quickly jumped up and confronted Kemp. USC's Rudometkin was the first to join the fray to defend Kemp. Both benches emptied in one of the most intense brawls of the rivalry. Before the melee ended, fans and coaches had joined the players on the court. A total of eight technical fouls were called in the game, which was won by UCLA, 72–70, on a last-second basket by Pete Blackman.

USC was determined to get back at the Bruins in 1960–61.

With Rudometkin stepping up as a big-time player, averaging 24.8 points to lead the AAWU in scoring, the Trojans won the conference title, thanks to two victories in three games against the Bruins.

Wooden's team was his best in four years, with forward Ron Lawson leading the team in scoring at 13.7 points a game. The Bruins and Trojans ended up in a battle all season, and it came down to a third-game rubber match at the Sports Arena in which Rudometkin scored from inside and out and Ken Stanley added just enough support for the Trojans to pull out an 86–85 overtime victory.

The 1961–62 season brought the first of an incredible stretch of 17 conference titles in 18 years for UCLA. John Green was the Bruins' top scorer, Fred Slaughter the top rebounder and Walt Hazzard the team's young floor leader. UCLA rolled to a 10–2 record in the AAWU and 18–11 overall. (One of the Bruins' conference losses came against the Trojans, who beat them, 74–60, in the second meeting of the season.)

Wooden had another strong team in 1962–63. With Hazzard taking over as UCLA's top scorer and Slaughter being more of a force inside, the Bruins finished tied for first in the AAWU but lost in the first round of the NCAA tournament.

Hazzard scored 27 points in each of UCLA's two victories over the Trojans in their first two matchups of that season. But in the third contest, UCLA got turnover-happy in the second half and blew a 13–point halftime lead in a 62–60 loss. It would be the last time for five years a Wooden-coached team would lose to the Trojans.

UCLA, 56–28 in the three previous seasons, began to find the answer to the big puzzle in 1963–64.

Led by the explosive scoring duo of Gail Goodrich and Hazzard, the Bruins rushed

■ **Gail Goodrich dribbles around Trojan John Zazzaro en route to the basket in 1964. Opposite: Bruin coach John Wooden and his 1964 NCAA championship team.**

through their opposition on the way to a 30–0 record and the program's first national title with a 98–83 victory over Duke.

The Bruins' national success changed the dynamics of their rivalry with the Trojans, who fell to 10–16 in 1964. It was only the second time in Forrest Twogood's career at

USC that the Trojans finished under .500.

In the 1964–65 season, UCLA swept USC again but did not go through the schedule undefeated. The Bruins were trounced by Illinois, 110–83, in the season opener, then won 28 of their next 29 games, including a 91–80 victory over Michigan in the NCAA title game.

After playing for so many years in the campus men's gym, Venice High School and Pan Pacific Auditorium, UCLA moved into state-of-the-art Pauley Pavilion for the start of the 1965–66 season.

But the Bruins failed to duplicate their success of the two previous seasons. Poor late-season outings against the Oregon schools cost UCLA as the Bruins (18–8) not only failed to win their third NCAA title in a row but did not even win a share of a league title. The highlight for the rivalry was sophomore Mike Warren's 35 points scored for the Bruins in a 99–62 victory over the Trojans at the Sports Arena to complete the season.

The real interest on the UCLA campus was the star-studded freshman class, led by Lew Alcindor, the highly recruited prep star from Power Memorial High School in New York.

No previous player, not

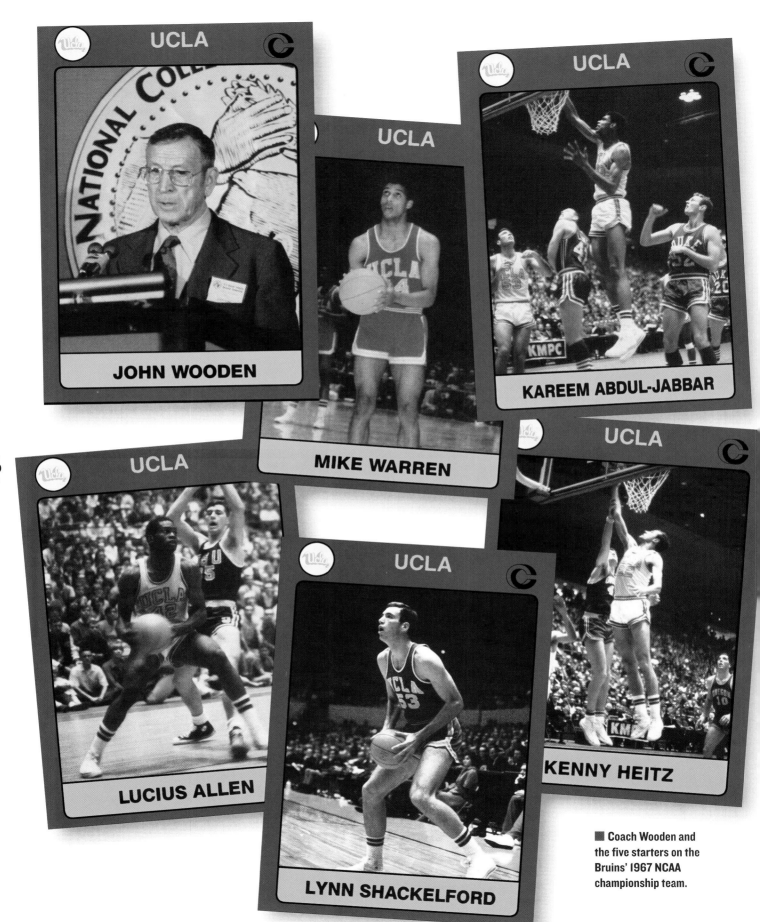

UCLA

JOHN WOODEN

UCLA

MIKE WARREN

UCLA

KAREEM ABDUL-JABBAR

UCLA

LUCIUS ALLEN

UCLA

LYNN SHACKELFORD

UCLA

KENNY HEITZ

■ Coach Wooden and
the five starters on the
Bruins' 1967 NCAA
championship team.

even Wilt Chamberlain or Oscar Robertson, had attracted as much attention while in high school as Alcindor, who was 7 feet 1, quick, graceful and polished.

The freshmen gave a hint of things to come when they beat the two-time defending champion varsity before the start of the season. (Freshmen were not eligible to play varsity at the time.)

After the Trojans finished 12–14 under Twogood in 1965–66, USC made a coaching switch and hired Bob Boyd. It was his misfortune that Alcindor and the rest of UCLA's talented freshman class, including Lucius Allen and Lynn Shackleford, were ready to make their mark on the college game.

It was only fitting that Alcindor made his collegiate varsity debut against Boyd and the Trojans.

Alcindor destroyed the Trojans in a 105–90 UCLA victory, finishing the game with a school-record 56 points. He made 23 of 32 shots from the field and grabbed 14 rebounds. Alcindor's performance overshadowed a strong game by USC's Bill Hewitt, a junior college transfer who led the Trojans with 39 points.

The next time USC faced the Bruins, UCLA and Alcindor again enjoyed a big win, 107–83, which made Boyd rethink his game plan for the Bruins. After USC had given up more than 100 points in their first two meetings, Boyd ordered

■ **Lew Alcindor as a freshman in 1965.**

a stall in the third game, at the Sports Arena.

The tactic worked enough to send the game into overtime. But again, the Bruins won, 40–35. UCLA completed the city series sweep with an 83–55 victory in the final regular-season game for the Trojans. The Bruins ended their season by defeating Dayton for the NCAA championship.

Wooden's 1967 championship team had a lot more talent than just Alcindor. As a junior captain, Warren was the veteran of a young team that included sophomores Allen and Shackleford.

Song Girls Come to USC

Trojans fought on (and on) to get them

In 1967, at college campuses across the nation, students were protesting the war in Vietnam and the military draft that was sending thousands of young men there.

The times were a-changin' at USC, as well.

That year, the campus administration, under pressure from students and even some alumni, allowed a campus referendum on whether to create a squad of song girls to cheer on Trojan teams.

The outcome of the student vote was overwhelming, and later that year some 70 contenders tried out for the first squad. Seven were chosen, and they gave their first performance at a basketball game in January 1968.

Why USC had never enjoyed the benefits of female spirit raisers in its previous 88 years remains a bit fuzzy. One story has it as being the wish of Trojan coaches who did not want anything to distract players' attention from the game. An account in the Los Angeles Times by Celeste Fremon, who was one of those initial seven Song Girls, as they were called then, says a wealthy alum had given USC a sizable gift along with orders that no women, except band members, were to be allowed on the playing field. Whatever the reason, until 1968, only male yell leaders were admitted to USC's school spirit department.

But although it took USC a while to get its "Song Leaders," as they are now called, it didn't take long for those USC squads to establish themselves as the gold standard against which all other teams were to be judged. Just a few years after their creation, USC squads won several consecutive national championships until the school decided to stop competing.

Some squads have toured Europe and Japan; some have appeared on Johnny Carson's "Tonight Show." The first team was introduced to all of America on a Bob Hope special. And, according to Ann Bothwell, whose late husband, Lindley, was the squad's first coach, USC's Song Leaders were the inspiration for another high-water mark of sports entertainment: the Laker Girls of L.A.'s most prominent NBA franchise.

In 1997, the USC Song Leaders were voted best cheerleaders in America by Sports Illustrated.

■ USC's first song girl squad. Front row from left: Celeste Fremon, Penny Ward, and Claudia Paulon. Back row from left: Susan Wright, Linda Hauf, Charlene Gonzales and Susanne Knolle.

losing to Houston in the Astrodome two weeks before they faced the Trojans for the first time in 1968.

Boyd was having more success in his second season, and the Trojans thought they would be able to stay close to UCLA and even pull out a win down the stretch. But it didn't turn out that way. The Bruins swept both games, 101–67 and 72–64, to extend their winning streak over USC to 16 games.

The final year of the 1960s again featured Alcindor and Shackleford, now teaming with sophomores Curtis Rowe and Sidney Wicks. UCLA opened the season with 25 consecutive victories, including a tough, 61–55, double-overtime win over USC on March 7 at the Sports Arena. The next night, the same two teams met again at Pauley Pavilion. Only this time, Boyd's squad accomplished what everyone said couldn't be done: The Trojans beat Wooden and the Bruins in their new gym.

Ernie Powell, USC's leading scorer, and point guard Mack Calvin played strong games, and the Trojans' inte-

Lucius Allen in 1968.

With three national titles in four years, UCLA's basketball program was just picking up steam. The next season, the Bruins extended their winning streak to 47 games before rior players held their ground against Alcindor just enough in USC's 46–44 upset victory. It was UCLA's first loss at Pauley Pavilion since it opened for the 1965–66 season.

TRACK AND FIELD

Heading into the 1960 season, USC's track program was in somewhat of a slump, at least by its lofty standards. The Trojans had won nine consecutive NCAA team titles from 1935 to 1943 and seven in a row in the 1950s, but they

had won only one in the previous four seasons.

Still, USC was the class of the West Coast. With weight thrower Dallas Long and triple jumper Luther Hayes leading the way, USC dominated league competition and extended its dual-meet winning streak to 85. Against UCLA, the Trojans rolled to an 81–51 victory at East Los Angeles College.

But again, USC fell short of an NCAA championship when the Trojans failed to produce any points in running events to add to victories by Hayes and Long.

UCLA had one national champion in high hurdler Jimmy Johnson and finished third at the 1960 NCAA meet. But later that summer, at the 1960 Rome Olympics, the Bruins of Coach Ducky Drake finished 1–2 in the decathlon when Rafer Johnson defeated teammate C.K. Yang and broke the

■ **Shot putters Dallas Long, left, and Dave Davis at 1960 meet.**
■ **Center: C. K. Yang with Coach Ducky Drake.**
■ **Bottom: Coach Vern Wolfe.**

Olympic record for the event.

In 1961, the Trojans extended their dual-meet victory streak to 92, including an 81.5–to-49.5 victory over the Bruins. Long set a dual-meet record of 63 feet in the shot put and Rex Cawley broke a 22-year-old record in the 440 in 47.1 seconds. USC went on to win its first NCAA title since 1958 behind Long's victory in the shot put, Hayes' win in the triple jump and Jim Brewer's first-place tie in the pole vault.

The title was the seventh in 11 years for Coach Jess Mortensen, who died before the start of the 1962 season of a pulmonary embolism.

With Athletic Director Jess Hill acting as interim coach, the Trojans finally lost a dual meet when Oregon defeated USC, 75–56, at the Coliseum on April 21, 1962, the Trojans' first defeat since 1945.

Before the NCAA meet that season, *The Times'* Al Wolf wrote that he believed the age of USC's domination might be nearing an end: "Track teams are getting better all over the country. Where USC formerly was one of the sport's few strongholds, improved coaching and brisker recruiting have produced a leveling effect."

■ USC's 1967 world record relay team; from left: Earl McCullouch, Fred Kuller, O.J. Simpson and Lennox Miller.

John Smith UCLA

Running for bragging rights

In 1969, freshman John Smith ran the second leg on UCLA's winning mile relay team at the NCAA championship meet, and over the next three years he would go on to win five more national titles. But for Smith, the pressure of the NCAA meets was never as intense as it was when UCLA met USC.

"The UCLA–USC meet is always special," Smith said. "Throw records and previous marks out the window. Scholarships are won, jobs are lost and careers are born on that meet. Whenever the Bruins and Trojans compete against each other, anything can happen.

"When I was growing up in Los Angeles, I had a lot of USC influences around me. Charlie Dumas, who competed on the Trojan track team years ago, was my junior high coach. I always heard from him about the rivalry. Once I got to high school and began attending Fremont, I had a couple of teachers from UCLA. So things always seemed to balance out. It's always been a flavorful rivalry to me.

"No matter what professional teams are in the city, there's always going to just be UCLA and USC. It could be the Dodgers and Angels; the Rams and Raiders; Lakers and Kings. The UCLA vs. USC rivalry has always owned L.A.... When I was coming up, everything stopped when UCLA and SC played. It was like a holiday or the Super Bowl. It was contagious.

"It went through every sport. People divide when it comes to UCLA vs. USC. You see families split up. You can be friends afterward, but during regulation time when the two schools met, you are on totally opposite ends of the spectrum.

"When I was growing up in South-Central Los Angeles, everyone was for UCLA basketball and USC football. But when it came to track, it was a combination of both. USC had more tradition and history. But by the time I was ready to go to college, the Trojans had the feel of an elitist camp.

"I was one of those who went to UCLA to prove a point. I knew I could beat those guys, and a lot of the guys on my team felt the same way because many of them were rejected by SC. It was great to kick USC's butt. We wanted to show them that we were a top team.

"Another thing is that most of us were Southern California kids, so when we hooked up, there was always something special at stake. Many of us had to flip between UCLA and USC. We grew up in the same neighborhoods, so it was always great to go tooth and nail against each other. Talking trash was always part of the experience. If you won, you had bragging rights the rest of the year.

"The one dual meet that stands out the most to me is the one we lost to them. It was 1971, and it basically was the UCLA–USC Olympic Games. After the meet was over, there were over 10 best-in-the-world marks set that day. We all did well, but the Trojans took it to us. Jimmy Hines had the day of his life. He won the long jump and, although he had not triple-jumped all season, he won that event to win the meet. The crowd was just crazy, and it was at UCLA. The stadium holds 11,000, and it was packed with people standing outside. You could feel the energy on the track.

"It's too bad that we lost. I still remember that to this day."

The Trojans finished third in the meet, but Wolf's dire prediction was a bit premature.

Vern Wolfe, a former Trojan pole vaulter, took over the USC program in 1963 and directed the team to an 11–0 dual-meet record, which included the Trojans' 30th consecutive victory over UCLA. A month later, Wolfe and the Trojans were back on top of the college track world, using depth to win the NCAA team title.

USC swept its 10 dual meets again in 1964, including another one-sided victory over UCLA, a program that had been struggling since its last NCAA title less than a decade before. Coach Drake stepped down after the season to concentrate on his role as athletic trainer.

Jim Bush succeeded Drake, a move that would result in an almost immediate upgrade in the program, and his first order of business was to put together a team to defeat USC.

He couldn't accomplish that immediately, losing in the 1965 matchup, 83–62. But in 1966, Bush and the Bruins accomplished their goal. For the first time, UCLA defeated USC in a track and field dual meet.

A balanced, talented UCLA team ran off with an 86–59 victory at the Coliseum behind sprinters Tom Jones and Norman Jackson, and hurdlers Ron Copeland and Roger Johnson, ending USC's 33-dual-meet winning streak over UCLA. The Bruins completed a perfect season by winning their second NCAA championship. UCLA won the 440-yard and mile relays, Jones won the 220 and Copeland the high hurdles. With points in 12 events, UCLA displayed the type of depth the Trojans lacked. In just two seasons, Bush had turned the Bruins' track program into one of the nation's strongest.

The Trojans responded to UCLA's success by turning to their football program. They grabbed standout athletes such as Earl McCul-

■ **Kermit Alexander was a sprinter, broad jumper and football star at UCLA.**

louch and O.J. Simpson to build the depth they had been missing.

But it wasn't enough. The Bruins handed the Trojans their second dual-meet defeat in 1967. With Copeland dominating the hurdles and Gerald Lee the triple jump, UCLA defeated USC, 83–62.

USC got its revenge at the

■ **Right: Earl McCullouch pulls ahead of Ron Copeland in the high hurdles in 1967. Below: Lennox Miller leads the way to the tape.**

NCAA championship level; the Trojans won the indoor title and finished tied for first outdoors with McCullouch and pole vaulter Bob Seagren winning national titles.

It was the Trojans' 440-relay team that really made news at the 1967 NCAA championships. After having watched UCLA equal the world record of 39.6 seconds in the Bruins' dual-meet victory a month earlier, Lennox Miller, Fred Kuller, Simpson

MEETS WON
The 1960s

TRACK & FIELD

USC 8 - UCLA 2

and McCullouch broke that mark by a full second with a winning time of 38.6.

In 1968, the Trojans repeated as NCAA champions, with Miller becoming USC's first winner in the 100 since Mel Patton won three consecutive times in the late 1940s. McCullouch won the high hurdles for the second year in a row, and the Trojans again took home the 440–relay title.

USC also ended a two-year losing streak to UCLA in a big way. The score: 108–36.

The next year, USC routed UCLA, 94–60, but the Bruins won the Pacific-8 Conference championship and finished fifth in the NCAA meet, ahead of USC. Bush's 1969 team was loaded with talented young runners, led by Wayne Collett and John Smith. The Bruins won the NCAA mile relay with Len Van Hofwegen and Andy Young joining Collett and Smith.

BASEBALL

Heading into the 1960 season, USC Coach Rod Dedeaux figured his Trojans had a good shot at winning their second national championship in three years.

Led by pitcher Bruce Gardener, catcher Bill Heath, outfielder Bob Levingston and third baseman Tom Satriano, USC was 16–6 heading into a four-game series against UCLA, which was in last place in the California Intercollegiate Baseball Association. The Trojans won the first game, 5–2, but were upset, 4–0, in the second game in Westwood. USC then swept the final two games at Bovard Field by a combined score of 22–5 on its way to the College World Series, where the Trojans reached the finals before losing, 2–1, to Minnesota in 10 innings.

In 1961, UCLA Coach Art Reichle's team, which had finished last in the CIBA in every season since 1958, reached respectability. Sophomore pitchers Tim Bottoms and Tom Sapp helped the Bruins finish third in the league, 25–15–5 overall. But they still couldn't catch up to the Trojans, who swept their four games.

USC pitcher Jim Withers was nearly unbeatable, winning 12 of 13 decisions, and Larry Hankammer and Ken Yaryan combined to go 15–4. Mickey McNamee, who had a team-high eight home runs, and Willie Ryan, who batted .373, led the Trojan offense.

Still, UCLA had hopes of a College World Series berth until a three-game series against the Trojans late in the season. In the first game, Reichle called on Ezell Singleton, normally an infielder, to start at pitcher. Singleton baffled the Trojans for eight innings but tired in the ninth. USC's 3–1 victory ended the Bruins' chances of a postseason spot.

Meanwhile, the Trojans won 20 of their final 23 games to win their third national championship under Dedeaux.

Both teams struggled in the 1962 season, with USC finishing second to Santa Clara in the conference and UCLA last. One team the Trojans had no difficulty with was the Bruins, who were outscored, 39–16, in their five losses.

It was a one-year slump for USC, which picked up the nickname "Yankees of College Baseball" when they won their fourth College World Series championship in 1963. Willie Brown, who played tailback on the football team, pitcher Walt Peterson and Kenny Washington Jr. were the key players for USC, which finished first in the CIBA with a 10–6 record and 35–10 overall.

But UCLA had its moments that season too. With Singleton leading the way, the Bruins had their best season in 20 years, finishing 30–17–2. UCLA was ranked in the top 10 in the nation most of the season.

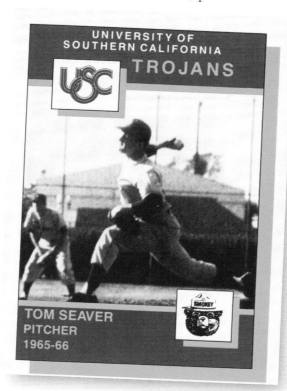

UNIVERSITY OF SOUTHERN CALIFORNIA

TROJANS

USC

TOM SEAVER
PITCHER
1965-66

They split four games with USC, which won its second consecutive CIBA title behind Peterson's 17–3 record but fell short of another national title.

The next season, a young pitcher emerged for USC, one who would go on to a Hall of Fame career in the big leagues. Tom Seaver finished 10–2 in his only season with the Trojans, but even with the dominating Seaver, USC struggled late in the season and finished fourth in the CIBA at 9–11, just the second time a Dedeaux-coached Trojan team finished below .500 in conference play

The Bruins finished third again, behind Bill Macri and Colletto, split four games with the Trojans and ended up a strong

■ Top: The Trojans' multi-talented baseball team in 1964 included football stars, from left: Willie Brown, Mike Garrett and Fred Hill. Right: Rod Dedeaux, left, gives a few base-running tips to Willie Brown, center, and Ken Walker.

UCLA's Randy Schwartz led the CIBA in batting with a .388 average and helped the Bruins win the first three games of their four-game season series against the Trojans, outscoring them 27–6. The second game of that series, at USC, was played in terrible conditions.

After losing, 11–2, in their third game, the Trojans put things together and won 14 of their final 17 games, including a 1–0 victory over UCLA at Westwood.

In 1964, the Bruins had another strong team with Schwartz and Jim Colletto, and again finished third in the CIBA with a 13–7 league record, 35–16–2 overall.

33–15 overall.

In 1966, the Trojans rebounded to win the CIBA title but failed to reach the College

World Series championship game, losing to eventual champion Ohio State.

After going 7–5 against USC the previous three seasons, UCLA was swept by the Trojans in 1966. The Bruin offense wasn't the problem; they scored 24 runs in the series. But their pitchers gave up 33.

UCLA finished second and USC third in the CIBA the next season, but the Trojans won the season series, two games to one. Colletto led the Bruins to a 43–19 overall record and a 10–6 mark in the league, second to Stanford.

The Trojans ran away with the CIBA title in 1968 with a 16–2–1 record. Behind pitchers Bill Lee, Bob Vaughn, Jim Barr and Brent Strom, USC dominated opponents and won 17 of its last 19 games to finish 42–12–1.

In 1968, UCLA had another solid team, 35–20 overall and 11–9 in league play, and defeated USC, 7–4, in the first meeting between the schools. But the Trojans came back to win the final two games to take the season series and eventually another national title.

A year later, the Trojans won 14 of their first 17 games and appeared ready to win back-to-back national championships for the first time in school history. Led by the hitting of first baseman Bill Seinsoth and the pitching of future major leaguers Jim Barr and Dave Kingman, USC was a heavy favorite to win the

CIBA heading into the second half of league play.

The Bruins thought otherwise. Behind the hitting of first baseman Chris Chambliss, a future star in the majors, and shortstop Gary Sanserino, UCLA swept the final three games of their four-game season series against the Trojans to win its first league title since 1944.

In his only varsity season with the Bruins, Chambliss batted .340 with a team-high 15 home runs and 45 runs batted in. It was his hitting over the second half of the season that led UCLA to a 17–4 record in the conference, 42–12–1 overall.

It was a fitting way to end the decade for the Bruins, who had taken more than their share of lumps in the early 1960s.

1960s UCLA Olympic Medalists

BASKETBALL			
Walt Hazzard	1964		Gold
SWIMMING			
Mike Burton	1968	400m Freestyle	Gold
		1500m Freestyle	Gold
Donna deVarona	1964	400m Individual Medley	Gold
		4x100m Freestyle Relay	Gold
Debbie Meyer	1968	200m Freestyle	Gold
		400m Freestyle	Gold
		800m Freestyle	Gold
Lillian Watson Richardson	1968	200m Backstroke	Gold
Zac Zorn	1968	4x100m Freestyle Relay	Gold
TRACK AND FIELD			
Rafer Johnson	1960	Decathlon	Gold
Marilyn White	1964	4x100m Relay	Silver
C. K. Yang (Republic of China)	1960	Decathlon	Silver

GAMES WON
The 1960s
BASEBALL
USC 26 - UCLA 14

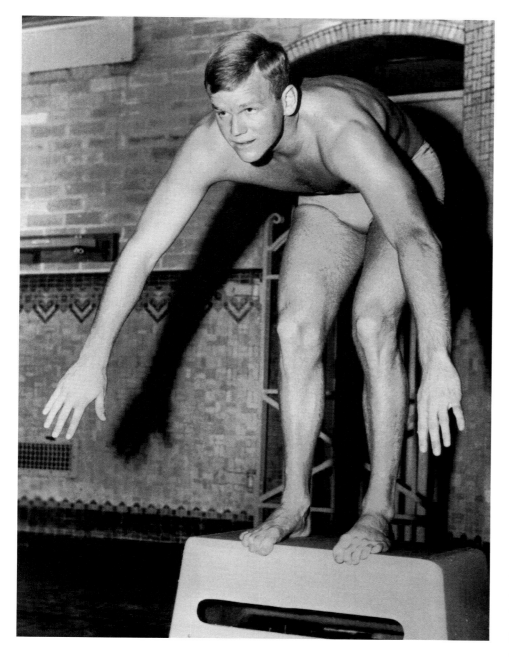

■ **Roy Saari**

110 consecutive meets.

With swimmers such as Charles Bittick, who set American records in the 100- and 200-yard backstroke in 1960; John Konrads, an Olympic gold and bronze medalist; and Roy Saari, who won nine NCAA individual titles, set four world records and won two Olympic medals, USC was hugely successful.

In 1963, UCLA made a move to elevate its swimming program when it hired Bob Horn as full-time coach. But the Bruins were still unable to catch the Trojans in the '60s.

But UCLA and USC were very competitive in another discipline in the pool: water polo.

Neill Kohlhase, the U.S. Olympic team water polo coach in 1956 and 1960, led USC to AAWU championships in 1962 and 1963. But the first recognized national water polo championship went to Bob Horn and the Bruins in 1969. The rivalry was spirited throughout the decade.

In 1964, for example, USC needed to beat UCLA to win the conference championship. In a heated battle, USC blew open a tight game with 10 third-period goals to defeat the Bruins, 16–9. Roy Saari led the Trojans in scoring and was a unani-

SWIMMING AND WATER POLO

USC in 1960 became the first West Coast school to win the NCAA swimming championship and began a decade of domination. Under Coach Peter Daland, the Trojans added NCAA titles in 1963 through 1966 and won an incredible

MEETS WON
The 1960s
SWIMMING
USC 10 - UCLA 0

Arthur Ashe UCLA

A hero on and off the court

Arthur Ashe, the world's first prominent African American male tennis player, burst onto the international sports scene while still a student at UCLA.

As a Bruin freshman in 1962, Ashe was a member of the American Junior Davis Cup team. The next year, he reached the third round at Wimbledon and as a junior at UCLA was the No. 3-ranked player in the U.S.

But it was in his senior season when Ashe put everything together. He won the NCAA singles and doubles titles while leading UCLA to a national championship.

In 1965, Ashe won 36 of 40 collegiate singles matches. He and doubles partner Ian Crookenden were nearly as good, with a 14–3 record. Ashe also won the Athletic Association of Western Universities singles title along with the Southern California Intercollegiate and Ojai tournament championships.

After college, Ashe became one of his generation's most recognized athletes. He won three Grand Slam singles titles (1968 U.S. Open, 1970 Australian Open and 1975 Wimbledon) and two doubles crowns (1971 French Open and 1977 Australian Open).

Ashe, who graduated from UCLA in 1966, told The Times in 1987 that his college experience helped prepare him for the professional tour: "I turned pro when I was 26, after I'd been to college and spent two years in the Army. I don't know how I would have done if I'd turned pro at 19."

Ashe, who had a lifetime record of

106–28 in Grand Slam competition, also played on the U.S. Davis Cup team for 10 years, producing a 28–6 record while playing on four championship teams.

His proudest moment as a player may have come in 1975 when he beat fellow UCLA alumnus Jimmy Connors in the Wimbledon final.

In 1969, at a time when tennis' popularity had reached an all-time high, prize money being offered to the players was lagging disproportionately behind. Ashe and several other players formed the present-day Association of Tennis Professionals.

Ashe will always be remembered for his lifelong fight for human rights and racial equality. He had a peaceful yet forceful approach, perfectly enunciated when he said: "True heroism is remarkably sober, very undramatic. It is not the urge to surpass all others at whatever cost, but the urge to serve others at whatever cost."

Ashe retired in 1980 and was elected to the Tennis Hall of Fame in 1985.

In 1988 he discovered he had AIDS, most likely the result of a tainted blood transfusion during heart surgery in 1983. Ashe revealed his illness at a 1992 news conference and died the next year.

mous all-conference player.

UCLA, led by All-Americans such as Dave Ashleigh, Bruce Bradley, Stan Cole, Kenny Smith and Russ and Torey Webb, then went on a tear, going undefeated for three consecutive seasons, from 1965 through 1967.

In 1968, USC ended UCLA's 51–game winning streak and tied the Bruins for the conference championship. But the following year, in the inaugural national championships, All-Americans Jim Ferguson and Torey Webb led UCLA through three difficult tournament games, including a 4–3 victory over USC in the first round, then to the title.

TENNIS

If you wanted to play for an NCAA championship tennis program in the 1960s, there was only one place to go to school: Los Angeles.

USC and UCLA, with rosters filled with players who were destined to become some of the biggest names in international tennis, teamed to win 12 consecutive national titles, starting with UCLA's back-to-back victories in 1960 and '61.

Sophomore Larry Nagler, who won the NCAA singles title and doubles with Allen Fox, led UCLA Coach J.D. Morgan's 1960 team. He had plenty of great players behind him. Fox, Norman Perry, and Roger Werksman each earned multiple All-America honors, and they helped the Bruins sweep the Trojans that year. USC had a solid team with Greg Grant, Bobby Delgado,

■ **Top: Trojan great Stan Smith.**

■ **Bottom: Bruin tennis coach J.D. Morgan.**

Allan Tong and Dick Leach, but the Trojans struggled against UCLA's top players.

In 1961, the Bruins again were loaded with Nagler, Fox, Perry and Paul Palmer. UCLA rolled through league play, with Nagler repeating as the Athletic Association of Western Universities singles champion. Nagler, however, failed to repeat as the NCAA champion, but at least his place was taken by a teammate. Allen Fox capped off a standout collegiate career with his first NCAA singles title. USC's Rafael Osuna and Ramsey Earnhart rallied to take home the Trojans' ninth doubles title.

After having won 13 of

17 league titles since 1945, the Bruins were overtaken by the Trojans in 1962. USC swept the AAWU and NCAA championships under Coach George Toley.

It was Toley's third NCAA title and the Trojans' fifth. Despite playing with an injured right knee, Osuna won the NCAA singles championship and the doubles title with Earnhart. The season was highlighted by the emergence of such quality players as Bill Bond and Dennis Ralston.

UCLA fielded another strong team in 1962 with Arthur Ashe and Charlie Pasarell—names that would one day almost transcend the sport itself. But the Bruins still couldn't defeat the Trojans, losing for the sixth time in a row to a team that was strong from top to bottom.

USC easily won its second consecutive NCAA title in 1963. Osuna and Ralston were nationally ranked, with Bond and Earnhart pushing them at every step. This time it was Ralston who won the singles title, and he teamed up with Osuna for the doubles crown.

USC's 1963 yearbook, El Rodeo, put it simply: "Toughest competition came from cross-town rival, UCLA, as the best tennis across the nation was centered in the Southern California area."

Big things were expected from UCLA in 1964, and the Bruins were determined to prevent USC from winning the NCAA title for a third consecutive year.

Ashe won the AAWU singles title, but Ralston claimed the NCAA title for the second consecutive year. He also repeated as doubles champion, with Bond replacing Osuna, who had graduated.

In 1965, Ashe and the Bruins ended USC's run of three consecutive NCAA and AAWU titles. UCLA finished the season 11–0, with Ashe losing only four singles matches and only three doubles matches with partner Ian Crookenden. Ashe won both the NCAA singles and doubles titles as Morgan won his seventh national title.

Toley had fielded a young team in 1965, one that had matured by the time the 1966 season started. The Trojans finished 17–0 overall and 6–0 in the conference behind Stan

1960s USC Olympic Medalists

SWIMMING			
Robert Bennett	1960	100m Backstroke	Bronze
	1964	200m Backstroke	Bronze
Bill Craig	1964	400m Medley Relay	Gold
		400m Medley Relay	Silver
Hans Klein (Germany)	1964	100m Freestyle	Bronze
		800m Free Relay	Silver
		4x100m Relay	Silver
John Konrads (Australia)	1960	1500m Freestyle	Gold
		400m Freestyle	Bronze
		800m Free Relay	Bronze
Lance Larson	1960	100m Freestyle	Silver
		400m Medley Relay	Gold
Sharon Finneran Rittenhouse	1964	400m Individual Medley	Silver
Murray Rose (Australia)	1960	400m Freestyle	Gold
		1500m Freestyle	Silver
		800m Free Relay	Bronze
Roy Saari	1964	400m Individual Medley	Silver
		800m Free Relay	Gold
Tsuyoshi Yamanaka (Japan)	1960	400m Freestyle	Silver
		800m Free Relay	Silver

DIVING			
Paula Jean Meyers	1960	Platform	Silver
		Springboard	Silver
Gary Tobian	1960	Platform	Silver
		Springboard	Gold
TRACK AND FIELD			
Rink Babka	1960	Discus	Silver
Rex Cawley	1964	400m Hurdles	Gold
Michael Larrabee	1964	400 meters	Gold
		1600m Relay	Gold
Dallas Long	1960	Shot Put	Bronze
	1964	Shot Put	Gold
Lennox Miller (Jamaica)	1968	100 meters	Silver
Ron Morris	1960	Pole Vault	Silver
Parry O'Brien	1960	Shot Put	Silver
Bob Seagren	1968	Pole Vault	Gold
PENTATHLON			
David Kirkwood	1964	Modern Team	Silver
ROWING			
Conn Findlay	1960	Coxed Pair-Oared	Bronze
	1964	Coxed Pair-Oared	Gold

USC its only loss during the season, but the Trojans emerged to win their second NCAA title in a row. USC clinched the title by beating UCLA in both doubles and one of the singles matches in semifinal competition. The Trojans' third-seeded Bob Lutz upset UCLA's second-seeded Crookenden and then went on to win his first NCAA singles title.

In doubles, Stan Smith and Lutz defeated the Bruins' Roy Barth and Tidball, and USC's Jim Hobson and Loyo-Mayo knocked off UCLA's Rose and Crookenden to reach the finals. Smith and Lutz won the final.

In 1968, UCLA fell short of the Trojans in the NCAA finals. Stan Smith took the singles final over Lutz and then teamed up with him to win the doubles championship over UCLA's Tidball and Barth, and the Trojans rolled to their third consecutive national championship.

The Trojans closed out the 1960s with their seventh NCAA title of the decade behind a dominant season from Loyo-Mayo, who played on the Mexican Davis Cup team. Loyo-Mayo had to step up after Lutz was knocked out in the quarterfinals, and he did. Loyo-Mayo won the singles title and teamed with fellow Mexican Marcello Lara to win the doubles crown. ■

Smith, Tom Edlefsen and Joaquin Loyo-Mayo. Despite not having a singles or doubles champion, the Trojans won their fourth national title in five years.

UCLA, which had lost Ashe to graduation, did not have the depth to stay with the Trojans in 1966, but they did still have Charlie Pasarell, who won the NCAA singles title. Pasarell served notice of his skills all season but had to raise his game to defeat USC's Smith at the AAWU championships.

The Bruins moved closer to the Trojans in 1967 behind Steve Tidball and Gary Rose. UCLA handed

MATCHES WON
The 1960s
TENNIS
USC 7 – UCLA 4

The 1970s

Decade OF Dominance

The athletic programs at USC and UCLA in the 1970s were filled with some of the most recognizable names in college sports history, individuals who led their teams to unheard-of heights and whose names have remained synonymous with athletic excellence for decades.

John McKay, John Robinson, Charles White, Rod Dedeaux, Ronnie Lott at USC and John Wooden, Bill Walton, Terry Donahue and Jimmy Connors at UCLA are only a few of the coaches and players who helped elevate the rivalry between the two schools to almost mythic status and helped the two schools amass an astounding combined total of 54 national championships during the decade. (USC won 22 while UCLA earned 32).

The Trojans dominated in the decade in football; the Bruins ruled college basketball under Wooden in a way that will in all likelihood never be duplicated. Championship baseball at USC almost seemed a given, as was volleyball at UCLA.

During the decade, UCLA also grew into a dominant force in both tennis and track and field, two areas once regarded as exclusive properties of USC. The Bruins also got a jump on the Trojans in soccer, which helped change the landscape of college athletics in Southern California.

But perhaps even more important, the 1970s marked the beginning of across-the-board competition in women's sports. With the advent of Title IX, the federal law requiring schools to provide equal athletic opportunities for women and men, the landscape of sports competition expanded. Bolstered by the school's early entry into women's athletics, UCLA teams dominated their cross-town rivals during the decade.

FOOTBALL

In the week leading up to the 1970 game, the atmosphere around UCLA was unusually flat. The Bruins were 5–4 and fighting to stay above .500, and they had lost three years in a row to the Trojans. Even the Daily Bruin sports editor, John Sandbrook, tried to downplay the game: "Let's face it. USC is not the big game this year. Supposedly, it's for the victory bell, the city championship. I'm in my fourth year and I have never seen the bell yet on this campus: How am I supposed to get excited about the bell when I have never seen it?"

UCLA's annual Westwood Parade, a regular component of Bruin week, was canceled because of lack of interest, and Bruin students bought only 6,600 of the 26,000 tickets available for the game. A good part of the apathy of the early 1970s was in no doubt due to the growing counterculture spirit on campuses throughout the nation, sparked by student protests over the war in Vietnam and the draft.

Even the mood around USC was down. After playing in the Rose Bowl the preceding four years, the Trojans were having a sub-par 1970 season by Coach John McKay's standards. Any hope of returning to the Rose Bowl

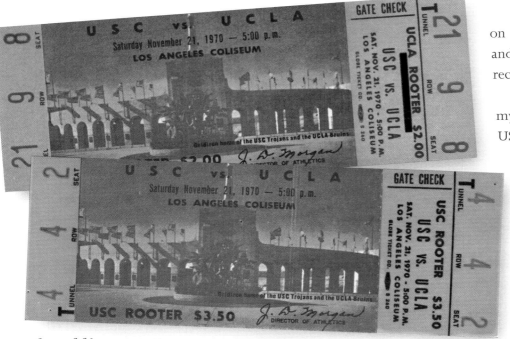

on 19 completions in 30 attempts, and Wilkes set a UCLA single-game record with 11 catches.

It was James Thompson "Tommy" Prothro's final game against USC, and he left the rivalry with a 3–3 mark. After the season, he signed a long-term deal to coach the Los Angeles Rams.

UCLA turned the program over to Pepper Rodgers, a one-time assistant to Prothro who had turned Kansas' lowly program into a Big 8 Conference power in just four years.

Rodgers' inaugural season, 1971, got off to an awful start. UCLA lost its first four games, the program's worst start since 1943. By the time the USC game rolled around, the previous year's triumph over USC was a distant memory.

The 2–7 Bruin record was bad enough, but the program was also beset by an academic scandal. Highly publicized recruit James McAlister, a standout running back and Olympic-class long jumper, had been ruled academically ineligible by the NCAA.

McAlister, who had played on UCLA's freshman football team in 1970 and competed on the varsity track and field team, did not play a down in 1971 after the NCAA determined there were irregularities in his college entrance test scores. Without McAlister, the Bruin season never got going.

As in the previous year, USC was also having some difficulties. The Trojans lost four of their first six games but at least were on a four-game winning streak as the big game arrived.

for a fifth consecutive season was wiped away by a 3–3 Pacific 8 conference record and a 5–3–1 mark overall.

USC was clearly the favorite as the game began, but UCLA quarterback Dennis Dummit had other ideas.

Still smarting from the heartbreaking loss the year before, when the Wild Bunch roughed him up and sacked him nine times, Dummit was determined to have his revenge.

Dummit completed eight of 11 passes for 148 yards, including touchdown passes to Rick Wilkes and Bob Christiansen, to give UCLA a 17–7 lead after one quarter. And thanks to two effective squib kickoffs that led to USC turnovers, the Bruins led, 38–14, at halftime.

In the second half, UCLA turned to tailback Marv Kendricks, who set a Bruin record of 182 yards rushing in 28 carries. The Bruins won easily, 45–20, the most points they had ever scored against the Trojans. Dummit finished with 272 yards passing

Top: Same game, why not the same price?

Below: UCLA Coach Pepper Rodgers.

UCLA entered as a two-touchdown underdog, but by relying heavily on a blitzing defense, the Bruins stymied the Trojans' offense.

With McKay alternating senior Jimmy Jones and junior Mike Rae at quarterback, USC sputtered on offense and managed only one touchdown, its lowest output of the season.

Rodgers had put in a wishbone attack for the first time that week, and although USC held an advantage of 295–158 in total yardage, Kendricks' touchdown run was all UCLA needed to come away with a 7–7 tie.

■ **Right: Anthony Davis runs against the Bruins in 1973.**

■ **Below: Mark Harmon tries a quarterback sneak in 1972 game against the Trojans.**

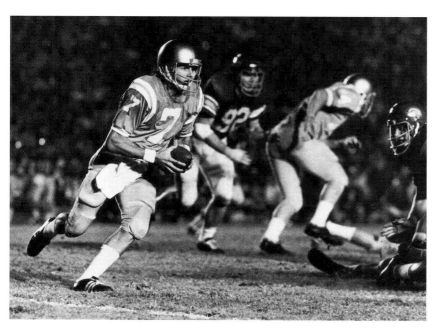

Kendricks told the *Los Angeles Times*: "Getting a tie with them was like winning."

The Trojans stormed out of the gate in 1972 with Rae at quarterback. After defeating Arkansas, 31–10, to open the season, USC became the nation's No. 1 team and kept the position with eight consecutive victories heading into its annual matchup against UCLA.

For Rodgers, the 1972 season was a season of redemption. By making the wishbone the Bruins' offensive staple and adding speed on defense, Rodgers turned UCLA's program around. Quarterback Mark Harmon directed the offense, and Kermit Johnson and McAlister were the team's starting halfbacks.

The Bruins won eight of their first nine games and, going into the game against USC, had a chance to win both the conference title and a trip to the Rose Bowl if they could beat the Trojans. Adding to the game's story line was the debate over which team featured the better offense: McKay's shifting I-formation, which averaged almost 40 points a game, or Rodgers' wishbone, which averaged nearly 35.

As it turned out, the Trojan offense powered past UCLA, 24–7. Sophomore tailback Anthony Davis dominated the game with 178

John McKay USC

"Student body" run creator

Not much was known about John McKay when he replaced USC football coach Don Clark in 1960.

He had joined the staff as an assistant a year earlier, and his previous coaching experience had been as an assistant at Oregon. For USC President Norman Topping, it was a difficult sell to the alumni, who were none too happy about the program's three-game winless streak against UCLA.

But McKay turned out to be an inspired choice. In his 16 seasons, the Trojans won four national championships, five Rose Bowl games and had a 127–40–8 record that included nine conference titles.

He also coached Heisman Trophy winners Mike Garrett and O.J. Simpson and 40 All-Americans.

The Los Angeles Times' Jim Murray wrote of the 1975 Rose Bowl: "If you're ever in a shipwreck, do yourself a favor and try to get in the same lifeboat as John McKay."

McKay earned a reputation as an innovator for perfecting the I-formation, which he installed in his first year at USC. His power running game became known as "student body right" and "student body left," masses of big blockers clearing the way for talented backs. His offense produced a long line of outstanding tailbacks

that included Willie Brown, Clarence Davis, Anthony Davis and Ricky Bell, as well as Garrett and Simpson.

McKay was 10–5–1 against UCLA. In 1975, in his final regular-season game coaching the Trojans, USC lost to UCLA, 25–22, extending the Trojans' losing streak to four games and sending the

Bruins to the Rose Bowl. The Times' Charles Maher wrote about the scene in the USC locker room after the game:

"It was John McKay's last Coliseum news conference as coach at USC, and his voice seemed to quaver a little at the start.

"But you couldn't tell whether it was because he was sorry to say goodbye or sorry to have lost. He has cashed in on a big financial opportunity offered by the new Tampa team in the NFL....

"A reporter asked McKay if he could sum up his 16 seasons at USC.

"'Well, they've been the happiest days of my life,' McKay said. 'We've had some losses but in between we've had tremendous success with some tremendous players. Somebody said something about me being a father image and it got the team down when I said I was leaving. I told the players I'd be happy to be their father image. But now I'm going into the sunset—and taking the seniors with me.'"

Within three years of becoming coach of the Tampa Bay Buccaneers in 1976, McKay had them playing in the NFC Championship Game. He was elected to the College Football Hall of Fame in 1988 and died at age 77 in 2001.

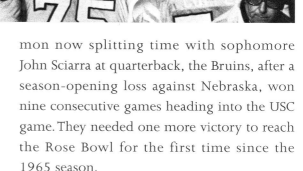

yards rushing in 26 carries, scoring the Trojans' first touchdown on a 23-yard run.

UCLA's wishbone got off to a good start when the Bruins took nine minutes off the clock with a 17–play drive to cut USC's lead to 10–7 in the first quarter. But that was the highlight of the night for the Bruins, who struggled once they fell behind because of their lack of a passing game.

USC went on to win the 1972 national championship and began the next season as the favorite to repeat. Although All-American tight end Charles Young, who was elected to the College Football Hall of Fame in 2004, tackle Pete Adams and fullback Sam Cunningham had moved on to the NFL and sophomore Pat Haden lacked the veteran leadership of Rae at quarterback, the Trojans were still formidable.

But their repeat title hopes were dashed with a tie against Oklahoma and a loss at Notre Dame. The Trojans headed into their matchup against UCLA needing a victory over the Bruins to make their second consecutive Rose Bowl appearance.

Rodgers and the Bruins believed that they were ready for the Trojans in 1973. With Har-

mon now splitting time with sophomore John Sciarra at quarterback, the Bruins, after a season-opening loss against Nebraska, won nine consecutive games heading into the USC game. They needed one more victory to reach the Rose Bowl for the first time since the 1965 season.

But the Bruins took their lumps. UCLA turned the ball over six times and again had trouble passing, gaining only 82 yards in the air. Trojan defenders Monte Doris, Dale Mitchell and All-American Richard Wood had a field day disrupting the Bruins' offense.

Anthony Davis led USC with 145 yards rushing in 27 carries, and Haden made enough big plays to send the Trojans to a 23–13 win and to the Rose Bowl, where they would eventually lose to Ohio State, 42–21.

After the season, UCLA found itself looking for a new coach when Rodgers returned to coach his alma mater, Georgia Tech. In three seasons, he had failed to defeat the Trojans, but he did help turn UCLA into an offensive powerhouse.

UCLA did not look far for Rodgers' replacement, hiring Dick Vermeil, a former Bruin offensive coordinator who was an assistant coach for the Los Angeles Rams.

Vermeil brought a sense of toughness to

 Top: Bruin coach Dick Vermeil.

Below: Trojan quarterback Pat Haden, right, with Coach John McKay and his son, J.K.

the program and immediately turned the Bruins into one of the hardest-working teams in the Pac-8. Vermeil got rid of the wishbone and began using a pro-style veer offense that featured split running backs, two wide receivers and a tight end, the versatile offense adding a good passing game to the option attack.

With Vermeil in charge, the Bruins would never be caught one-dimensional again.

The Bruins were 6–2–2 heading into the 1974 game against USC. And despite losing starting quarterback Sciarra and his backup, Jeff Dankworth, to injury, they were still in Rose Bowl contention.

But the 7–1–1 Trojans, with Haden, Davis and wideout J.K. McKay leading USC's bal-

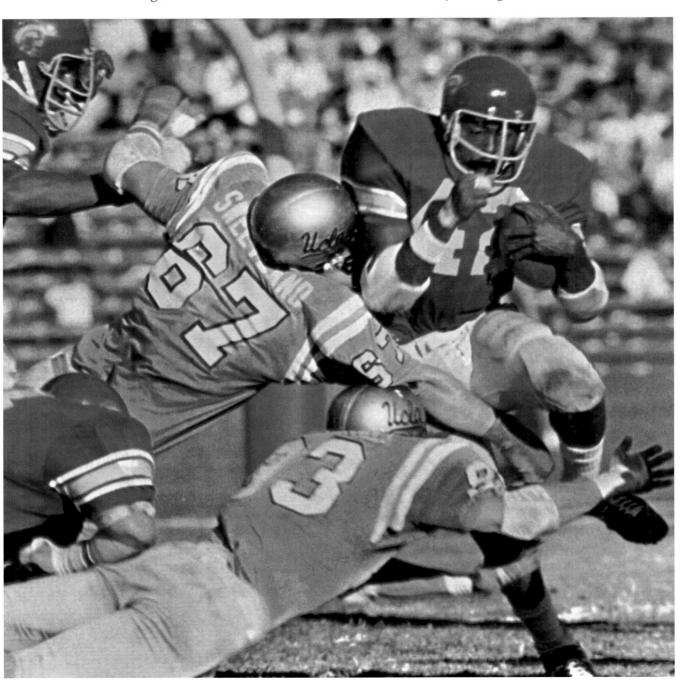

■ Top: USC coach John Robinson flashes the victory sign after 1976 win over the Bruins.

■ Below: UCLA coach Terry Donahue in 1977.

■ Opposite: USC running back Ricky Bell.

anced offense and Wood and defensive back Charles Phillips toughening the defense, were heavily favored.

The game wasn't even close. Davis ran for 195 yards in 31 carries to lead USC to a 34–9 victory, the Trojans' largest margin of victory in the rivalry since 1944. The victory was USC's fifth in a row over UCLA when the Rose Bowl was on the line for both teams. The Trojans went on to beat Ohio State in the Rose Bowl, 18–17, gaining revenge for the 21–point beating at the hands of the Buckeyes a year earlier.

USC and UCLA expected big things at the start of the 1975 season. With a deal to become the first head coach of the NFL expansion Tampa Bay Buccaneers already in place, McKay wanted to go out on top with the Trojans. He was excited about converted fullback Ricky Bell, who took over from Davis at tailback, and USC's big-play defense.

Although rumors ran rampant around Los Angeles that McKay had accepted the NFL job, he kept his decision a secret while the Trojans opened the season with seven consecutive victories, outscor-

ing opponents 174–66.

However, by the time the Bruins met the Trojans, USC's program was in disarray because McKay had announced that he would depart at season's end. The news unsettled the team, and the Trojans lost three games in a row heading into the game against the Bruins.

Still, there was motivation for the Trojans, since a USC victory would keep UCLA from winning the conference title and its first Rose Bowl berth in 10 years.

The Bruins tried their best to give the game away, but they overcame eight fumbles to spoil McKay's final game at the Coliseum, 25–22. Wendell Tyler fumbled four times but still finished with 130 yards in 17 carries. For a change, the key to the Bruins' victory was their defense, which was led by linebackers Ray Bell and Terry Tautolo and nose guard Cliff Frazier.

Ricky Bell had a big game with 136 yards rushing in 36 carries, but USC quarterback Vince Evans, who at one point threw 14 consecutive incompletions, had a miserable outing.

After upsetting then–No. 1 Ohio State in the Rose Bowl, Vermeil and the Bruins could rightfully claim they owned Los Angeles. McKay was now an NFL coach, and USC's control of the West Coast college football world seemed to be coming to an end.

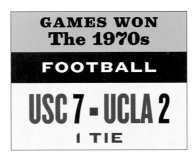

GAMES WON
The 1970s
FOOTBALL
USC 7 - UCLA 2
I TIE

Then one month after defeating the Buckeyes, Vermeil decided to leave UCLA to accept an NFL head coaching job with the Philadelphia Eagles.

Heading into the 1976 season, both USC and UCLA had new coaches. Former Trojan assistant John Robinson replaced McKay; former Bruin assistant Terry Donahue was promoted to take over for Vermeil.

Donahue's Bruins played up to expectations from the start, winning nine of their first 10 games with a tie at Ohio State. UCLA's undefeated record in the Pac-8 had the Bruins one victory away from making their first back-to-back trips to the Rose Bowl.

The Trojans were the only team in their way. After losing to Missouri to open the season in Robinson's USC debut, the Trojans ran off 8 consecutive victories with Evans emerging as a multi-dimensional quarterback.

UCLA entered the game ranked No. 2 while USC was No. 3. Both teams featured great defenses and strong ground attacks with ailing running backs.

USC struck first on safety Dennis Thurman's 47-yard fumble return for a touchdown, and the defense smothered UCLA's attack in a 24–14 victory.

In 1977, the teams were moving in opposite directions as the big game approached. USC had won its first four games to move to No. 1 in the nation, then lost four of its next six.

UCLA began the season 2–3, then won

five consecutive games. With Freeman McNeil emerging as an effective runner in UCLA's new pro-style offense, the Bruins still had an outside chance to reach the Rose Bowl.

UCLA began by taking a 10–0 lead, but USC scored 26 unanswered points to take a 26–10 advantage midway into the third quarter.

Then the Bruins rallied behind quarterback Rick Bashore, who played despite a broken rib and collapsed lung. Bashore led three long scoring drives to give the Bruins a 27–26 lead with 2:51 remaining in the game.

USC, however, responded with quarterback Rob Hertel, who completed 15 of 24 passes for 254 yards and three touchdowns, including two to wide receiver Kevin Williams. With time running down, Hertel put the Trojans into field-goal range, and kicker Frank Jordan won the game with a 38-yarder with two seconds left.

The Rose Bowl was again on the line for

■ Bruin quarterback Rick Bashore in 1979.

Charles White USC

Beating UCLA was such sweet pain

Charles White is one of the lucky ones.

In his four years of playing football against UCLA, the Heisman Trophy winner's USC teams went 4–0 against their major rival. In his final two games against the Bruins, White rushed for a combined 339 yards in 68 carries, earning every little bit of that yardage the hard way.

"They always had a bunch of guys talking trash, telling everyone what they were going to do with us. So by the time the game started, everyone was ready to play.

"I remember my first carry against them. I got the ball and got hit, and I said to myself, 'Ooooh, this is going to be one of them loooong days.'" says White, who now works in administrative information services at USC. "I will give UCLA this: They came out and played physical.... At least their defense was physical.... At the end of every game, I was worn out. Beat up and bruised."

Growing up in San Fernando, White heard about the USC–UCLA rivalry from Anthony Davis and Manfred Moore, two Trojan players who lived in his neighborhood. "I just couldn't wait to play UCLA," he remembers. "It was the championship game of the city."

In his freshman year, White didn't play much because he backed up Ricky Bell. Still, he calls even that game "overwhelming."

"I had a great experience standing on the sideline. I just took in the scenery and the ambience of the Coliseum. One side blue and gold and the other cardinal and gold. It was quite a sight to see the Coliseum with no empty seats."

In White's senior season, the 1979 Trojans were 9–0–1 entering the UCLA game, and it was White's final chance to impress Heisman Trophy voters.

He made certain that his message was understood, rushing for 194 yards in 35 carries and scoring four touchdowns in USC's 49–14 victory.

"I just wanted to finish on a good note. It was the last game before going to the Rose Bowl. What better way to end your career than to beat the crap out of UCLA?"

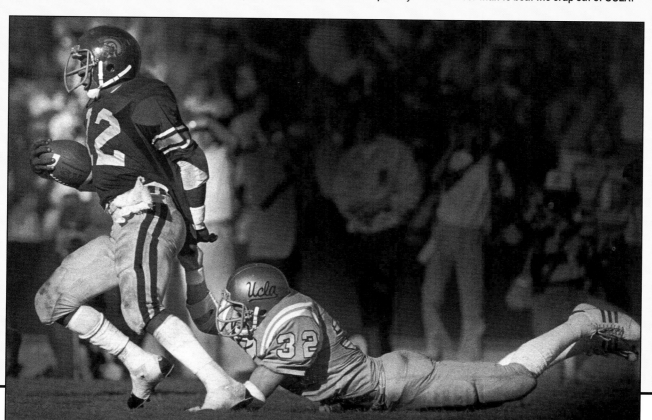

The McNeill Brothers

A collegiate sibling rivalry

One of the most unusual matchups in the history of the UCLA–USC football rivalry occurred in the early 1970s, when Fred and Rod McNeill faced off against each other.

Rod, the older of the two brothers, played tailback for USC from 1970 to 1973; Fred played defensive end for the Bruins from 1971 to 1973.

"When Rod graduated from high school, he looked at UCLA and USC and figured where he would best fit in," Fred McNeill told the Los Angeles Times. "At first, I was going to USC because Rod was there. Then I got some advice from people who are much wiser than I am.

"They told me to make up my own mind and not to go to USC just because Rod was there. They said I should go where I would be the happiest. After considering all the factors, I thought I'd be happier here. I'm not saying USC isn't a good school, but UCLA was best suited for me."

Rod told the Daily Trojan that he chose USC over UCLA because of the conservative nature of the school. "There is something about the atmosphere at USC. There is more of a conservative attitude. Fred is more of a radical or liberal than I am, so he chose UCLA."

The first time the brothers faced each other on the field was Nov. 18, 1972, and The Times' Mal Florence interviewed the McNeills before the game and wrote: "With UCLA meeting USC with the Rose Bowl bid at stake Saturday, you'd expect Fred and Rod McNeill to be snarling at each other....

"Not so, says Fred McNeill, the UCLA defensive end who lives with Rod, the USC tailback, at another brother's home in Baldwin Hills. 'If anything, this game has brought us closer together,' Fred said."

Rod McNeill's Trojans won in 1972 and 1973, outscoring the Bruins, 47–20. In USC's 24–7 victory in 1972, Fred McNeill was matched against his brother on one play in the first half and missed the tackle.

After the game, the UCLA defender explained the play to The Times: "I knew it was him. He just got to the outside and put a move on me—a move I didn't know he had."

both teams when they met in 1978. UCLA was 8–2 overall, USC 8–1. Both had 5–1 conference records.

The Trojans took a 17–0 lead, but UCLA tried to make the game interesting by collecting 10 points in the second half. Trailing by just a touchdown with just more than a minute left, the Bruins forced USC into a third-and-six play. But Charles White, who would finish with 145 yards rushing in 33 carries, stepped up with an 11-yard run to clinch the game and send the Trojans to the Rose Bowl for the fifth time in seven years. USC would win a share of the national championship by beating Michigan.

In 1979, the Bruins suffered through one of their worst seasons

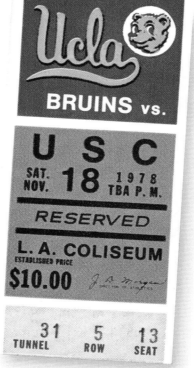

under Donahue, entering the USC game with a 5–5 record.

Adding to UCLA's woes was an injury to Bashore, who had been the Bruins' No. 1 quarterback since his sophomore season. Bashore, a senior, missed three games because of a chipped bone in his foot.

Donahue gave the starting nod to freshman Tom Ramsey, who had led UCLA to victories over Arizona State and Oregon leading up to the USC game.

With a Trojan secondary that featured future NFL stars Ronnie Lott and Dennis Smith and a linebacking group led by Dennis Johnson, Ramsey never had a chance.

In the 49–14 loss, Ramsey completed only three of 13 passes for 34 yards and was intercepted twice by Lott, who returned one for a touchdown.

Charles White again played a big role for the Trojans, running for 194 yards and scoring four touchdowns.

The victory over Donahue and the Bruins was John Robinson's fourth in four tries. It also gave the Trojans a 10–0–1 record and sent them to the Rose Bowl again, where White, who was the Heisman Trophy winner, rushed for a Rose Bowl–record 247 yards in a win over Ohio State.

BASKETBALL

UCLA might have begun the 1970s in the middle of their seven-year run as NCAA champions, but the Bruins also entered the decade having lost their last game against the Trojans.

As Wooden's Bruins were running over the rest of the college basketball world, USC Coach Bob Boyd's Trojans had gained a reputation for

having the number of their cross-town rivals. This dichotomy held up when the teams met for the first time in the 1969–1970 season.

With the Bruins ranked No. 1 in the country, the Trojans stretched their winning streak over UCLA to two with a nail-biting 87–86 victory on a free throw by Don Crenshaw in the final minute of play at Pauley Pavilion. They turned out to be the only two losses Wooden would experience at Pauley.

The next night at the Sports Arena, UCLA rolled to a 91–78 victory behind Sidney Wicks' 31 points and 16 rebounds.

When the schools met for the first time the next season, UCLA didn't have any trouble taking the Trojans seriously. Behind Paul Westphal, Mo Layton and Ron Riley, USC had a 16–0 record and was ranked ahead of the defending national champions in the latest national poll because of UCLA's loss to Notre Dame two weeks earlier.

Although the Trojans took a 59–50 lead, they scored only one point in the last nine minutes, 30 seconds and lost 64–60.

After that victory, the Bruins continued to win and took a 24–1 record into their rematch with the Trojans. USC matched the Bruins' record, setting up a crucial regular-season finale to decide the conference championship.

As they had a month earlier, the Trojans played the Bruins close in the rematch but again could not get the job done down the stretch. The Bruins wore down the Trojans and won, 73–62, leaving USC as the nation's No. 2 team and eliminated from postseason play.

■ Trojan coach Bob Boyd in 1972.

After the game, USC's Layton criticized the Pac-8 rule that would not allow the second-place team in the conference to even participate in the NIT. Layton told *The Times*: "It's a terrible rule, a bad rule. Here we are—24–2. We've lost only twice—to the No. 1 team."

In the first game between the schools in the 1971–1972 season, the Bruins attacked the Trojans early at Pauley Pavilion. With sophomore center Bill Walton spearheading UCLA's defense, the Bruins ran USC off the court in an 81–56 victory.

By the time UCLA traveled to the Sports Arena for the rematch on March 10, the Bruins had already clinched the Pac-8 title and took a relaxed approach to the game. UCLA took the floor for pregame warm-ups to the tune of "Sweet Georgia Brown" and started tossing the ball around in a fashion reminiscent of the Harlem Globetrotters.

Once the game began, USC stayed close to the Bruins until 10 minutes remained in the second half. That's when UCLA pulled away, winning, 79–66.

Both programs remained strong in 1972–1973. UCLA entered the game against USC undefeated and on a 61–game winning streak. With Walton dominating the middle and forwards Keith Wilkes and Larry Farmer carrying the offense from the perimeter, the Bruins, six-time defending NCAA champi-

■ **Larry Farmer in 1973**

ons, were 16–0 for the season.

Behind guard Gus Williams and big man John Lambert, USC got off to a strong start, winning 13 of its first 17 games and taking a six-game winning streak into the game against the Bruins at the Sports Arena.

The Bruins won easily, 79–56, with Walton dominating the Trojans' front line. Although Boyd used a lineup that had plenty of height with Lambert and Mike Westra, both 6–10, and 6–8 big men Clint Chapman and Bruce Clark, Walton went over and around every player USC planted in the paint.

Gene Bartow UCLA

Now, this guy had a tough job!

UCLA basketball coach John Wooden retired after the Bruins' 1975 national championship season, and Gene Bartow was hired as his replacement. Before UCLA played the Trojans for the second time on March 6, 1976, The Times' Jim Murray wrote:

"Like to sing on the bill after Caruso, would you? Share a scene with Cagney? Take a part Spencer Tracy once played?

"Maybe you'd care to hang your oils next to Rembrandt? Play duo piano with Paderewski? Debate with Winston Churchill? What does the world hear about Stephen A. Douglas?

"If Gene Bartow had a live agent, he would never have let Gene take the spot. It's worse than coming on after a talking dog.

"John Wooden was a certified American divinity when he relinquished the basketball coaching job at UCLA. Most people were positive they would have to draft somebody for the job. He had 10 national championships in 12 years. To top that, Gene Bartow would have to change water into wine at halftime, or feed 20,000 people with two carp.

"Replacing a legend is the most thankless pastime in the annals of the Republic. In 1931, Heartley (Hunk) Anderson took over a football team from Knute Rockne, dead in a plane crash earlier that year. He won six games, lost two and tied one. And Notre Dame sat up nights figuring a way to get rid of a coach with such a catastrophic record. Rockne had not lost a game in several years. In 1865, Andrew Johnson replaced Abraham Lincoln as President. Within a year, they were trying to impeach him."

Turned out, Murray was a little optimistic about how the new coach might fare. Bartow led the Bruins to the Final Four in his first season and got to the tournament again the following year, but he didn't win a national title. He lasted only two seasons at UCLA before moving on to the University of Alabama-Birmingham. He finished with a 52–9 record, which included a 4–0 record against USC, but for Bruin followers grown accustomed to nothing short of NCAA championships, it simply wasn't good enough.

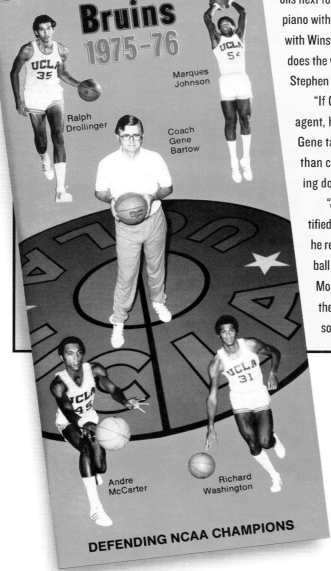

UCLA BASKETBALL Bruins 1975-76

Ralph Drollinger

UCLA 35

Marques Johnson

UCLA 54

Coach Gene Bartow

Andre McCarter

UCLA 45

Richard Washington

UCLA 31

DEFENDING NCAA CHAMPIONS

By the time the teams played again that season, the Bruins had won the Pac-8 Conference title and a berth in the NCAA Western Regional with a 25–0 regular-season record. And the Trojans, with the old restrictive rule now gone, had secured a berth in the NIT, their first postseason tournament since 1961.

Nine minutes, 30 seconds of Trojan Hell

Hoop loss still smarts

UCLA Coach John Wooden's success over USC is undeniable. Wooden's teams were 61–23 against the Trojans, 28–2 in his last 30 games against USC.

But on Feb. 6, 1971, the Bruins faced an undefeated USC team that was actually ranked higher. With guard Paul Westphal leading the way, Coach Bob Boyd's Trojans were 16–0 and favored over the 15–1 Bruins.

With Kareem Abdul-Jabbar (then Lew Alcindor) gone, people around Los Angeles questioned UCLA's dominance. Critics said that Wooden's team lacked teamwork and that the money of professional basketball had become a distraction.

But the Bruins felt differently, and behind the leadership of Sidney Wicks, Curtis Rowe and Steve Patterson, they wanted to prove it against the Trojans.

In front of a sellout crowd of 15,307 at the Sports Arena, USC played a near-perfect game and took a 59–50 lead midway into the second half. Everything was working for the Trojans, and they had the Bruins on the ropes with their fans starting to smell victory.

But USC couldn't hang on. UCLA held the Trojans to one point over the final nine minutes, 30 seconds and won

going away, 64–60. It was a total collapse by the Trojans.

When the teams met again on March 13 at Pauley Pavilion, UCLA ran up a 19-point lead in the first half, won 73–62, and went on to a fifth consecutive NCAA title.

When asked by The Times in 1985 what he thought would have happened if USC had held that nine-point lead in the first meeting in 1971, Westphal said: "I don't think it would have changed very much.... SC had a great recruiting year the next year: Gus Williams, John Lambert.

[But Bill] Walton had already been recruited [by UCLA]. And no matter who USC got, they wouldn't have beaten Walton."

Walton had a big first half, finding Larry Hollyfield with back-door passes for easy layups, and the Bruins led 32–25 at intermission. UCLA opened the second half with eight consecutive points and never looked back in an easy 76–56 victory as Keith Wilkes scored 15 of his 17 points in the second half and Walton finished with 17 points and 20 rebounds. The Bruins went on to beat Memphis State in the NCAA title game, their

seventh consecutive national championship.

At the start of the 1973–74 season, the Bruins were the undisputed kings of the college basketball world. With Walton providing great senior leadership, UCLA won its first 13 games to extend its winning streak to an NCAA-record 88 games before losing to Notre Dame.

The Bruins' next game after that loss was against USC, which was 14–2 and loaded for

■ Bill Walton, left, and Marques Johnson soar past the Trojans.

■ Opposite: Henry Bibby, left, and Paul Westphal in 1971.

bear. Before a sellout crowd at Pauley Pavilion, the Trojans battled Wooden's Bruins but ran out of gas down the stretch and lost, 65–54. All-American forward Keith Wilkes, who would later change his first name to Jamal, led UCLA with 20 points.

After their victory over USC in their first meeting of the season, the Bruins lost twice to mediocre Oregon teams while the Trojans won eight in a row and needed a victory over UCLA in their second season matchup for the league championship. And with forward/center Clint Chapman, who did not play in the first meeting because of a knee injury, back in the lineup, the Trojans had high hopes for their regular-season finale against the Bruins at the Sports Arena.

UCLA and USC entered the rematch with identical conference (11–2) and overall (22–3) records. A USC victory would give the

Trojans a berth in the NCAA tournament and end the Bruins' streak of seven consecutive conference titles.

USC's biggest concern was Walton. But the Trojans couldn't do anything about him.

Walton led the Bruins to an 82–52 trouncing of the Trojans at Pauley. UCLA dominated from the start, taking a 47–13 lead at halftime. Walton had seven more points and four more rebounds than the entire USC team at the half and finished with 26 points and 20 rebounds.

Despite a nine-game losing streak against the Bruins heading into the start of the 1974–75 season, Boyd still was feeling optimistic about beating UCLA. Walton had graduated, and the USC coach was hearing rumors that Wooden was about to retire.

With Gus Williams and John Lambert back, along with Bob Trowbridge from the previous year, Boyd had reason to expect big things. His team had won their first eight games and were ranked sixth in the nation with a 13–2 record when they faced the Bruins for the first time.

The Times reported: "This one figured to be one of the best of the 158 games the teams have played over the years. It might have been the best."

In winning their 77th consecutive game at Pauley Pavilion, by a score of only 89–84, the Bruins never led by more than seven points and were out-rebounded by the Trojans. But UCLA rode Dave Meyers' 23 points and nine rebounds to move ahead of USC in the conference race.

In the second meeting, at the Sports Arena, UCLA again showed it was a notch above USC. After trailing UCLA, 45–32, at halftime, the Trojans came back in the second half to take a 63–58 lead with 5:11 remaining. That's when UCLA turned to Pete Trgovich, who shot, stole and hustled the Bruins to their ninth consecutive Pac-8 title.

UCLA's 92–85 defeat of Kentucky in the NCAA title game gave the Bruins their 10th title under Wooden, who went into retirement at the end of the season, bringing to a close the most successful run of college basketball supremacy in history. In the end, Wooden had amassed a stretch of 10 NCAA championships in 12 seasons, including a run of seven in a row. Those numbers will likely never be matched, as more players are turning pro early and the talent base of collegiate players is spread among so many strong programs.

Gene Bartow, who had an 82–32 record at Memphis State, including a trip to the 1973 NCAA championship game against UCLA, became the first in a series of UCLA coaches who had the misfortune of following in

■ **Kiki Vandeweghe, left, and James Wilkes reach for the rebound in a 1979 game.**

Wooden's footsteps and failing to duplicate the Hall of Fame coach's success.

Bartow's job was to keep the Bruins as the nation's dominant team. Wooden had left him considerable talent in Marques Johnson and Rich Washington, the team's top two scorers, and UCLA was still considered the premier team in the Pac-8 in 1975–76.

Over at USC, Boyd had an inexperienced lineup. But the Trojans again started strong, winning 11 of their first 12 games. With guard Marv Safford filling the scoring role left by Williams' graduation, USC even started talking about beating UCLA once again.

But once Pac-8 play began, USC lost five close games, while the Bruins won three of four.

Even without Wooden, the Bruins discovered they still had the right answers against the Trojans, winning, 68–62, at Pauley Pavilion. When the teams came together for the rematch, the Bruins had already earned a berth in the NCAA regional with a 23–3 record and a 12–1 mark in the Pac-8. USC was a miserable 0–13 in the conference.

The game, however, wasn't a total mismatch—at least for the first half. UCLA led by only two, 35–33, at intermission before pulling away for an 87–73 victory.

The Bruins finished 28–4 in Bartow's first season, but the team lost in the NCAA semifinals to the eventual champion, Indiana.

After coaching UCLA to a Pac-8 title and 24–5 record in 1976–1977, Bartow decided he'd had enough after the Bruins' second-round loss in the NCAA tournament, and he resigned to start a program at Alabama Birmingham. Although he took the Bruins to the Final Four in 1976 and was 52–9 at UCLA

(Wooden was 54–7 in his last two seasons in Westwood), Bartow never could live up to the standards set by Wooden's championship teams.

And so UCLA turned to former Wooden assistant Gary Cunningham. Under Cunningham, the Bruins continued to win in 1977–78, going 14–0 in conference play as they took home their 12th consecutive Pac-8 championship. In their two victories over USC, UCLA outscored the Trojans by 25 points.

UCLA's continued domination of Trojan teams, even after Wooden's retirement, finally got the best of USC coach Boyd. Three days after the Trojans lost, 89–86, to the Bruins on Jan. 13, 1979, Boyd announced he would resign at the end of his 13th season at USC. Boyd made the decision after suffering his 18th consecutive loss to the Bruins.

Boyd's announcement gave his players even more motivation to defeat the Bruins at their next meeting. With the Bruins ranked fourth in the nation and winners of 16 of their first 19 games, the Trojans were a determined bunch when they faced the Bruins next at Pauley Pavilion.

With a lineup made up of underclassmen Clifford Robinson, Purvis Miller, Barry Brooks, Don Carfino and Dean Jones, USC pushed UCLA to the limit. But every time the Trojans made a run, the Bruins had an answer with Roy Hamilton, Kiki Vandeweghe, Brad Holland and David Greenwood taking turns stepping up.

After the Trojans sent the game into overtime, the Bruins pulled away in the extra period to win, 102–94, extending their winning streak to 19 over USC and capping a frustrating decade of rivalry for Trojan basketball teams.

**GAMES WON
The 1970s
BASKETBALL
UCLA 19 - USC 1**

TRACK AND FIELD

Arguably the fiercest competition in the USC vs. UCLA rivalry at the start of the decade was in track and field. After ending USC's 33-meet winning streak in 1966, Coach Jim Bush's Bruins were now the new bullies of Los Angeles and the college track world. UCLA would go on to win four NCAA championships in the decade, three straight from 1971 through 1973, while USC captured just one title, in 1976. (The Trojans also won an indoor crown in 1972.)

Behind quarter-milers John Smith and Wayne Collett, the deep and talented UCLA squad entered its dual meet against USC in 1970 on a roll. The Bruins talked about scoring as many as 100 points even on the Coliseum's dirt track.

And they were justified in being so cocky; the meet wasn't even close.

Collett equaled a Coliseum record in the 440 yards at 45.8 seconds and anchored the 440-yard relay team to victory in 39.6, tying the UCLA school record. Bruin sprinter Reggie Robinson won both the 100- and 220-yard dashes, and UCLA distance runner Mike Mullins won the mile over USC's Ole Oleson at 4:05.8.

From *The Times*' account of the meet: "It was possibly the darkest day in Trojan track and field history as UCLA, a school which went 32 years before scoring its first win over USC in 1966, pranced to a 100–54 victory to wrap up the Pacific 8 dual meet championship. It had been almost a half a century, 49

years to be exact, since anybody had scored 100 points on a USC track team."

At the Pac-8 championships a month later, the Bruins rolled on, setting a school record with 111 points in taking home first place for the second year in a row.

In 1971, Bush had another strong team. Collett and Smith seemed to be chasing

records every week in the 440, and long jumper James McAlister, pole vaulter Francois Tracanelli and javelin thrower Peter Jones were heavy favorites in their field events.

Many figured the key to the meet would be the 440, with USC's Edesel Garrison going against Collett and Smith.

In front of a record crowd of 12,584 at Bruin Track Stadium, the Trojans and Garrison did come to run, defeating UCLA, 75–70, in what many considered the best dual meet in the history of the rivalry.

Garrison won the 440 in a lifetime best and school-record 45.4, with Smith second at 45.5, followed by Collett's third-place finish at 46.7. The victory was one of several impres-

■ **USC's Vern Wolfe, left, and UCLA's Jim Bush: friends and rivals.**

**MEETS WON
The 1970s**

TRACK & FIELD

UCLA 7 ▪ USC 3

135

lost by 46 points to the Bruins in 1970.

Sprinter Willie Deckard won the 100- and 220-yard dashes, establishing the fastest sprint double of all time. Deckard tied a school record in the 100 when he ran down UCLA's Warren Edmonson to win with a time of 9.2. Deckard, who also anchored the Trojans' winning 440–relay, set a Trojan record in the 220 with a mark of 20.2.

The race that actually clinched the victory for the Trojans was the two mile, the second-to-last event of the afternoon. USC's Jeff Marsee passed the Bruins' Joe Balasco coming down the stretch and placed second behind UCLA's Ruben Chappins to score the three points for the Trojans that gave them their 36th victory over the Bruins in 39 years.

The Trojans, however, did not have much time to enjoy their victory. The Bruins bounced back and won their third conference championship in a row and first NCAA title since 1966.

In 1972, the two programs were at it

■ **John Smith after breaking the world record in 440-yard run in 1971.**

sive efforts from the Trojans, who ended UCLA's 17-meet winning streak.

USC athletes established 10 personal lifetime bests, broke five school records, set five world bests and tied or broke four conference marks. Wolfe considered the victory his most satisfying dual meet win after having again. In the annual dual meet, the Bruins ran to a 76–69 victory, with John Smith having a big day in the 220 and 440 at the Coliseum. After finishing second to USC in the Pac-8 championships, UCLA won its second consecutive NCAA title, with USC finishing second.

It was more of the same for the Bruins in 1973. Bush's squad had an easier time with the Trojans, winning convincingly, 89–55, at Westwood behind long jumper James McAlister, who defeated Olympic champion Randy Williams.

UCLA's Harry Freeman broke stadium and meet records in the triple jump at 53 feet, 2 inches, and the Bruins' Benny Brown ran a world-best 45.0 in the 440. USC's Don Quarrie won the 100 and 220 in wind-aided times of 9.4 and 20.3 seconds.

UCLA followed that victory with its fourth conference title in five years and third consecutive NCAA championship.

Early in the 1974 season, Bush hinted that the Bruins' run was about to end and even predicted the Bruins might lose a couple of meets. Still, even with shot putter Jim Neidhart and sprinter Maxie Parks out with injuries, the Bruins cruised to an 82–63 win over the Trojans, their 26th consecutive dual-meet win.

In the weeks leading up to a rematch at the

1974 Pac-8 finals, *The Times* covered the two track teams as if they were in the Rose Bowl game. Readers knew all about UCLA javelin thrower Rory Kotinek's injured arm and Parks' hamstring strain. They also were told about how USC's Williams was taking acupuncture treatments for a back ailment that put pressure on the sciatic nerve.

USC didn't win an event, but the Trojans

■ Heisman Trophy winner Charles White was a Trojan track star, too.

Willie Banks UCLA

Triple jumper smoked '75 dual meet

In the 1970s, to say that the UCLA vs. USC track and field dual meets were competitive would be an understatement. One of the most memorable meets took place on May 4, 1975, and this is The Times' Harley Tinkham's report: "When was the last time you saw an organized rooting section at a track meet? When's the last time you saw a triple jumper actually cheered as he ran down the runway? When's the last time you saw a man carried off the field after winning his event?

"It all happened at UCLA Saturday. The man they carried off was Willie Banks after the 19-year-old freshman from Oceanside carried UCLA to its fourth straight victory over USC with an astonishing leap of 55-1 on his final attempt in the triple jump that bettered his previous best by almost two feet.

"The score was 75–70, clinching the national collegiate dual meet championship for the Bruins for the fourth

straight year. The turnaway crowd was a record 15,069 on hand to see the best dual meet in memory.

"Most track fans have always rated the 1971 USC–UCLA meet as the greatest ever—and it was a big one with such people as Willie Deckard, Edesel Garrison, John Smith and Wayne Collett—but look at some of the performances Saturday:

"— Mike Tulley of UCLA set a school record of 17-10 in the pole vault and came within a whisker of clearing 18-2 when the bar finally toppled after he had landed in the pit.

"— Rory Kotinek of UCLA won the high jump at 7-3.5, breaking the school record of 7-3 he shared with Dwight Stones. Kotinek earlier won the javelin with a seasonal best of 226-10.

"— James Gilkes of USC won the sprints in 9.3 and 20.4, his mark moving him to No. 1 in the nation this year.

"— Tom Andrews of USC won the 440 hurdles in 50.2, equaling the meet record and handing UCLA's Lynssey Guerrero his

first defeat in four years of dual meet competition. Guerrero fell over the last hurdle but Andrews already was long gone.

"— USC ran a nation-leading 39.1 in the 440 relay and set a school record of 3:07.2 in the mile relay even though Ken Randle did not run on the quartet."

"Here's the picture as Banks, who already had won the long jump with a wind-aided 26-2.5, took his final jump: UCLA would have led only 71-69 if Banks didn't improve. The Bruins were in deep trouble, going into the mile relay against a USC team that had run four seconds faster this year.

"As Banks moved to the head of the runway, suddenly four Bruin students appeared from the stands and led rooters in a U-C-L-A spellout. When Banks started his run, the rooters burst into cheers urging the freshman on as he moved determinedly toward the takeoff.

"'I love it,' Banks said. 'I jump on emotion. It was just what I needed because, believe me, I was scared. When I heard those cheers, it really pumped me, and I told myself, 'Give it everything you have. Go for broke.'"

still were able to hand UCLA its first Pac-8 meet loss in two years. At the Coliseum on May 5, 1974, USC scored 134.5 points to UCLA's 130.5.

By 1975, it was impossible to predict which team had the advantage going into their dual meet. Both teams were strong and laden with record holders. Expectations ran high.

The meet lived up to the hype. Five meet records were set or equaled. Each school broke or equaled three school records. Four events produced the best marks in the nation that year, and the Bruins won, 75–70, behind an inspirational effort from Willie Banks, a 19-year-old freshman, who was carried off the field after a leap of 55 feet, 1 inch in the triple jump.

In 1976, USC finally ended the Bruins' dual-meet win streak at 42 in their matchup at Drake Stadium. Gilkes won the 100 and 200 meters, Randle won the 400 and USC won big, 83–62. USC's Mike Budincich put the shot 19 inches farther than he ever had on his first effort and upset Neidhart with a throw of 63 feet, 5.75 inches.

In 1977, the teams met in front of a record crowd of 15,514, which did not include a few thousand more pressed against fences and hanging on walls at Drake Stadium. They saw Greg Foster bring home UCLA's sprint relay team to a school- and stadium-record time of 39.29 seconds early in the meet.

But that would be the highlight of the day for UCLA. USC turned the meet into a romp, 91–63, behind Clancy Edwards' wins in the 100 and 200 meters and other Trojan wins in nearly every key event.

Both programs took a hit in 1978 after the NCAA adopted a rule to limit track and field to 14 scholarships a year. For dominant pro-

■ UCLA's Drake Stadium in 1974.

■ USC sprinter Don Quarrie

grams, such as USC and UCLA, the change hurt their dual-meet performances because more athletes would have to compete in multiple events.

Wolfe's 1978 team was one of his best ever, defeating UCLA in a dual meet and winning the Pac-10 and NCAA championships. But two years later, the Trojans had to forfeit their victories because of the use of an academically ineligible athlete, quarter-miler Billy Mullins. Although UCLA had lost on the track, after the scores were retabulated, the Bruins were later credited for winning both the 1978 dual meet, 83–71, and the NCAA championship.

USC had many top scorers back in 1979 with Sanford, Mullins and Williams leading the way, along with solid sprinters Mike Simmons, Colin Bradford and Timmy White. But Edwards was gone and triple- and long-jumper Ken Hays was injured, leaving USC to start the season short-handed.

UCLA's top gun was hurdler Greg Foster, who had won the NCAA 110-meter hurdles title in 1978. Foster also was the Bruins' top sprinter in the 100 and 200 meters and anchor leg on the sprint and mile relay.

And with Foster as its leading scorer, UCLA smashed the Trojans, 93.5 to 60.5, on April 28, in their final dual meet of the decade.

■ Bill Bonham, left, and Bob Pifferini.

BASEBALL

After winning its first league title in 25 years to close out the 1960s, UCLA began the 1970 season with high hopes along with several good hitters, including catcher Bob Pifferini, and a couple of solid starting pitchers in Bill Bonham and Rick Pope. But Coach Art Reichle's team struggled to a 26–24–1 record.

The Bruins lost all five games they played against USC by a combined score of 35–13. USC simply had the stronger team with Dan Stoligrosz and Dave Kingman, who were two of college baseball's best hitters, and a pitching staff that included aces Jim Barr and Brent Strom. In fact, USC went on to win its sixth College World Series championship in 1970, outlasting Florida State 2–1 in 15 innings.

The next season, USC swept UCLA again, this time in three games. Coach Rod Dedeaux's 1971 team was one of his best, with future American League MVP Fred Lynn leading a powerful lineup.

To close the regular season, UCLA had a chance to keep the Trojans from becoming the first team in Pac-8 history to finish conference

play undefeated in a home-and-home series.

In the first game, USC shortstop George Ambrow hit Rick Pope's first pitch of the game for a home run, and Trojan pitcher Steve Busby made the run stand up with a six-hit, 1–0 victory.

The victory was Busby's sixth consecutive complete game. Busby, who finished the season with an 11–2 record, was at his best in the ninth inning when he struck out the last two hitters after the Bruins had put two runners on.

The next day, USC came from behind for a 6–3 victory as Craig Perkins and Ambrow each hit home runs in the sixth inning to give

GAMES WON
The 1970s
BASEBALL
USC 43 - UCLA 13

USC a 3–2 lead and Mark Sogge pitched 7 2/3 innings for the victory.

USC, which finished first in the conference for the fourth time in six seasons, went on to win its second consecutive College World Series title and seventh overall.

After back-to-back championships, USC was clearly the top program in the nation and was 25–9 when it faced the Bruins for the first time in 1972.

UCLA headed into the three-game set against USC beset by injuries to Mike Gerakos, Dan Guerrero, Tim Doerr and Bill Susa, and had lost 11 of 12 games.

The Trojans won the opener, 2–1 with Daryl Arenstein's two-run homer. USC then swept a doubleheader, 5–2 and 10–0.

The next time the teams played, the Trojans won two of three games. With the Pac-8 Southern Division title clinched, USC defeated UCLA, 8–6 and 9–2, in the first two games of the series, extending the Trojan win streak to 13 games against the Bruins. Then UCLA snapped the streak, 7–6, against a lineup primarily of reserves.

Rick Pope, above, and Fred Lynn.

UNIVERSITY OF SOUTHERN CALIFORNIA
TROJANS
USC

FRED LYNN
OUTFIELDER
1971-73

Roy Smalley Jr., above, and Bruin Tim Leary.

The Trojans would go on to win a third consecutive College World Series.

In 1973, the Trojans won five of six from the Bruins. Roy Smalley Jr., Rich Dauer and Ed Putman led an effective offense that scored just enough for a dominant pitching staff that included Mark Barr, Russ McQueen and Randy Scarberry.

The Bruins, who finished 29–24 and third in the conference, won the opener of a four-game series near the end of the season, 6–5, behind pitcher Frank Panick. But USC didn't lose again on its way to

its fourth national title in a row.

In 1974, on their way to a fifth consecutive national title, USC swept through the regular season behind the hitting of Steve Kemp, Marvin Cobb, Ken Huizenga and Dauer, winning five of six from UCLA and defeating Miami in the championship game of the College World Series.

The Bruins, meanwhile, slipped further from their cross-town rivals, falling to 26–35, and Reichle, after 747 victories over 30 seasons coaching the Bruins, left the dugout to become an assistant athletic director.

Reichle was replaced by Gary Adams. A former UCLA captain who had played three seasons as an infielder for the Bruins, Adams had coached UC Irvine to NCAA small-college championships in 1973 and 1974.

In his first season, Adams led the Bruins to a 31–22 record and third place in the Pac-8. It was a good season that could have been better if UCLA had not lost five of six games against the Trojans in 1975.

Heading into the first three-game series, USC trailed UCLA and Stanford in the Pac-8 by one game. UCLA, at 23–11, had been getting great hitting from outfielders Dave Penniall, Venoy Garrison and Steve Connors. But USC swept the series.

The following year, the Trojans won four of the six matchups with UCLA. But the Bruins won the game that counted on May 15.

Heading into that game, USC was leading in the conference by half a game and had a 6–4 lead in the bottom of the ninth inning. It needed only three outs to claim the conference title.

But the Bruins rallied to score three runs for a 7–6 victory and took home their first conference title since 1969. Around Westwood, the game was dubbed the "Miracle of Sawtelle Field."

Unfortunately for the Bruins, the CIBA champion did not have an automatic berth into the NCAA playoffs, and UCLA was passed over for the Region 8 at-large berth in favor of Northern Colorado. The Bruins ended the season with a 35–25 record.

Despite losing 12 lettermen from the 1976 team, Adam's Bruins were still competi-

Left: Gary Adams, holding bat, with teammate Ezell Singleton. Below, Mark Barr.

tive in 1977, finishing second in the conference with a 10–8 record, 31–30 overall.

It was back to form for the Trojans, who won their seventh conference title in eight years behind dominant pitchers Bill Bordley (14–0) and Brian Hayes (11–3). USC finished 16–2 in conference play and 46–20 overall, including five victories in six games against UCLA.

In the 1977 NCAA playoffs, the Trojans fell short with back-to-back losses to Cal State Los Angeles, but that only gave them more motivation for the next season.

While the 1978 Trojans did not have any marquee players, they established a school record with 54 wins and only nine defeats. With pitchers Rod Boxberger (12–1), Brian Hayes (11–2), Ernie Mauritson (11–0) and Bordley (12–2), USC had four players with at least 11 wins, becoming the first team in NCAA history to accomplish the feat. Arizona State was beaten for the third time by the Trojans in the title game, 10–3.

After the Trojans' NCAA championship winning season in 1978, the Bruins were hoping for a turnaround in 1979 as they had a decade earlier. In 1968, USC won the national championship, and the next season, UCLA swept the Trojans and won the conference title.

In 1979, the Bruins proved that history does repeat. With the conference expanding to 10 with the addition of Arizona and Arizona State, the Bruins cruised through league play behind Tim Leary and Jim Auten.

The Bruins overwhelmed their crosstown rivals, winning five of the six games they played against the Trojans that spring.

Leary, who established school records for innings pitched and victories, and Auten, who set an NCAA record with 29 home runs and a school-record 78 runs batted in, led the Bruins into the West Regional at Fresno State, where they finished second to eventual NCAA champion Cal State Fullerton.

■ **USC tennis coach George Toley in 1979.**

TENNIS

After winning four consecutive NCAA championships to close out the 1960s, USC had another strong team in 1970. Coach George Toley still had the talented Erik Van Dillen and Tom Leonard, even though he had lost No. 1 singles player Marcello Lara, who was ruled academically ineligible for the season. The Trojans went 20–1 during the season and probably would have won another national title if not for Coach Glenn Bassett's UCLA Bruins.

When the teams met for the first time, the Bruins were considered heavy favorites. Although both teams were 12–0, the Bruins had All-American Haroon Rahim and were regarded as the nation's top team. Toley had to face the Bruins without injured senior Steve Avoyer (broken hand) and with Van Dillen limited by a rib injury. But the underdog role fit the Trojans well as they defeated UCLA,

■ **Bruin ace
Peter Fleming**

1971 NCAA singles title and eventually emerge as one of the most successful and well-known tennis professionals in history.

Connors opened the season as UCLA's No. 3 singles player behind Borowiak and Rahim and helped the team to a 17–0 record that included three victories over USC, which would slip to 17–5 and only 2–4 in conference play.

In the first meeting, USC's No. 1 player, Marcello Lara, was leading in the first set when he fell and injured his right thumb, eventually defaulting. The Bruins, even without three of their top six players, won, 5–4.

The Bruins defeated the Trojans in the rematch and again in the Pac-8 championships en route to their second consecutive NCAA title.

After having combined to win national team titles for six consecutive years, USC and UCLA suffered down seasons in 1972. The Bruins finished 13–4–1 and third in the Pac-8; the Trojans were 17–5 and second in the league.

After splitting their regular-season matches, USC won the rubber match at the Pac-8 championship semifinals before losing to Stanford in the finals.

In 1973, Toley had his best team in years with Raul Ramirez, John Andrews, Sashi Menon and Mike Machette. During the regular season, the Trojans swept two matches from the Bruins and finished second in the Pac-8 conference behind Stanford.

In the conference tournament, the Bruins got hot at the right time. Behind freshman Brian Teacher, UCLA defeated Stanford in the semifinals to set up a showdown against heavily favored USC, which had won 13 of its previous 14 matches.

But UCLA rode Bob Kreiss'

6–3, with Van Dillen and sophomore Dick Bohrnstedt each winning key singles matches.

In the rematch three weeks later, UCLA jumped all over the Trojans, 7–2, with Rahim and Jeff Borowiak winning key feature singles matches and sweeping doubles.

UCLA defeated the Trojans again, 7–2, in the Pac-8 championship match and then went on to win its ninth national team title, with Borowiak winning the singles championship.

The next season, UCLA may have been the best ever at the collegiate level. The 1971 Bruins had proven veterans such as seniors Rahim and Borowiak, along with the Kreiss brothers, Mike and Bob, and a talented freshman named Jimmy Connors, who would win the

**MATCHES WON
The 1970s
TENNIS
UCLA 13 - USC 5**

The Kreiss Brothers UCLA

Triple threat at the net

In the early 1970s, UCLA's tennis program kept a roster filled with outstanding players, from Jimmy Connors and Jeff Borowiak to Brian Teacher and Billy Martin. The Bruins also had the Kreiss brothers: Mike, Bob and Tom.

Mike, the oldest, and Bob began playing as freshmen together in 1970, and Tom started his Bruin career as a 16-year-old freshman in 1972. Although none of the brothers made it big as professional players—as Connors, Borowiak, Teacher and Martin did—they left their mark on the UCLA–USC rivalry.

Growing up less than a quarter-mile from the northern border of campus in Bel-Air, the Kreiss brothers were natural fits for the Bruins.

In 1970, Mike and Bob had one of the best seasons in doubles history at UCLA as they went 8–0 in dual matches, including wins over the Trojans. In 1971, they played on the Bruins' national championship team, then were joined by Tom the next season.

In his first collegiate match, on April 15, 1972, Tom faced USC's Sashi Menon and, despite the pressure of the match, he played well in a tough three-set loss. The third member of the Kreiss Brothers took the first set 7–5 and was leading in the second, 4–3, on his own service.

"I was very nervous, especially when I was ahead," Tom Kreiss told reporters after losing to Menon, who broke serve in the second and won, 5–7, 7–5, 6–3.

"What a spot to throw him into—against USC and probably the best No. 6 man in the country," UCLA Coach Glenn Bassett said about the 16-year-old's collegiate debut. "He played beautifully. The pressure got to him a little, but considering everything, he played just great."

In 1972, Mike and Bob won a team-high 14 doubles matches for the Bruins, and one of their best victories came over USC's Raul Ramirez and Marcello Lara in UCLA's upset victory over the Trojans.

After his brothers turned pro, Tom Kreiss became one of UCLA's top doubles players. In 1974 and 1975, he teamed with Ferdi Taygan to win 21 of 23 doubles matches and played a key role on the Bruins' 1976 national championship team.

■ **Left to right: Tom, Bob and Mike Kreiss.**

upset victory over Ramirez in the top singles match to a 6–3 victory, to give the Bruins their fourth conference title in five years.

After the season, Bassett was selected to receive the NCAA's first tennis coach-of-the-year award, having led UCLA to two national championships and a 114–14 record in seven seasons.

Bassett had a difficult challenge in 1974 as the Bruins entered the season without Jeff Austin and Bob Kreiss, who had graduated. Stepping in as the Bruins' top two singles players were sophomores Teacher and Tom Kreiss, who became the third Kreiss brother to play for UCLA.

Teacher and Kreiss led a balanced team that split its two regular-season matches with USC and then finished second in the Pac-8 tournament behind Stanford.

In 1975, behind sensational freshman Billy Martin, UCLA easily defeated USC in two regular-season matches on its way to Bassett's third NCAA team title.

In the first match, Martin needed only 35 minutes to defeat Butch Walts in the featured singles, 6–1, 6–2. Walts won only 14 points.

The Bruins finished the season 17–0, with Martin taking home the NCAA singles title.

In 1976, Peter Fleming stepped in for Martin, who turned pro after his freshman season, and the Bruins continued to beat up on Pac-8 teams. UCLA went 17–1, with its only loss coming against the Trojans to close out the regular season.

After Fleming led UCLA to an easy 7–2 victory over USC, the Trojans ended the Bruins' 36–match winning streak with a 5–4 victory, thanks to strong efforts from Chris Lewis and Bruce Manson.

In the conference tournament, UCLA won its second title in a row and sixth in eight years. In the NCAA team finals, the Bruins won a piece of their 12th national championship when they finished tied for first with the Trojans.

USC had a chance to win the title outright, but UCLA's Ferdi Taygan and Fleming defeated Lewis and Manson in the doubles final. With Taygan filling in for Teacher, who was injured, the UCLA duo won easily, 6–0, 6–2, 6–4, to create the first split national championship in the rivalry. The Bruins won the coin toss to see which team took home the first-place trophy.

1970s USC Olympic Medalists

SWIMMING			
Joe Bottom	1976	100m Butterfly	Silver
Robin Corsiglia (Canada)	1976	400m Medley Relay	Bronze
Bruce Furniss	1976	200m Freestyle	Gold
		800m Free Relay	Gold
Steve Furniss	1972	200m Individual Medley	Bronze
Nancy Garapick (Canada)	1976	100m Backstroke	Bronze
		200m Backstroke	Bronze
Tom McBreen	1972	400m Freestyle	Bronze
John Naber	1976	100m Backstroke	Gold
		200m Backstroke	Gold
		200m Freestyle	Silver
		800m Free Relay	Gold
		400m Free Relay	Gold
Steve Pickell (Canada)	1976	400m Free Relay	Silver
Keena Weisbly Rothhammer	1972	200m Freestyle	Bronze
		800m Freestyle	Gold
Laura Siering	1976	400m Medley Relay	Silver
Rodney Strachan	1976	400m Individual Medley	Gold
TRACK AND FIELD			
Lennox Miller (Jamaica)	1972	100 meters	Bronze
Don Quarrie (Jamaica)	1976	100 meters	Silver
		200 meters	Gold
Bob Seagren	1972	Pole Vault	Silver
Randy Williams	1972	Long Jump	Gold
	1976	Long Jump	Silver
YACHTING			
Conn Findlay	1976	Tempest	Bronze

In 1977, UCLA swept both matches from the Trojans for the second time in three years on their way to finishing first in the conference for a third consecutive year.

The next year, UCLA further distanced itself from its rival with a three-match season sweep that included a 9–0 victory at Westwood. The Bruins' John Austin and Bruce Nichols, who won the 1978 NCAA doubles' title, highlighted a 23–3 season for Bassett, whose team lost to Stanford in the NCAA finals. Meanwhile, the Trojans finished the 1978 season 11–10 overall and 0–6 in the conference.

In 1979, the Trojans ended a five-match losing streak to the Bruins with a 5–4 victory at USC in the first meeting between the schools.

SWIMMING

Over the 1970s, UCLA grew into a dominant force in both track and field and tennis, two areas once regarded as exclusive properties of USC. The Bruins also got a jump on the Trojans in volleyball and soccer, which helped change the landscape of college athletics in Southern California.

But the one sport the Trojans still controlled was swimming, under Coach Peter Daland. USC won four NCAA team swimming titles and eight conference championships over the decade.

When the teams met in 1971, the Bruins were primed to beat the Trojans, and Daland expected a difficult battle. UCLA had defeated

■ **USC swimmers, from left: Joe Bottom, Bruce Furniss, John Naber and Scott Findorff.**

But UCLA crushed USC, 9–0, in the rematch.

Nichols completed a solid season with 22 dual-match singles victories, but he did not win the Pac-10 title for the third year in a row. Teammate Fritz Buehning gave the Bruins their fifth individual conference winner of the decade.

Stanford, which had given the Trojans all they could handle a week earlier.

Daland's concerns proved to be valid when the Bruins upset USC, 59.5 to 53.5, their first-ever dual meet victory over the Trojans.

UCLA's top swimmer was Steve Ginter,

■ **Bruin diver Susie Kincade.**

who set a school record in the 1,000-yard freestyle and also won the 500-yard freestyle.

Two weeks later, the Bruins again defeated the Trojans, this time at the Pac-8 championships. Ginter established two conference records and had three first-place finishes and a second to lead the Bruins to a 433–426 victory over the second-place Trojans. The key for UCLA was diving, where the Bruins outscored USC, 30–5.

But at the NCAA championships, USC finally beat the Bruins with their best effort of the season. The Trojans finished second behind Stanford but ahead of third-place UCLA.

In 1972, the Trojans swept through the regular season, going 9–0 in the Pac-8, including an easy victory over the Bruins. In the conference meet, USC won by a record 50 points.

The next season, the Trojans were defeated twice in dual meets for the first time under Daland, including a tight loss to the Bruins. With Kurt Krumpholz anchoring UCLA's winning 400 medley and freestyle relays, the Bruins upset the Trojans, 59–54.

UCLA might not have won the meet without diver Susie Kincade, who swept both the one- and three-meter diving events. Because the Bruins had no women's swimming program, Kincade was allowed to compete on the men's team.

The defeat wrapped up a 5–2 regular season for the Trojans, but behind James McConica and Steve Furniss, they bounced back to win their 11th conference title in 14 years. At the NCAA championship meet, USC finished third.

For 1974, USC added one of the best freshman classes in the history of the rivalry. John Naber, Joe Bottom, Rod Strachan, Marc Greenwood and Scott Brown gave the Trojans' program an instant boost.

In what would be his final season as head swimming coach, Bob Horn's team was outmatched by the Trojans. After losing to the Bruins in 1973, USC saw to it that history did not repeat itself and cruised to a 92–21 victory. USC then won its first NCAA title since 1966.

MEETS WON
The 1970s
SWIMMING
USC 7 - UCLA 3

So thorough was the Trojans' domination of UCLA that the only first-place points recorded by the Bruins came in the diving events, where Kincade bested USC's Carl Rankin in the three-meter event.

At the end of the 1974 season, the Bruins hired George Haines, a four-time U.S. Olympic swimming coach and coach of the national powerhouse Santa Clara Swim Club, to take over as coach. His principal job was to get the Bruins to compete more effectively against the Trojans.

But in his first three seasons at UCLA, Haines watched USC go 31–0 and win three consecutive national and conference championships.

Finally in 1978, Haines and the Bruins accomplished their goal by ending two major USC winning streaks. Led by freshman Brian Goodell's victories in the 500- and 1,000-yard freestyle events and a win by Kip Virts in the 200-yard breaststroke, UCLA defeated USC, 60–53.

The Bruins' win not only ended USC's overall winning streak at 49 but handed the Trojans their first defeat in the USC North Gym pool (known as the Dungeon) since 1957.

Before the start of the 1979 season, Haines retired, and the Bruins hired Ron Ballatore, who also made defeating USC a priority. "There's a big rivalry, no question," Ballatore told *The Times*. "Our guys really hate SC and want to beat them real bad. I don't mean to use the word 'hate.' It sounds better when you say 'rivalry.' But basically, that's what it is."

Yet, it was still USC who was the powerhouse, finishing the 1979 season 12–2 in conference play and winding up as runners-up for the NCAA title.

VOLLEYBALL

After winning two U.S. Volleyball Association national titles and four league championships in the 1960s, UCLA's volleyball team kept on rolling into the new decade. The team won the NCAA's inaugural national championship in 1970, a preview of achievements to come during the rest of the decade.

Coach Al Scates' Bruins survived a season-ending round-robin tournament and then swept Long Beach State in the finals behind Dane Holtzman, Kirk Kilgour and Ed Becker at Pauley Pavilion.

USC's program was restarted during the 1970 regular season under Coach John Smith. Although the Trojans had teams in previous years, winning two national USVBA titles in 1949 and 1950, they had not fielded a team since 1951.

Smith's first team was 1–6 overall and 0–4 in its first season in the Southern California Intercollegiate Volleyball Association, which included a blowout loss at UCLA.

In 1971, Dick Montgomery took over as USC's coach, but the Trojans still struggled at 2–9, with two of their defeats coming against UCLA. The Bruins went on to win their second consecutive NCAA title with Kilgour, Larry Griebenow and Ed Machado leading UCLA over UC Santa Barbara in the finals.

In 1972, the Bruins beat the Trojans again in their only regular-season match but needed four games to do it at Pauley Pavilion. John Zajec, a senior middle blocker, controlled the net for the Bruins and finished the night with 25 kills in 29 attempts.

USC lost to UCLA in the NCAA West Regional at San Diego and ended the season with a 3–7 overall record and 1–5 in the league.

The Bruins were runners-up to San Diego State in the SCIVA during the regular season but bounced back to win their third NCAA title in a row with a come-from-behind victory over the Aztecs in the finals.

In 1973, UCLA's NCAA championship run came to an end, and so did the Bruins' winning streak over the Trojans. With setter Carlos Fonseca, USC became a more competitive team, finishing with a 9–5 record, including an 8–3 mark in the league.

In USC's third match of the 1973 season, the Trojans ended a five-match losing streak to the Bruins. Behind Fonseca's perfect sets, USC won in five games at Pauley Pavilion.

Less than a month later, UCLA avenged the loss with a victory at USC.

At the NCAA West Regional, the teams met each other again in a rubber match that went five games. With Fonseca and fellow Brazilian Celso Kalache clicking together, the Trojans won two of the first three games heading into the fourth. That's when UCLA got serious, winning that game and the clinching one.

After the 1973 season, Ernie Hix replaced Montgomery as USC coach, but the Trojans still could not defeat UCLA when it counted. The Bruins, who lost to San Diego State in the NCAA playoffs in 1973, were determined to peak late in the season in 1974 and lost to the Trojans twice early in the season, with USC winning six of seven games.

But it was a different story when they faced each other in the NCAA playoffs. The Trojans had finished second in the SCIVA race behind UC Santa Barbara but ahead of third-place UCLA.

MATCHES WON
The 1970s
VOLLEYBALL
UCLA 18 - USC 5

Joe Mica UCLA

He did the little things that count big

One of the most lopsided aspects in the USC–UCLA rivalry is men's volleyball. UCLA Coach Al Scates' Bruins have dominated the Trojans, winning 81 of the 110 matches while winning 18 NCAA titles through the 2003 season.

The Trojans have had their moments over the years, as they did in 1980, when they defeated UCLA in the NCAA championship match. But most of the time, the Bruins have had more players like Joe Mica, who did the little things to help them win when it counted.

The Times' Elizabeth Wheeler wrote about Mica after UCLA's victory over USC in the 1979 NCAA championship match:

"Joe Mica figured he was going to watch the UCLA volleyball team complete its undefeated season by winning the national championship from the same perspective that he had seen it win most of his matches—the bench.

"The Most Valuable Player of the 1976 NCAA tournament and an All-American his first three years with the Bruins, Mica (6 feet, 2 inches; 185 pounds) redshirted the 1978 season, came back in 1979, lost his starting position during a midseason illness and found himself entering the NCAA championship in a new and none-too-pleasing position. He was more used to being a star than a sub, but this Bruin team was winning without him.

"And many thought that Saturday night at Pauley Pavilion would be no exception. The Bruins were playing USC for the national championship. The Trojans had an excellent team—against everyone but UCLA. They were 23–0 against other teams and 0–4 against UCLA. In fact, USC had not won a game from the Bruins.

"Saturday night the Trojans ended their streak. They came out aggressively and, despite an injury to setter Dusty Dvorak in the first game, won the game and had the momentum. Methodical Al Scates, the Bruin coach, had to reconsider his attack.

"'I think if it had gone according to plan,' Mica said, 'I never would have had a chance to go in there. But they were stopping up the middle and we had to [look] elsewhere.'

"Elsewhere was to Mica—a skilled outside hitter. Bruin middle blocker Steve Salmons grabbed Mica during the court change after the first game and said, 'Hey, Joey, we need you out there.' Scates agreed and Mica started the second game.

"'I was really fired up,' Mica said.

"UCLA rallied to win the next three games and the title as Mica served the final point—an ace—and he was named an all-tournament player."

Scates, however, had the Bruins playing their best volleyball, with Bob Leonard, Mike Norman and Jim Menges.

At Pauley Pavilion after USC appeared to have the match wrapped up with a 2–0 lead, the Bruins won the final three games. UCLA went on to defeat UC Santa Barbara in the NCAA finals.

In 1975, the Trojans again swept two regular-season matches from the Bruins by neutralizing UCLA's hitters.

Still, the regular season is not the playoffs, where the Bruins won another national title with a victory over UC Santa Barbara in the finals.

The next season, the Bruins ended a four-match regular-season losing streak to the Trojans with a four-game victory at USC. When the teams met again, the Trojans were in disarray with only one win in their previous 11 matches, and UCLA added to their problems with an easy victory.

UCLA, which won its third consecutive NCAA title in 1976, started out strong again the next year, defeating the Trojans again in four games at Pauley Pavilion early in the season.

But Hix turned things around the next time the Trojans played the Bruins. With Brazilian Celso Kalache, Dusty Dvorak and Bob Yoder stepping up, USC won back-to-back matches over the Bruins.

1970s UCLA Olympic Medalists

BASKETBALL			
Ann Meyers	1976		Silver
SHOOTING			
Vic Auer	1972	Small Bore Rifle, Prone Position (English Match)	Silver
TRACK AND FIELD			
Benny Brown	1976	4x400m Relay	Gold
James Butts	1976	Triple Jump	Silver
Wayne Collett	1972	400m Dash	Silver
Millard Hampton	1976	4x100m Relay	Gold
	1976	200m Dash	Silver
Maxie Parks	1976	4x400m Relay	Gold
Kate Schmidt	1972	Javelin	Bronze
	1976	Javelin	Bronze
Dwight Stones	1972	High Jump	Bronze
	1976	High Jump	Bronze
WATER POLO			
Bruce Bradley	1972		Bronze
Stan Cole	1972		Bronze
Jamie Ferguson	1972		Bronze
Eric Lindroth	1972		Bronze
James Slatton	1972		Bronze
Russ Webb	1972		Bronze

The late-season victories propelled the Trojans into the NCAA playoffs, where they won their first national championship and finished the season 18–1.

Scates and the Bruins must have taken USC's success in 1977 to heart because they swept three matches from the Trojans the next season.

In 1979, the Bruins returned to championship form after a two-year national title drought. UCLA became college volleyball's first undefeated team, finishing the season

UCLA Olympic Medalists

SWIMMING			
Shirley Babashoff	1972	4x100m Freestyle	Gold
	1972	4x100m Medley Relay	Gold
	1972	100m Freestyle	Silver
	1972	200m Freestyle	Silver
	1976	4x100m Freestyle	Gold
	1976	200m Freestyle	Silver
	1976	400m Freestyle	Silver
	1976	800m Freestyle	Silver
	1976	4x100m Medley Relay	Silver
Tom Bruce	1972	4x100m Medley Relay	Gold
	1972	100m Breaststroke	Silver
Mike Burton	1972	1500m Freestyle	Gold
Clay Evans (Canada)	1976	4x100m Medley Relay	Silver
Steve Genter	1972	4x200m Freestyle Relay	Gold
	1972	200m Freestyle	Silver
	1972	400m Freestyle	Silver
Brian Goodell	1976	400m Freestyle	Gold
	1976	1500m Freestyle	Gold
Dana Schoenfield Reyes	1972	200m Breaststroke	Silver
Karen Moe Thornton	1972	200m Butterfly	Gold
DIVING			
Jenny Chandler	1976	3-meter Springboard	Gold

OTHER SPORTS

UCLA's water polo program was regarded as the nation's best in the early 1970s. Over a four-year stretch, the Bruins won three NCAA titles and finished second once behind such talented All-Americans as Paul Becskehazy, Scott Massey, Eric Lindroth, John Reese and Bob Neumann.

By 1972, USC began to challenge the Bruins. The Trojans handed UCLA a rare defeat early in the season (14–11 in overtime) and the Bruins squeezed out a 7–6 nonconference victory over USC in the finals of the UC Irvine tournament.

A lot was on the line when the teams met for the third time. USC needed a victory to win the Pac-8 title and end UCLA's reign as conference champion. The Bruins needed a win to gain a high seeding in the NCAA playoffs.

In a defensive struggle, UCLA pulled away in the second half and later went on to win its third NCAA title.

In 1973, UCLA defeated the Trojans again during the regular season, but the Trojans won the second meeting at USC heading into the NCAA playoffs. The victory placed the Trojans in second place in the Pac-8 and marked the first time since 1963 that the USC water polo team finished above UCLA in the conference standings.

31–0, including five victories over the Trojans.

USC's only losses during the season came against UCLA. The first four times they played, UCLA swept in three games, but when the teams played in the NCAA championship match, the Trojans started strong by winning the first game, 15–12, at Pauley Pavilion. The Bruins responded behind MVP Sinjin Smith along with Peter Erhrman, Joe Mica and Steve Salmons to win the final three games to give Scates his seventh NCAA title of the decade.

THIS HOLE
MARSHALED BY
GLENDORA
COUNTRY CLUB

With Robert Webb and Garth Bergeson leading the Bruins' offense, UCLA bounced back to reach the NCAA semifinals but lost to California. In the third-place consolation game, the Bruins faced the Trojans in the rubber match. USC won, 7–5, behind Scott Newcomb and Curt Caldwell.

Over the rest of the decade, neither UCLA nor USC won a national title, but the Bruins were runners-up in 1976 and 1979.

In golf, USC began the decade with a streak of seven consecutive individual Pac-8 champions and a dual-match winning streak of 39.

USC, the defending Pac-8 champions in 1969, needed four more dual-match victories to tie its own record of 51 in a row when the Trojans faced UCLA at Brentwood Country Club. But Coach Stan Wood's golfers could not hold off the Bruins, who snapped the Trojans' winning streak at 47 with a 34–20 victory. Behind the steady play of Pete Lazzlo, UCLA took advantage of a couple of bad holes by the Trojans.

At the Pac-8 championships, four players finished tied for the conference title. USC's Allan Tapie and Gary Sanders shot a 291, along with UCLA's Lazzlo and Oregon's Craig Griswold.

In 1971, the Trojan team featured not only Sanders and Tapie but also Harry Fischler and Joe Batyko. USC swept both matches against the Bruins, including a 37–17 victory at Brentwood Country Club, to close regular-season play. With the wins, Wood improved his dual-match record to 28–4 against UCLA.

At the 1971 Pac-8 championships, USC won its seventh title in 10 years with Sanders posting the Trojans' low score, finishing ahead

MATCHES WON
The 1970s
WATER POLO
UCLA 18 – USC 7

of UCLA's Don Truett but behind Oregon State's Scott Massingill.

It was more of the same for the Trojans in 1972 as they won the Pac-8 dual-match crown with a 42–12 victory over UCLA to close the regular season at Los Angeles Country Club. USC's Craig Stadler, a future star on the PGA Tour who finished second at the Pac-8 tournament, shot a one-under par 71 to defeat Truett by six strokes. Warren MacGregor was the only Bruin to win a singles match.

USC won consecutive Pac-8 team titles in 1972 and 1973. Stadler finished second to Oregon's Griswold in 1972, but the Trojans' Mark Pfeil took home the individual championship in 1973, the year Stadler won the U.S. Amateur.

In 1975, Wood's Trojans were deep and talented with Stadler, the senior leader, and Scott Simpson, the Pac-10 individual champion who also would become a longtime standout as a professional. In 1975, USC also won its fourth Pac-8 team title of the decade and finished third at the NCAA championship.

Behind Simpson, who won the individual national championship, USC won the Pac-8 title again in 1976 and finished seventh at the NCAA championships. The next year, Simpson became the first Trojan to win the Haskins Award, presented to the nation's top collegiate golfer, after he won his second NCAA individual title in as many years.

For the Bruins, things began to improve with the arrival of Corey Pavin in 1978. As a freshman, Pavin finished fourth in the Pac-8 championship and 23rd at the NCAA finals. In 1979, Pavin and Tom Randolph helped lead the Bruins to a third-place finish in the Pac-10 and 13th at the NCAA championships.

■ Opposite: Trojan golf great Craig Stadler in his 1977 rookie year on the pro tour.

WOMEN'S SPORTS

When Title IX went into effect in 1972, some women's athletic programs at UCLA and USC were already thriving. By 1974, when UCLA launched 10 varsity programs under the Department of Women's Intercollegiate Athletics, the Bruins already had one of the best women's volleyball programs under Coach Andy Banachowski, who led UCLA to a 46–2 record, from 1970 to 1972

The Bruins, who began their women's volleyball program in 1965, finished 23–1 in 1970, including a three-game season sweep over the Trojans. The next season, UCLA did not play USC, but the Bruins won the Division of Girls and Women's Sports national title with a victory over Long Beach State.

From 1972 to 1975, the Bruins won eight in a row over the Trojans, extending their volleyball winning streak to 11 heading into the 1976 season. UCLA also added two Association of Intercollegiate Athletics for Women national titles.

Terry Condon and Nina Grouwinkel led UCLA's 1974 championship team, which gave up only 11 points to the Trojans in sweeping both matches in straight sets.

In 1975, USC finally won a game from the Bruins but still lost both matches. UCLA went on to win its second consecutive title behind Leslie Knudsen and Condon.

In an effort to improve USC's program, Barbara Hedges was promoted to assistant athletic director to oversee women's sports in July 1974, and in April 1975, Judith Holland was named director of women's intercollegiate sports at UCLA.

After her appointment, Hedges told *The Times*: "There have been things wrong with the program, no doubt. For one thing, the budget last year was $11,000, which is inadequate. For another, the alumni, who are very active in men's sports, have been totally unaware of the women's program."

In 1976, with Chuck Erbe taking over as coach, USC's volleyball program ended a six-year losing streak to UCLA with a four-game

victory. Erbe's team won its first 24 matches before losing to the Bruins in the first match of the AIAW West Regionals.

But USC won the next two against the Bruins to advance to the AIAW championships. After sailing through the first three rounds, the Trojans met UCLA again in the championship match on Dec. 11 at the University of Texas at Austin.

USC took an early lead behind the strong net play of Paula Dittmer-Goodwin, and the Trojans won the first game, 15–6, and led 3–0 in the second before the defending AIWA champion Bruins rallied.

Behind Condon, UCLA wore down the Trojans to win the second game,

■ Bruin volleyball coach Andy Banachowski with player Terry Condon, left. Opposite: Ann Meyers with older brother Dave, another Bruin hoop star.

MATCHES WON
The 1970s
WOMEN'S VOLLEYBALL
USC 14 - UCLA 6
(1976-1979)

Ann Meyers UCLA

Never lost to USC, rarely to others

Some great high school athletes fade away in college; some have mediocre careers. Only a very few excel in the way Ann Meyers did at UCLA.

Meyers, a four-year All-American from Sonora, Calif., became the first high school student to play for the U.S. national basketball team in 1974. The next year she followed older brother Dave to UCLA, where she took her game to the next level.

From 1975 through 1978, Meyers was a first-team Kodak All-American, the first male or female to be named four consecutive years. She was a starter on the 1976 silver-medal team in the Montreal Olympics. And she never lost a game to USC, winning by at least 10 points each time.

"We had some really good teams at UCLA, while USC wasn't exactly at our level," said Meyers, the widow of Baseball Hall of Fame pitcher Don Drysdale.

"It wasn't much of a rivalry when we played USC. The thing I remember most is playing games against them at the Sports Arena and not having too many people there to watch."

With Meyers dominating play on both ends of the floor, UCLA had one of the nation's top programs in the mid-1970s under coaches Kenny Washington, Ellen Mosher and Billie Moore. The Bruins defeated Maryland in the national championship game in 1978. After that season, Meyers was awarded the Broderick Cup as the nation's top women's college athlete.

Meyers, a member of the Basketball Hall of Fame, also competed on Bruin volleyball and track and field teams.

"Basketball may have still been developing at USC when I was at UCLA, but not volleyball," said Meyers. "We had some great competitions against them.... But probably the most pressure I felt was watching my brother, Dave, play against USC. Those games along with the football games are what I remember the best about the rivalry."

She graduated from UCLA with 12 of 13 school records in basketball but did not get a chance to compete in the 1980 Moscow Olympics because of the U.S. boycott. She did, however, sign a contract and participate in training camp with the Indiana Pacers, becoming the first woman to do so in the NBA.

Meyers, who played in the short-lived World Professional Basketball League, has worked as a television sports analyst for the last 20 years.

16–14. In the final game, USC turned to Debbie Landreth and Julie Morgan to win going away, 15–5, for the AIWA title.

In 1977, the Trojans repeated as national champions with a 38–0 season. USC defeated the Bruins five times, including a memorable five-game match at Pauley Pavilion in October.

The Trojans outlasted the Bruins in five games behind All-Americans Star Clark, Sue Woodstra and Lynn Luedke.

The last time USC faced UCLA in 1977, it was in the finals of the AIAW Regionals at Long Beach. After defeating the Bruins in three games in the round-robin tournament, USC defeated them in the finals in four games.

The Bruins rallied under Banachowski in 1978. With All-Americans Denise Corlett and former Trojan Lindy Vivas emerging as two of the best players at UCLA, the Bruins ended a nine-match losing streak to the Trojans with a three-game victory.

UCLA followed that win with three more over the Trojans en route to the AIAW championship game. Although the Bruins lost to Utah State in the finals, the season proved to be a success for Banachowski, who ended a lengthy losing streak to the Trojans and finished the season with a 33–5 record.

In 1979, the Trojans won two of three matches against the Bruins and finished ahead of them in conference play. USC, however, played the season without seniors Debbie Green, Debbie Landreth and Sue Woodstra, who left school to train for the 1980 Olympics in Moscow, an event the U.S. ended up boycotting. USC failed to advance beyond the AIAW Regionals.

In basketball, UCLA took command over USC from the start.

UCLA ran all over the Trojans twice in the 1971–72 season, outscoring them 120–51. It

was more of the same in 1972–73, with UCLA winning twice, outscoring USC 138–68.

From 1975 to 1977, the Bruins, with Ann Meyers and Karen Nash leading the way, had one of the top programs in the nation.

Coach Billie Moore and the Bruins finally earned that elusive title in 1977–78. With Denise Curry and Anita Ortega joining Meyers, UCLA won its final 21 games, including two lopsided victories over USC, and won the AIAW championship with a 90–74 victory over Maryland in the championship game.

UCLA's edge over the Trojans came to a halt in 1979, when USC ended a 10–game losing streak with a 78–68 home victory.

The tennis rivalry was also all-UCLA in the early 1970s. Under Coach Bill Zaima, the Bruins' women's program went 15–1 in dual matches in its first two seasons in 1972 and 1973.

In 1974, USC finally beat the Bruins, 6–3, at Westwood. For Coach Dave Borelli, the victory signaled a change in attitude for the Trojans' program. Although UCLA won the first Pac-8 title in 1976, USC became the first school in the rivalry to win a national title in women's tennis in 1977.

Behind senior Diane Desfor, plus Barbara Hallquist and Shiela McInerney, the Trojans swept two matches from UCLA during the season en route to a 17–0 record.

In 1978, the Trojans again swept the Bruins but lost to Stanford in the AIAW finals (but USC claimed the USTA national crown). The next year, UCLA ended a four-match losing steak to the Trojans with a split in two regular-season matches. But USC still went on to win its second AIAW championship in three years with a victory over Stanford. ■■

■ Ann Meyers, No. 15, pressures Trojan Lindy Vivas in 1976. Opposite: UCLA's Denise Curry makes a driving layup in a 1979 game.

Bringing Out

Although UCLA began to get an upper hand in some areas of the rivalry during the 1970s behind such legendary coaches as John Wooden, Al Scates, Jim Bush and Glenn Bassett, USC enjoyed enough success over the decade to keep the competition relatively close.

But in the 1980s, UCLA significantly widened the gap over the Trojans with national championships for men and women in volleyball, tennis and track and field, men's titles in swimming and gymnastics, and women's championships in softball.

Coaching stability played an important role in UCLA's success. With Scates and Bassett setting the pace by combining for six NCAA titles over the decade, UCLA continued to push its claim as one of the best all-around athletic programs in the nation. Athletic Director Peter Dalis, who took over in 1983, did his best to make sure that continuity was maintained on the UCLA campus.

But, across town, shakeup was the name of

the game, especially after Mike McGee took over as USC's athletic director in 1984. Although the Trojans managed to win national titles in men's volleyball and women's basketball, volleyball and tennis over the decade, Rod Dedeaux, Ted Tollner and Stan Morrison ended their USC coaching careers under McGee's watch.

In head-to-head matchups, UCLA had lengthy winning streaks over USC in volleyball, baseball, and track and field. The Bruins were stronger on the football field and continued to hold command on the basketball court, although the Trojans managed to sweep two hard-fought competitions in the 1984–85 season, matchups that were among the best games in the history of the rivalry.

■ ■ ■ ■ ■ ■ ■ ■
FOOTBALL

On Aug. 11, 1980, UCLA and USC got the bad news.

The presidents and chancellors of the Pacific-10 Conference ruled that USC, UCLA, Oregon, Oregon State and Arizona State were ineligible for the league title and any postseason bowl games for that one season. In other words, the Trojans and Bruins were eliminated from the Rose Bowl race before the season even started because of off-field violations, including falsified transcripts and unearned

■ **Opposite:**
Siblings Reggie and Cheryl Miller took their rivalry to the highest levels during their respective careers at UCLA and USC during the 1980s.

The Best

"Probation Bowl"

This one was played for pride

When UCLA and USC met Nov. 22, 1980, at the Rose Bowl, nothing but pride was on the line. Nothing but that could be at stake. This was "The Probation Bowl."

Before the start of the 1980–81 school year, both UCLA and USC were caught up in one of the broadest sets of sanctions in NCAA history. The presidents and chancellors of the Pacific-10 Conference put five universities—UCLA, USC, Oregon, Oregon State and Arizona State— on a one-year probation and banned them from the conference football championship and from participating in any bowl games that season.

Their ruling said that the schools had violated conference standards for essentially allowing their athletes to stay in school (and participate in sports) without going to class.

The investigation began in October 1979 following revelations that football players at Arizona State received credit for classes they hadn't attended. Later, investigators turned their sights on the Oregon and Los Angeles schools for similar infractions.

Throughout the first half of 1980, the Los Angeles Times uncovered academic improprieties at USC and UCLA that helped fuel the Pac-10 investigation.

The Times exposed three Bruin football players for having forged transcripts in their UCLA files from a junior college and 10 other Bruin players for getting credits for summer classes they never attended. In addition to being taken out of the conference race and postseason play for the 1980 football season, UCLA was forced to forfeit its five Pac-10 football victories from the 1977 season.

The Times and the Daily Trojan also revealed that 34 USC athletes, mostly members of the 1980 Rose Bowl championship team, were enrolled in speech classes in the fall of 1979 that they had not attended.

In addition, The Times disclosed how USC track standout Billy Mullins had picked up 28 units from four Los Angeles area community colleges during the summer of 1977, an accomplishment that USC administrators believed could not have been accomplished given how far apart those campuses were. (As a result of these revelations, the track and field team was separately sanctioned and made ineligible for conference and NCAA meets in 1981. Furthermore, the track team's totals for the 1978 conference meet were retabulated, eliminating scores by ineligible athletes that retroactively deprived USC of the 1978 Pac-10 track and field title.)

The 1980 Trojan football team was expected to be a contender for the national title, an honor that the Pac-10 sanctions would not have affected. But USC finished 8–2–1 and out of the national championship picture.

Meanwhile, UCLA finished at 9–2, second to Washington in the Pac-10, a solid season perhaps made more satisfying by its 20–17 victory over USC in that infamous "Probation Bowl."

credits for student-athletes.

UCLA Coach Terry Donahue told *The Times*: "That's going to take a little fun out of the race, isn't it?"

The mood was even darker at USC, which had been 11–0–1 and ranked No. 2 nationally in 1979, because 1980 was supposed to bring even more success to the Trojans.

The Bruins, who were coming off a 5–6 season, managed to open the season with six consecutive victories, including a 17–0 win at Ohio State. In fact, the Bruins were ranked No. 2 when they lost, 23–17, at Arizona and then suffered a 20–14 home loss to Oregon. Although the Bruins were 7–2 by the time they played USC, they still had a chance to finish with their best regular-season

SEC. ROW SEAT

5

USC

UCLA BRUINS

5 1:00 PM SATURDAY NOV. 22, 1980 $13.00 L.A. COLISEUM

USC

15

SEC. ROW SEAT

■ Bruin tight end Tim Wrightman, foreground, with fullback Jairo Penaranda.

record since 1976.

Sophomore quarterbacks Tom Ramsey and Jay Schroeder and tailback Freeman McNeil, though injured for part of the season, led a balanced Bruin offense that would finish with 1,401 yards passing and 1,980 rushing.

At USC, Marcus Allen had taken over from Charles White at tailback and led the Trojans to a 7–0–1 record until they lost to Washington, 20–10, the week before the UCLA game. That ended a 28–game unbeaten streak for the Trojans and took a little luster off the big game.

Still, at UCLA, Donahue's players had plenty of incentive and were determined to avenge a 49–14 loss to the Trojans in 1979.

"I've grown up with a lot of these [USC] guys," Bruin tight end Tim Wrightman told *The Times* before the game. "When I'm playing across from some guy at Washington, I'm blocking a number. Against USC, it's somebody I know. That's what makes it so big for me. That we're not playing for the Rose Bowl, I don't think that has much effect on how we feel. The thing, after all, is coming out of the tunnel and getting hit with that crowd—all blue and gold on one side, cardinal and gold on the other. I can't describe it."

Using an eight-man front to hold Allen to 72 yards rushing in 37 carries—93 yards under his season average—the Bruins won 20–17, giving Donahue his first victory in five outings against USC.

Schroeder, who replaced Ramsey in the first quarter, completed nine of 11 passes for 165 yards and two touchdowns, including

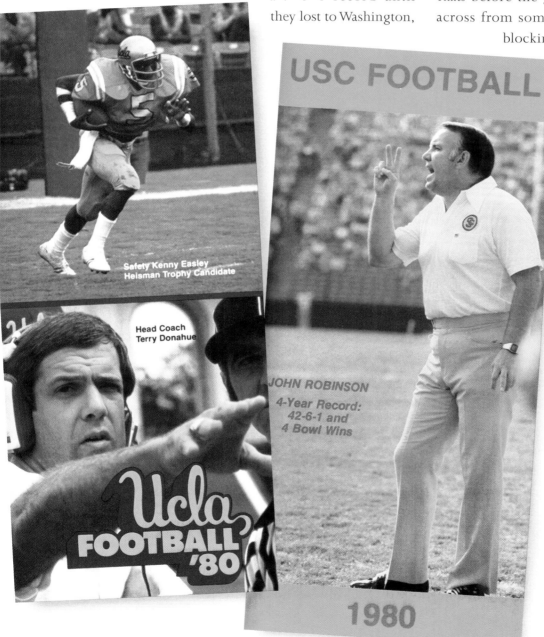

Safety Kenny Easley
Heisman Trophy Candidate

Head Coach
Terry Donahue

UCLA FOOTBALL '80

USC FOOTBALL

JOHN ROBINSON
4-Year Record:
42-6-1 and
4 Bowl Wins

1980

■ Bruin star running back Freeman McNeil.

■ Opposite: Trojan great Marcus Allen rushes in 1980 UCLA game.

catches heading into the UCLA game.

The Trojans and Bruins played a classic in the Coliseum that wasn't decided until the final play. USC nose guard George Achica blocked Norm Johnson's 46-yard field-goal attempt with four seconds remaining to preserve the Trojans' 22–21 victory, an outcome that knocked the Bruins out of the Rose Bowl picture.

With Washington State upsetting Washington, the Bruins would have gone to Pasadena if they had defeated the Trojans, but Achica's well-timed jump sent UCLA to the Bluebonnet Bowl in Houston's Astrodome on New Year's Eve and USC to the Fiesta Bowl at Tempe, Ariz., games both L.A. teams lost.

In his last collegiate game at the Coliseum, Allen rushed for 219 yards in 40 carries, but six turnovers left the Trojans trailing, 21–12, after three quarters.

USC kept pounding away and finally took the lead with 2:14 remaining when Allen scored on a five-yard run. The game appeared to be over when USC cornerback Joe Turner intercepted Ramsey's pass with 1:19 left, but linebacker August Curley was cited for roughing the UCLA quarterback, and the 15-yard penalty gave the Bruins a first down at the Trojan 44.

UCLA drove to the 29 with time running out and then called on Johnson for what the Bruins hoped would be the winning field goal. But Achica went through tackles Dennis Edwards and Charles Ussery to block the kick and cement the victory, USC's 11th over UCLA in 15 years.

After the 1981 season, USC and UCLA both had busy off-seasons. The Trojans had to deal with another investigation involving irregularities and ended up drawing another NCAA probation that included a two-year ban from bowl games.

the throw that won the game in the closing minutes, a 58-yard bomb to McNeil that was deflected by defensive back Jeff Fisher.

In 1981, Ramsey became the starting quarterback at UCLA when Schroeder left school to concentrate on baseball. Ramsey, who had not lasted past halftime in either of his two games against the Trojans, led the Bruins to a 7–2–1 record heading into the USC game.

Across town, it was all about Allen, who had rushed for a then NCAA record 2,123 yards in just 10 games and had been held under 200 yards only three times during the season. Allen, who would go on to win the 1981 Heisman Trophy, had led the Trojans to an 8–2 record overall and 4–2 in the Pac-10 and was determined to make up for his meager 72 yards against the Bruins the year before.

With John Mazur at quarterback, the Trojans rarely passed, and when they did it was usually to Allen, who led the team with 25

Meanwhile, UCLA made a decision to end the long-standing relationship it had had with the Coliseum, and after sharing the stadium with USC for 53 years, the Bruins entered into a five-year agreement with Pasadena to play at the Rose Bowl.

UCLA stormed through the regular season in 1982, going 8–1–1 into the USC game. Ramsey was an efficient quarterback, and Donahue's defense played with a knack of creating turnovers.

USC opened the season with sophomore Sean Salisbury at quarterback, but after he suffered a season-ending knee injury, senior Scott Tinsley took over. The Trojans' passing game remained strong with Jeff Simmons, Malcolm Moore and Timmy White as receivers, but Robinson never settled on a tailback. Still, the Trojans were good enough to head into their first UCLA game in the Rose Bowl with a 7–2 record.

In front of 95,763, the Bruins were up 20–13 late in the fourth quarter when Tinsley engineered a drive that ended with a one-yard touchdown pass to Mark Boyer with no time left, making it a 20–19 ballgame.

Instead of going for a tie, which would have kept UCLA out of the Rose Bowl, Robinson decided to go for

the two-point conversion. Tinsley dropped back to pass but never got the ball off. UCLA's Karl Morgan charged through the line to make the sack and gave the Bruins a dramatic victory. UCLA went on to defeat Michigan in

the Rose Bowl.

Although USC ended its season with a victory over Notre Dame, Robinson resigned as football coach and was replaced by little-known Ted Tollner, who had been an assistant under Robinson for less than a year.

Robinson explained his decision by saying he felt it was time for a change. "I kind of got to the point where I just wasn't enjoying it as much," Robinson told Steve Springer and Michael Arkush, authors of "60 Years of USC–UCLA Football."

Although Robinson remained on the USC campus in an administrative position, it wasn't for long. Within three months of giving up the Trojan coaching job, he had accepted a contract to coach the Los Angeles Rams beginning in 1983.

Tollner's first season with the Trojans—his first as a head coach—was a disaster, and the Trojans entered their game against the Bruins with a 4–5–1 record.

Donahue's Bruins were having an up-and-down season too. After opening 0–3–1, UCLA won five games in a row but was coming off a loss at Arizona. With USC's sub-par record and the Bruins' 5–4–1 mark, the 1983 rivalry game didn't generate a lot of buzz.

Things changed after Washington State upset Washington earlier in the day of the USC–UCLA game, which put the Bruins in position to go to the Rose Bowl with a victory. And that's exactly what the Bruins did.

After trailing, 10–6, at halftime, UCLA scored three third-quarter touchdowns to win 27–17. The victory was Donahue's third in his

■ A frustated Coach John Robinson yells at officials during 1980 Trojan loss to Bruins.

■ Opposite top: Karl Dorrell, now the Bruin football coach, as a player in 1985. Below: UCLA's Gaston Green struggles (and fails) to get the ball over the goal line in 1985 loss to USC.

last four games against USC, and UCLA then defeated Illinois in the Rose Bowl, a major accomplishment for a team that didn't win its first four games.

In 1984, the Trojans bounced back with their best season under Tollner and were 8–1 entering the UCLA game. The key to USC's success that season was its defense, led by linebackers Jack Del Rio, Duane Bickett and Neil Hope and safeties Tim McDonald and Jerome Tyler. The Trojans had a Rose Bowl berth already locked up when they traveled to Pasadena to play UCLA.

After winning back-to-back Rose Bowls, UCLA opened the season as one of the nation's top teams, then lost two of its first five games. But Donahue and the Bruins made up for that with a 29–10 victory over USC.

The story of the game was UCLA freshman running back Gaston Green, who replaced injured starter Danny Andrews in the second quarter. Green rushed for 134 yards, becoming the only player to rush for more than 100 yards against USC all season.

By 1985, Donahue had done his job: The Bruins no longer were considered underdogs to the Trojans.

With Green, James Primus and Eric Ball sharing carries at running back, and quarterback David Norrie ranked as the conference's passing efficiency leader—Karl Dorrell was his top receiver—UCLA had the most balanced offense in the Pac-10. And heading into its game against USC, UCLA was 8–1–1, including 6–1 in the Pac-10.

Although USC had beaten Ohio State in

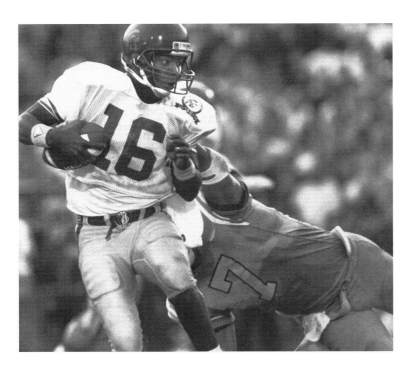

■ Trojan quarterback Rodney Peete.

the 1985 Rose Bowl, the Trojans struggled in the regular season later that year and were 4–5 heading into the UCLA game.

With a victory over the Trojans, UCLA would earn the conference's Rose Bowl bid, and even with a loss, the Bruins would still go to the Rose Bowl if Arizona defeated Arizona State.

The Times' Mal Florence wrote, "There is now a role reversal. UCLA was once identified as the 'gutty little Bruins,' a phrase not to be confused with the size of the team, just a prevailing underdog attitude.

"But UCLA has been the football school in the city, not USC, in recent years. The Bruins have won four of the last five games from the Trojans and will be favored to make it four straight for the first time since the series began in 1929.

"So, it's now the 'gutty little Trojans' trying to knock the Bruins out of the Rose Bowl. USC did it in 1977 and 1981 when it was out of the race. The Trojans also failed under the same circumstances in 1975, 1982 and 1983."

USC was outplayed by UCLA for most of the game, but in the waning minutes the Tro-

jans drove to the Bruins' six-yard line, trailing 13–10. Then on fourth and two, Tollner rolled the dice and went for the win.

Redshirt freshman Rodney Peete, who had replaced Sean Salisbury at quarterback, rolled out for three yards and a first down, then four plays later, he scored on a quarterback sneak to give USC a 17–13 lead. The Trojans clinched the victory when Tim McDonald intercepted a pass intended for Mike Sherrard.

Although USC had prevented UCLA from winning an unprecedented fourth consecutive rivalry game, the Bruins still gained a Rose Bowl berth when Arizona State lost to Arizona and the team defeated Iowa for its third Rose Bowl victory in four years.

The Bruins opened the 1986 season aiming for bigger things, with Donahue telling reporters he believed UCLA could win a national championship. But that thought didn't last after the Bruins were crushed, 38–3, by Oklahoma in their season opener.

UCLA was 6–3–1 and USC was 7–2 when the two teams met in 1986 in Pasadena. Neither was in the running for a berth in the real Rose Bowl.

If the game were a boxing match, it wouldn't have gone the distance. By halftime, the Bruins led, 31–0. And largely on the efforts of Gaston Green, who rushed for 224 yards and four touchdowns in 39 carries, UCLA delivered a 45–25 knockout.

Rodney Peete said after the game, "They just knocked us off the ball and kicked our butts. Everything we did was wrong, and everything

Rodney Peete USC

On the spot

One of the most bizarre weeks in the history of the USC vs. UCLA football rivalry happened in 1988 before the Trojans played the Bruins on Nov. 19 at the Rose Bowl. With the Pacific-10 Conference title on the line, all attention was on USC Heisman Trophy candidate Rodney Peete, who had contracted measles.

Throughout the week, the Trojans were vague about Peete's status, which only added to the drama of a game that featured two teams ranked in the top six and UCLA's own Heisman Trophy candidate, Troy Aikman.

Almost no one was sure whether Peete would play until kickoff.

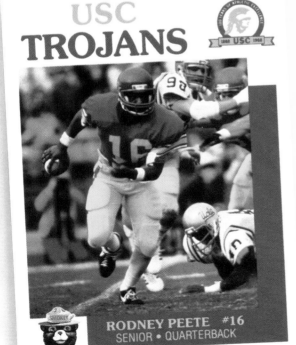

USC TROJANS

RODNEY PEETE #16
SENIOR • QUARTERBACK

But one person who knew about Peete's health was USC tight end Martin Chesley, who shared an apartment with the Trojan leader.

"I had just returned home from the hospital following surgery on my right knee and wasn't feeling well," Chesley said. "But I remember Rodney coming home and telling me that he also was feeling bad."

Chesley said he had taken some medication that actually made him feel worse, and the team's doctor, Richard Diehl, then came to the players' mid-Wilshire apartment.

"That's when all hell broke loose," Chesley said. "They brought an ambulance for me to be transported back to the hospital. When I came out, I said, 'What in the world is all this about?' There were cameras everywhere. People were in the hallways, on the front lawn, just everywhere. There were signs outside, with one, 'Go SC, for Peete's sake!'

"So, here I am going in the ambulance and people are thinking that it was Rodney. It's so funny to think people were outside our building singing and worried, and it was me."

Chesley's return to the hospital turned out to be a perfect diversion for Peete, whom USC medical staff moved to a local hotel so he could rest before the game.

When Chesley returned from the hospital, he was barraged by phone calls from people checking in on the quarterback's status.

"I remember [The Times'] Mal Florence calling looking for Rodney," Chesley said. "He kept trying to probe and then finally he asked me what did I think about Rodney's chances of playing. I told him, 'Knowing the type of guy he is, if I had to put my money on whether this guy is going to play, knowing him the way I know him, he'll be fighting to play.'

"Well, the next day in the newspaper, there's a story saying that Peete's going to play, using me as the source. I was so angry. But everything worked out in the end. Rodney lost his voice but was able to play and we won."

Peete did play and played well enough to lead the Trojans to a 31–22 victory. After watching Peete complete 16 of 28 passes for 189 yards and a touchdown, The Times' Scott Ostler wrote: "Come on Rodney, show us a splotch. One splotch. Show us a doctor's report, preferably notarized. Quick, now, describe the hospital where you supposedly spent the past week, fighting a courageous battle against the dreaded measles.

"Convince us, Rodney Peete, that you really were sick, that this wasn't just a great little practical joke you and your Trojans pulled off to throw the UCLA Bruins off-balance....

"If it all seemed weird and theatrical, remember that USC is the school that gave us George Lucas. At least they didn't have Rodney arrive at the Rose Bowl in a UFO."

Peete finished second in the Heisman voting that year to Oklahoma State running back Barry Sanders.

they did was right.... They just blew us out."

USC athletic director McGee decided before the Trojans' Citrus Bowl loss to Auburn to fire Tollner, who was 1–3 against the Bruins. So the 1987 season began

**GAMES WON
The 1980s
FOOTBALL
UCLA 5 ▪ USC 4
I TIE**

with UCLA coming off its fifth consecutive bowl victory under Donahue, a romp over Brigham Young in the Freedom Bowl, and USC starting over with a new coach, Larry Smith.

The Bruins picked up where they left off, winning nine of their first 10 games, thanks to the emergence of quarterback Troy Aikman, a transfer from Oklahoma. They were substantial favorites when they faced the Trojans, who were 7–3.

But the unexpected is sometimes the rule in this rivalry, and USC defeated the Bruins, 17–13, scoring all its points in the second half. The winning score came on a controversial juggling catch by Erik Affholter for a 33-yard touchdown. Whether Affholter had his feet in bounds when he finally gained control of the ball was heatedly debated.

Rodney Peete made a great hustle play to keep UCLA out of the end zone after throwing an interception late in the first half. Eric

Turner picked the ball off at the goal line, and Peete doggedly ran him down, catching him after an 89-yard chase that ended at the USC 11-yard line.

Peete also won his matchup against Aikman. Peete completed 23 of 35 passes for 304 yards and two fourth-quarter touchdowns; Aikman completed only 11 of 26 passes for 171 yards with three interceptions in the second half.

USC gained a Rose Bowl berth but lost to Michigan State, while the Bruins defeated Florida in the Aloha Bowl.

It was like old times in 1988 for both USC and UCLA. With Heisman Trophy candidates Peete and Aikman as the star players, the Trojans and Bruins ranked among the nation's top 10 teams all season.

USC entered the game ranked No. 2 with a 9–0 record overall and 7–0 in the Pac-10, while the Bruins were No. 6 at 9–1 and 6–1. The winner of the game would earn a berth in the Rose Bowl.

With Peete playing despite being ill with the measles all week, the Trojans played their best game of the season, defeating UCLA, 31–22, in front of 100,741 at the Rose

■ **Trojan Coach
Larry Smith.**

NFL, both teams started new quarterbacks, players who had been high school rivals in Orange County: freshman Todd Marinovich at USC and Bret Johnson at UCLA.

USC had already clinched a Rose Bowl berth when the teams met in the Coliseum, Marinovich on his way to becoming the fourth Trojan to pass for more than 2,000 yards in a season.

The Bruins were struggling at 3–7, and Johnson had not led the Bruins to a second-half touchdown in six games. The game had all the makings of a rout, but UCLA looked to the USC game to salvage a forgettable season. Linebacker Marvcus Patton told The Times: "The record will always be there, but we could say that we beat SC. Two of the most successful teams in the school's history didn't beat them the last two years, so if we beat them this year, it will make our season."

The teams played to a 10–10 tie. The Trojans took the tie like a loss.

USC finished with 387 net yards compared with UCLA's 202, and 20 first downs to the Bruins' 10. It was an ugly game with nine turnovers and 16 penalties. Each team was assessed two unsportsmanlike conduct infractions.

USC went on to defeat Michigan, 17–10, in the Rose Bowl. And UCLA looked with a hopeful eye to a new decade.

■ **Bruin quarterback and future NFL superstar Troy Aikman in 1988.**

Bowl, the largest crowd for a USC–UCLA game since 1954. Peete completed 16 of 28 passes for 189 yards and a touchdown, adding another on the ground. Aikman passed for 317 yards and two touchdowns. Although they lost to USC at the end of the season, the Bruins went on to the Cotton Bowl, where they defeated Arkansas and gave Donahue his NCAA-record seventh consecutive bowl victory.

It was a season of adjustments for both teams in 1989. With Peete and Aikman in the

BASKETBALL

Before the start of the 1979–80 season, UCLA named Larry Brown to replace Gary Cunningham as the school's basketball coach. Cunningham stepped down just days after the Bruins lost to DePaul in an NCAA tournament regional final, and it was clear that Brown was selected to return Pauley Pavilion to its glory days.

Brown didn't get off to a great start, losing back-to-back games to Notre Dame and DePaul and then suffering a road loss at Oregon State early in the Pac-10 season. Things hit a low point for Brown and the Bruins when they lost to the Trojans, 82–74, at the Sports Arena.

As expected, the victory was huge for the Trojans and first-year coach Stan Morrison, who had replaced Bob Boyd after the end of the 1978–79 season. In his first try, Morrison ended USC's 10-year, 19-game losing streak against UCLA.

With guard Don Carfino leading the way with 24 points, the Trojans enjoyed their first home victory over the Bruins since 1963. UCLA seniors—forwards Kiki Vandeweghe and James Wilkes and centers Darrell Allums and Gig Sims—were criticized for their lack of leadership in the loss.

Wilkes scored only eight points, had four rebounds and committed six of the Bruins' 25 turnovers. Vandeweghe scored all of his 15 points in the second half and had only five rebounds. Allums scored eight points in the first half but didn't score again. Sims had only four points in 18 minutes.

"In the biggest game of the year to date, our starting forwards didn't score in the first half," Brown said after the game. "Our experienced players are not accepting responsibility or leading and directing the team."

With an 8–4 record overall and 3–2 mark in conference play, Brown decided to shake up the Bruins, inserting four freshmen— guards Rod Foster and Michael Holton, forward Cliff Pruitt and swingman Darren Daye—into the lineup.

■ James Wilkes

Brown told the *Los Angeles Times* on Jan. 15: "Our older players, our so-called seniors, are like freshmen.... Coach Wooden told me that if you play as many freshmen as we do, they'll make mistakes. They're not supposed to win games, but I think we could be 8–4 now even if we started four freshmen."

In the rematch at UCLA, the four freshmen

played huge roles, and the Bruins were back in the thick of the conference race. The Trojans, meanwhile, had lost six in a row and were fighting to stay out of last place in the Pac-10. They didn't have much fight in them against the Bruins, getting trounced, 91–64.

Wilkes led the Bruins with 18 points,

■ UCLA's Kiki Vandeweghe guarded by USC's Maurice Williams in 1980 matchup.

making eight of nine shots from the field, and Foster added 14 on six-of-seven shooting.

"It was a combination of our home court and the fact we're a better team now, and we really wanted to stick it to them," Vandeweghe said afterward.

After the game, Brown said the team was inspired by fellow UCLA students. He and his players visited with overnighters lined up at Pauley Pavilion on Friday night. Then Brown stayed out till 2 a.m. to talk with the students.

After the game ended, UCLA students chanted, "We want Larry! We want Larry!" and the coach obliged. He came back onto the floor with his players for a quick pep rally.

UCLA then won nine of 11 games to reach the NCAA championship game, where the Bruins lost to Louisville.

The 1980–81 Bruins picked up where they left off, winning eight of their first nine games heading into their first game against USC. UCLA was ranked seventh in the nation, and Brown had his young team playing solid basketball.

The Trojans headed into their game with the Bruins on a mini-slide, having lost three of their previous four games. No one expected much from USC, since the game was being played at Pauley Pavilion, where the Trojans had not won in more than 10 years.

But USC's Maurice Williams made a last-second 20-foot shot from the corner that gave the Trojans a 68–66 victory.

Williams' game-winning basket gave USC only its third victory at Pauley Pavilion and only its fourth anywhere in the last 41 games between the cross-town rivals.

Again, the Bruins kept the Trojans from a rare season sweep in the rematch, winning 76–62, but this time they didn't make a run afterward. They lost to BYU in the first round of the NCAA tournament.

And just like that, Brown was gone too. The mercurial coach packed up and left Westwood to coach the New Jersey Nets.

UCLA suddenly found itself in a familiar position: sans coach. In the six years since Wooden had retired in 1975 after 27 seasons and 10 national championships, there had been three coaches for two years each—and now the school's program was in transition again.

UCLA turned to Larry Farmer, a low-profile assistant coach who had played under Wooden and survived three head coaching changes. Farmer had been with UCLA for every season but one since joining Wooden's program in 1970.

One of his priorities was regaining the Bruins' dominance of college basketball. Furthermore, Farmer had the Trojans in his sights. Although USC was anything but a national power, the Trojans had split their last four games with the Bruins and this was a problem in Westwood, because prior to 1980, UCLA had won 19 games in a row against their cross-town rivals.

When the teams met on Jan. 9, 1982, at the Sports Arena, the Trojans took the court with plenty of confidence and had an easy 86–71 victory, with Dwight Anderson and Jacque Hill dominating UCLA's backcourt. USC hadn't beaten UCLA so decisively since 1961. The win was Morrison's third in five games against the Bruins.

For the rematch, UCLA was on a six-game winning streak, with an average victory margin of more than 14 points in those games. The Bruins avoided being swept by the Trojans, holding on to a slim 69–66 victory at Pauley Pavilion.

In the 1982–83 season, the series returned to its roots and featured back-to-back games for the first time since 1970.

USC was 9–3 in the Pac-10 and 15–7 overall heading into the Thursday-Saturday matches; UCLA was atop the conference at 11–1.

In the first game, the Bruins made it look easy in a 77–60 victory. With most of their baskets coming on high percentage shots close to the basket, Darren Daye made 11 of 14 to score a team-high 24 points.

The lone bright spot for USC was Clayton Olivier, a 6–10 sophomore with bushy bright orange hair, who scored a career-high 16 points. With fans in the UCLA student section wearing clown masks and wigs and taunting him with chants of "Bozo, Bozo," Olivier led Trojan comebacks in the first and second half.

The Trojans shot a little better in the rematch two nights later but were never able to fully overcome a 16–0 deficit at the start of the game in the Bruins' 71–64 victory at the Sports Arena. UCLA needed two pressure free throws in the final 58 seconds from point guard Ralph Jackson, who had missed the front end of two one-and-one situations in the previous two minutes, to clinch the victory at the Sports Arena.

At the start of the 1983–84 season, grumbling could be heard around Westwood about Farmer. Although the Bruins had swept the Trojans and won their first Pac-10 conference title in four years the previous season, fans were not pleased with UCLA's first-round exit in the NCAA tournament.

The Bruins were 10–4 heading into the first game against USC, which was 8–11 after a slow start. Behind Wayne Carlander's 33 points and 13 rebounds, the Trojans took the Bruins to overtime before losing, 75–69, at Pauley.

Jackson, as he had the previous season, overcame his own mistakes—this time a pair of costly turnovers that helped the Trojans get to overtime—by making key free throws and a late basket to win the game.

GAMES WON
The 1980s
BASKETBALL
UCLA 13 • USC 7

■ Opposite: Reggie Miller shows his present and future greatness by dunking over USC's Larry Friend in 1986 match.

By the time the rematch came, both teams were on a decline. UCLA had dropped to 14–8, but still Farmer expressed some faith in his team. "I've seen them disappointed, angry, hurt and upset," he told *The Times*, "but I have not seen them turn on each other or give up."

USC was having even more difficulty at 9–17, but the Trojans got a measure of revenge with an 80–72 victory that helped keep the Bruins out of the postseason.

Days after UCLA's season ended, Farmer agreed to a three-year extension, then abruptly resigned a week later.

In transition again, the Bruins then turned to another former player in Walt Hazzard, who was on UCLA's first NCAA championship team under John Wooden in 1964. Hazzard, who was coaching at Chapman College, walked into a tough situation. The Bruins no longer had the best talent.

In the first game between the teams in the 1984–85 season at the Sports Arena, Morrison's Trojans defeated UCLA, 78–77, in double overtime.

It was a tense, lead-changing game between two evenly matched teams. The score was tied, 58–58, at the end of regulation, at 65–65 after the first overtime. USC's Derrick Dowell picked a good day to have a career game, with 24 points and 21 rebounds, one of which was a critical board with 37 seconds left in double overtime.

Heading into the second meeting, Hazzard had the Bruins playing their best basketball of the season. UCLA had a four-game winning

four overtimes in front of a stunned crowd at Westwood.

After the game, USC students danced around the Pauley Pavilion floor waving brooms to celebrate the victory that moved the Trojans into first place in the Pac-10.

The defeat took a lot out of Hazzard, who told *The Times*, "We've lost some tough games,

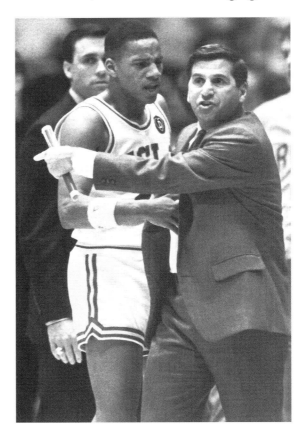

■ Left: UCLA coach Walt Hazzard with his star player Reggie Miller in 1986. Right: UCLA Coach Jim Harrick is restrained by Pooh Richardson after being hit with a technical foul in 1989 game.

streak and was coming off an impressive 75–65 victory over Louisville.

USC had not swept a season series from UCLA since 1942. The Trojans hadn't defeated the Bruins twice in a season since 1961, the last year they won a conference championship. The teams played three times that year, with UCLA winning the middle game.

The 1985 rematch was even better than the first game. Reserve Trojan center Charlie Simpson scored a wide-open layup with two seconds left to give USC an 80–78 victory in

and this is another one."

The ironman for the Trojans was Carlander, who played 59 minutes and scored a career-high 38 points on 14-of-19 shooting from the field and pulled down 13 rebounds.

The Trojans finished the season tied for first in the Pac-10 and lost to Illinois State in the first round of the NCAA tournament. UCLA ended up in the National Invitation Tournament and won the championship with a victory over Indiana in the finals.

In 1985–86, the rivalry took on a Philadelphia feel. Hazzard, a Philadelphia native, added point guard Pooh Richardson to the Bruin lineup, and the freshman point guard made sure that UCLA's three-game losing streak to the Trojans ended on Jan. 29, 1986, at Pauley Pavilion.

Two other freshmen from Philadelphia—center Hank Gathers and guard Bo Kimble—were playing for USC.

Richardson played all 40 minutes and scored 16 points in the Bruins' 66–56 victory. Richardson's 15–foot jumper put the game away with slightly more than three minutes to play. A key to the Bruins' victory was Reggie Miller's aggressive defense on USC's high-scoring forward, Tom Lewis, who was held to 12 points. Miller, who would go on to a stunning career in the NBA, finished with 21 points.

In the second meeting of 1986, the Trojans ended a seven-game Pac-10 conference losing streak with a 79–64 victory at the Sports Arena to gain a season split with the Bruins.

Hazzard called it "one of the worst efforts I've ever seen" from one of his teams.

At least Hazzard kept his job. Morrison didn't. He was fired after an 11–17 season and replaced by George Raveling.

Unfortunately for Raveling, the Trojans' top three players (Gathers, Kimble and Lewis) transferred before the start of the 1986–87 season, leaving USC with Dowell as the lone offensive threat.

The Trojans played like a short-handed team all season and were swept by a rejuvenated UCLA team, which finished 25–7 and won its first Pac-10 title since 1983.

In the first meeting at the Sports Arena on Feb. 14, the Trojans could not slow down the Bruins in a 77–65 UCLA victory.

Although the second match of the season was closer than the first, UCLA never was threatened as Miller scored 36 points in an 82–76 victory.

With the victory, UCLA won only its second conference title since 1978–79. In the NCAA tournament, the Bruins were defeated by Wyoming in the second round.

The Bruins easily swept the Trojans again the next season, 81–65, at Pauley and 85–70 at the Sports Arena, in down seasons for both programs. USC finished 7–21, and UCLA went 16–14 and did not qualify for the NCAA tournament. The team's performance cost Hazzard his job.

UCLA turned to former Pepperdine Coach Jim Harrick, and he led UCLA to a 21–10 record in his first season, 1988–89.

Harrick coached the Bruins to two victories over the Trojans in his first season in Westwood. In the first game, Richardson made a big jump shot from the top of the key with 11 seconds remaining to give UCLA a 67–66 win at the Sports Arena.

Richardson was not supposed to take that final shot. Don McLean was Harrick's go-to guy. But Richardson dribbled around a screen before making a shot that hit nothing but net.

Richardson, who scored only nine points, told *The Times*: "It was just a shot that I had to make. I'm not going to give those kinds of shots up. You take those."

BASEBALL

At the start of the decade, USC's once-solid baseball program was starting to show cracks. The Trojans ended the 1979 season by losing two of three games to UCLA and finished six games behind the first-place Bruins in the conference.

For USC Coach Rod Dedeaux, things did not get any better in 1980. Although UCLA

■ Future home-
run king Mark
McGwire as a
Trojan.

failed to repeat as Pac-10 champion, the Bruins again won their season series against the Trojans, 4–2.

In 1981, UCLA's program took a step forward when Jackie Robinson Stadium opened on the Westwood campus. Coach Gary Adams told *The Times*, "Before, we'd think that, yes, the program has improved…. But not many people noticed. Now, it's a visible improvement. People see the facility and say, 'Wow, UCLA has a good program … look at the field."

But Adams also was concerned about the Bruins' losing their edge in the lap of luxury. "UCLA players have been an unspoiled, hungry lot…. They came here because they liked the coaches, the program and the school.

GAMES WON
The 1980s
BASEBALL
USC 33 – UCLA 27

■ **UCLA's Jackie Robinson Stadium was dedicated in 1981.**

Now someone may want to come here and play just because of the facility."

The new field couldn't help an inexperienced team that finished last in the Pac-10 and was swept by USC in a three-game series in April.

At that time, Bruin pitcher Eric Broersma was none too complimentary in comments to *The Times*. "The only regret I have about this team is that I can't pitch against it."

USC also struggled in 1981, finishing third in the Pac-10 and failing to reach a post-season tournament for the third year in a row.

The next year, the Trojans and Dedeaux suffered through their first losing season in 37 years, when USC had a 23–36 record, including a last-place finish in the Pac-10 at 9–21. But despite their dismal season, USC won four of six against UCLA.

The Bruins, who finished 38–27 overall and 11–19 in the conference, lost their final two games of the regular season to the Trojans by a combined score of 30–17.

In 1983, it was more of the same in the rivalry. USC, which bounced back with a 32–23–1 overall record and second-place finish in the Pac-10, won five of six against the Bruins, who finished fifth in the conference.

UCLA's season was summed up in its final game against the Trojans. Right-hander Ken Bloom pitched a one-hitter, but the Bruins still lost, 5–4, at Dedeaux Field. USC's Mark McGwire, who would break Roger Maris' record by hitting 70 home runs in 1998, scored twice and had the only hit against Bloom, who was making only his third start.

In 1984, Dedeaux had his best hitting team in years, with McGwire belting a school-record 32 home runs with 80 runs batted in. USC also had football players Jeff Brown and Jack Del Rio, who provided more power to the lineup.

The Trojans swept all six games against the Bruins, including all three at Jackie Robinson Stadium, which had yet to provide the boost to the Bruin program Adams had hoped for.

Outfielder Shane Mack, a future major leaguer, was one of the few bright spots for the Bruins in 1984. "I like him," Dedeaux told *The Times*. "I think he's an outstanding ball player. He can hit, hit for power, field, run.... I really think he's one of the best players in the country."

The next season, Dedeaux's team finished 22–44 and last in the Pac-10 with a 5–25 mark, the worst season in Dedeaux's four-decade span as Trojan coach.

The Bruins were a much better team in 1985, with Torey Luvullo and John Joslyn emerging as a dependable hitters for Adams' improving program, which finished with a 34–30–1 record overall and 13–17 in the conference.

UCLA won five of six games against USC, including a three-game sweep to close the season. The Bruins' first victory came against lanky left-hander Randy Johnson, who would eventually become one of the most feared power pitchers in major league baseball.

At the start of the 1986 season, the Bruins had high expectations. Adams said he expected his team to contend for the Pac-10 title. The Trojans could confirm that after losing all six games to the Bruins, giving up 56 runs in the process.

"It is gratifying," Adams told *The Times* after his team won its first conference title since 1976. "I think I feel like our players do, that all the hard work paid off."

Dedeaux, who lost 11 of his final 12 games against the Bruins, retired after the 1986 season at the age of 71, with former USC player Mike Gillespie taking over the program.

In 1987, the Trojans struggled under Gillespie to a 12–18 conference record and 32–28 overall. They lost four of the six games against UCLA and suffered a three-game sweep when the teams met for the first time.

■ **Rodney Peete, the quarterback, was a Trojan infielder, too.**

In their sweep, the Bruins scored 25 runs with Luvullo doing most of the damage with several run-producing extra base hits. When the teams faced each other again near the end of the season, USC ended a 13-game losing streak to UCLA with a 7–6 victory on Don Buford Jr.'s bases-loaded single with two out in the bottom of the ninth inning at Dedeaux Field.

But in the second game of the series, Luvullo had four hits and drove in four runs, and Steve Hisey added a grand slam to lead UCLA to a 11–6 victory at Jackie Robinson Stadium. The Bruins hit three homers off USC pitching, giving UCLA 53 in 29 games.

For Luvullo, the game was special because he hit two home runs in a nine-run first inning.

■ **UCLA's Shane Mack**

The two schools split the six games in 1988 in seasons that weren't particularly successful for either program, as both teams had records under .500 in the Pac-10. Then in 1989, USC, though it finished only 16–14 in the conference, dominated UCLA, winning five of six games and scoring at least 10 runs in all but the first matchup.

TRACK AND FIELD

When Jim Bush took over as UCLA's track and field coach in 1965, his immediate goal was to beat USC. People told him plenty of times that UCLA would never win in the rivalry, considering that the Trojans had won all 32 dual meets between the schools up to that point.

Bush answered his critics in 1966 when the Bruins defeated USC and then, for good measure, beat the Trojans again in 1967.

By 1980, it was all UCLA.

Led by multi-talented hurdler/sprinter Greg Foster, the Bruins were stacked in nearly every event. Ron Cornell and Steve Ortiz headed a solid group of middle-distance runners; football wideout Dokie Williams was a world-class triple jumper, and Andre Phillips was one of the best 400-meter hurdlers in the country.

"UCLA has us outnumbered in athletes two to one," USC Coach Vern Wolfe said before the 1980 meet.

The Bruins lived up to their outsized billing and defeated the Trojans, 83–71. Foster, who had been hampered with a strained thigh muscle, won the 110-meter hurdles; Williams won the triple jump and Cornell won the 1,500 and 5,000 meters. It was Cornell and Ortiz's 1–2 finish in the 5,000 that gave the Bruins eight points to clinch the meet.

But the story of the meet was USC's James Sanford, whose wind-aided 9.88 in the 100 meters was the second-fastest time ever recorded in the event at the time.

In 1981, the Bruins took their beating of the Trojans to a new level. With USC ineligible for conference or NCAA meets because of Pac-10 violations for academic infractions, UCLA enjoyed an easy victory at Drake Stadium. The Bruins had the meet won after 13 events when they took a runaway 81–32 lead.

The next year, USC took steps to avoid another embarrassing defeat by having the 1982 meet held without team scoring. That did not please Bush, who told *The Times*: "It's a shame. It was one of the greatest rivalries in the United States in any sport."

If the meet had been scored, UCLA would have won, 42–40, with the Bruins' Chip Benson and USC's Ed Tave hooking up in the best competition of the day in the long jump. Benson won with a wind-aided leap of 25–11 (he had a legal jump of 25–9), with Tave a close second at 25–10, also wind-aided.

In 1983, UCLA and USC agreed to return to a scoring dual-meet with a twist. With the addition of New Mexico, the teams competed in a triangular double-dual meet at Drake Stadium, which lessened further the sense of rivalry.

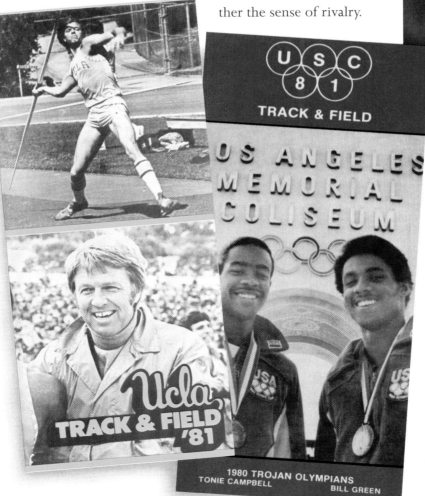

1980 TROJAN OLYMPIANS
TONIE CAMPBELL   BILL GREEN

"The annual USC–UCLA track meet has taken a different form in the 1980s. World-class performances by world-class athletes, enhanced by the intense rivalry between the schools, is now the stuff of scrapbooks," wrote *The Times*' Mal Florence.

UCLA crushed USC, 88–55, with USC not entering anyone in the steeplechase, 5,000 meters and hammer throw.

An era came to an end when, before the start of the 1984 season, both Bush and Wolfe announced they would be retiring after the NCAA Championships.

Without much fanfare, the teams hooked up and again UCLA won, 93–68, at Drake Stadium. With John Brenner dominat-

seven-meet losing streak against UCLA, the Trojans thought they were ready for the Bruins. Bullard's team was deeper and entered with a 6–0 dual meet record.

UCLA also was unbeaten at 8–0 and remained that way, winning 12 of 19 events for a 104–59 victory.

With freshman Henry Thomas sidelined because of a foot injury, UCLA teammate Mike Marsh stole the spotlight by winning the 200 meters and finishing second in the 100 behind USC's Luis Morales. UCLA also received

■ Ed Tave, above, and Andre Phillips.

■ Opposite: Greg Foster.

ing the discus and hammer throws, the Bruins completed Bush's run against the Trojans with an impressive victory.

The next year Bob Larsen took over at UCLA and Ernie Bullard at USC.

Although Bullard worked to increase the size of the 1985 Trojans' team, they still did not have enough athletes to cover 21 events. That was not a problem for Larsen, who didn't have many elite athletes but still had enough talent to defeat the Trojans, 89–73.

The 1986 dual meet was moved to the Coliseum for the first time since 1974. With a big performances from Mark Junkermann, who led a UCLA sweep in the 1,500 and 5,000 meters, and Danny Everett, who won the 400 meters and anchored the Bruins' winning 1,600-meter relay team.

"UCLA is a tremendous team," Bullard said after the meet. "They are definitely the best dual meet team in the country. They don't give you any breathing room."

in 1988 and defeated USC again at the Coliseum, 97–66. The victory was the Bruins' 10th in a row over the Trojans and 14th out of the last 16 dual meets in the cross-town rivalry.

Before the teams met in 1989, Larsen was concerned about the Bruins' health. With several of his top athletes sidelined because of injuries, UCLA wasn't as confident heading into the meet at Drake Stadium.

■ The 1987 Bruin track and field team that won both the NCAA and Pacific-10 championships.

In 1987, the Bruins swept everyone in winning the Pac-10 title for the first time since 1982 and ending a nine-year drought in the NCAA championship meet.

The Trojans never had a chance when the teams competed against each other at Drake Stadium. For the second year in a row, the Bruins cruised to a 104–59 win.

UCLA repeated as conference and national champions

MEETS WON
The 1980s
TRACK & FIELD
UCLA 9 ▪ USC 0

But with USC having only token entries in the shot put, discus and hammer throw, Bullard knew the Trojans were in trouble. "We got a track team but not a field team to go with it," Bullard told *The Times*. "We also have two fine relay teams, but no spare parts."

With Marsh and 400-meter specialist Steve Lewis getting the job done on the track, the Bruins won going away, 93–68.

■ Bruin volleyball ace Sinjin Smith shows his form at the beach in 1982.

At the start of the decade, USC had the upper hand over UCLA in volleyball, winning the 1980 NCAA championship. The title was the Trojans' second in four years, and they did it behind the play of setter Dusty Dvorak.

But USC struggled at times during the regular season. UCLA beat the Trojans in three games at Westwood, and the Bruins won again when the teams met to close the regular season. But in the NCAA championship match, Dvorak and his teammates took advantage of UCLA mistakes to win, 15–7, 6–15, 15–13, 15–8.

In 1981, USC and UCLA played each other seven times, including a conference playoff game that decided the league champion. The Trojans beat the Bruins twice, including the league title playoff game, but came up short against UCLA in the NCAA championship match.

The Bruins had to overcome injuries throughout the

■ ■ ■ ■ ■ ■ ■ ■ ■ ■

VOLLEYBALL

UCLA and USC dominated men's volleyball in the 1980s. The Bruins won six national championships (including four straight from 1981 to 1984) and the Trojans got two national titles (in 1980 and 1988) and were No. 2 in the nation for three consecutive seasons from 1985 to 1987.

tournament to beat the Trojans in a five-game match at Santa Barbara. USC led 5–1 and 9–7 in the fifth game, but Steve Salmons, who spent most of the season rehabilitating his knee, rallied the Bruins. Tournament MVP Karch Kiraly had a great game setting, and Steve Gulnac joined Salmons to make key plays around the net to give Al Scates his eighth NCAA title.

In 1982, the Bruins beat up on the Trojans

six times in six matches. And USC had a pretty solid team that was good enough to finish third at the NCAA tournament.

In becoming Scates' second undefeated team, the 1982 Bruins never were really tested. At the NCAA championships, Kiraly and the Bruins needed only 45 minutes to beat Ohio State in the semifinals and then swept Penn State to take home the title.

The next season, Scates' team overcame a slow start to win its second consecutive league title, defeating the Trojans three times during the season. At the NCAA championship, the Bruins defeated Pepperdine for Scates' 10th NCAA title.

UCLA's volleyball program reached a new height in 1984 when the Bruins won 38 consecutive games to establish an NCAA record for victories in a season. The Bruins extended their winning streak over USC to 13 with three wins over the Trojans, who won only one game in three matches.

The national championship gave UCLA four consecutive titles and Scates his 11th championship in the 15-year history of the sport.

The Trojans got a chance to give it back to the Bruins in 1985. After losing to UCLA twice early in the season, USC beat the Bruins the final three times they played, including a three-game victory in the NCAA West Regional at Cal State Northridge.

With Adam Johnson and Bill Yardley con-

trolling play at the net, the Trojans beat UCLA, 15–13, 15–11, 15–7, ending the Bruins four-year reign as national champions and preventing them from playing in the Final Four at Pauley Pavilion. USC lost to Pepperdine in the NCAA championship match.

Before the start of the 1986 season, USC Coach Bob Yoder felt that the Trojans were

■ Karch Kiraly was one of the players responsible for the Bruins' multiple NCAA volleyball championships in the 1980s.

slighted by being ranked third behind Pepperdine and UCLA. With Johnson returning to the lineup along with Chao Ying Zhang and Tom Duke, the Trojans believed they were the best team in the country when they faced the Bruins in a nonconference season opener.

But the Bruins gave the Trojans a lesson, handing them a sound defeat in the Kilgour Cup at UCLA. "The team's confidence was shattered," Yoder told *The Times*. "I think we

Al Scates UCLA

18 national titles—and counting

If ever anyone nurtured a college program from infancy to adulthood, it is UCLA volleyball coach Al Scates.

When Scates took over as coach in 1962, volleyball was not a sanctioned NCAA sport and money was scarce. His teams would play one or two matches a week, and it wasn't uncommon for Scates to pile the entire eight-man team into his 1947 Mercury woody station wagon, purchased for $25, for away games.

"We didn't have money for food, so it always was a big treat for us to go to a tournament that had boxes of oranges," Scates told The Times in 1996.

If not for the generosity of UCLA basketball coach John Wooden, the volleyball team wouldn't have had any uniforms either.

"Budget-wise, we didn't have money, so when we got new uniforms they took our old ones," said Wooden, who watched UCLA volleyball teams play in hand-me-down basketball uniforms until the early 1970s. "But if the [volleyball] team had been losing, I don't know if I would have let them."

Under Scates, losing has never been a problem. Heading into the 2005 season, Scates' teams had won 18 NCAA titles, the most ever won by a coach in a single sport.

That run of success almost never happened. In 1964, Scates tried to step down after he had allowed basketball standout Keith Erickson to play in a key volleyball match.

"Coach Wooden and Athletic Director J.D. Morgan didn't want Erickson to play for fear that he would get injured," Scates said. "But he showed up one day with his basketball uniform and helped us win a match."

A guilty Scates returned to school the next day and handed a resignation letter to Morgan because he felt that he had betrayed Wooden and the school. The request was never granted.

After volleyball became an official sport in 1970, UCLA won six of the first seven national titles. Scates' versatile teams featured tournament MVPs Dane Holtzman, Kirk Kilgour and Dick Irvin.

In 1979, a Sinjin Smith–led team became the first to finish undefeated, at 31–0, with a four-game victory over USC in the final.

"I try to recruit highly competitive players who have a history of winning, and if they are on [a losing team], they look like they are winning," said Scates. "Then it's a matter of peaking at the right time. I've learned how hard to work a team. Some coaches overwork their teams and some others under-work them. I've found the right combination of hard work and rest."

In addition to his 18 NCAA titles, Scates also won U.S. Volleyball Association collegiate championships in 1965 and 1967. During his five decades at UCLA, Scates has coached 49 first-team NCAA and 26 USVBA All-Americans, 37 U.S. national team members, 21 Olympians and seven national players of the year.

He is a five-time national coach of the year and the first active coach inducted into the USA Volleyball Hall of Fame.

overrated ourselves."

The Trojans responded to the loss by winning the rest of their games heading into the NCAA tournament, including a 20–0 mark in the California Intercollegiate Volleyball Association.

"[The UCLA loss] did shake us up," Yoder told *The Times*. "We worked real hard after the loss, we made some lineup changes which allowed our outside hitters to hit more from the right side. We discovered that we hit better from the right side, particularly Adam Johnson."

By moving Duke into a middle blocking role and keeping Dave Yoder, the coach's brother, and Chris Martz as left-side hitters, USC developed into a balanced team, defeating

MATCHES WON
The 1980s
VOLLEYBALL
UCLA 31 - USC 15

UCLA the final three times in 1986. The Trojans went on to lose to Pepperdine in the NCAA championship match for the second year in a row.

After a slow start to the 1987 season, UCLA dominated opponents in the second half. The Trojans, who were led by Duke and Yoder, played well against nearly every team on their schedule in 1987. But they simply could not beat the Bruins.

During the regular season, USC lost six times to UCLA. The Bruins not only won but they also won convincingly over the Trojans, who defeated every other team in the Western Intercollegiate Volleyball Association at least twice.

UCLA and USC met for the seventh time in the NCAA finals. USC didn't have a chance at Pauley Pavilion. The Bruins, who started a line-up with only one player under 6 feet, 4 inches, beat the Trojans in straight sets, 15–11, 15–2, 16–14, to win their 12th NCAA title.

In 1988, the Trojans had another strong season, going 34–4 and winning their second WIVA title in three years. Yoder's team also swept all four games against UCLA during the regular season.

In the NCAA championship finals, USC rallied behind former walk-on setter Mike Lauterman to defeat UC Santa Barbara in five games at Fort Wayne, Ind.

The Bruins responded to their disappointing season in 1988 with a fresh championship run the next year. Behind the brilliant play of Matt Sonnichsen and seniors Anthony Curci and Matt Whitaker, UCLA won three of four matches against the Trojans in 1989.

UCLA went on to finish the decade with an NCAA championship.

MATCHES WON
The 1980s

TENNIS

UCLA 14 - USC 11

TENNIS

In the 1980s, USC had several great teams under Coach Dick Leach, winning at least a share in three Pacific-10 Conference titles. But the Trojans did not win an NCAA championship. That left them playing second fiddle in Los Angeles to UCLA, which won five conference titles and a pair of national championships in that span.

The Bruins stood out, thanks to a long line of great players, from Marcel Freeman and Michael Kures to Brian Garrow and Pat Galbraith.

Without a doubt, the three USC–UCLA matches in 1984 stand out as some of the best-ever collegiate tennis and demonstrate how much the rivalry between the two schools often represents the highest level of college competition.

For most of that season, the Bruins were unbeaten and on top of the ratings in the Intercollegiate Tennis Coaches Association poll. USC, which was usually ranked second, was also unbeaten until it ran into UCLA in the semifinals of the Head/ITCA National Collegiate Team Championships in late January.

UCLA won the first meeting, 5–4, but it took six hours over two days and a comeback doubles victory on the second day by Kures and Mark Basham. The pair won the deciding doubles match over Todd Witsken and Jorge Lozano after play was suspended by darkness on the first day.

When the teams met again, it was a Pac-10 match, and both teams were unbeaten in league play. This time, USC outlasted the Bruins, 5–4, in 6 hours, 35 minutes.

It came down to the No. 3 doubles, the last match of the

day under the lights at USC. USC's Matt Anger and Antony Emerson edged Jimmie Pugh and David Livingston, 7–6, 6–7, 6–4.

Leach told reporters that the second meeting was the greatest USC–UCLA match he had ever seen. UCLA Coach Glenn Bassett, who played at UCLA and had coached the Bruins for 17 years, said he had never seen anything like it.

After beating the Bruins, USC went on to clinch the league title with a 9–1 record, while UCLA dropped two other matches. Heading into the final regular-season match between the schools, the match between USC, ranked No. 1, and UCLA, No. 2, was a hot topic in the tennis world.

With a top seeding in the NCAA team championships at stake, Bassett was confident that the Bruins would win the rubber match. He was right.

Behind Jeff Klaparda and Craig Venter, UCLA rolled over the Trojans, 6–3, and the momentum carried the Bruins for the rest of the season as they won their second NCAA title in three years with a victory over Georgia in the finals. USC lost to Georgia in the semifinals.

The decade began with the Trojans making a run for the national team title after finishing tied for first in the Pac-10 in 1980. During the regular season, USC swept two matches from UCLA behind dominant doubles teams with Doug Adler, Roger Knapp, Bill Nealon and Robert Van't Hof.

But the Trojans fell short in the NCAA playoffs, dropping a tough match to California in the semifinals.

In 1981, the Bruins turned things around on the Trojans, sweeping them in the regular season and winning the Pac-10 title. But in the NCAA finals, the Bruins lost to Stanford.

The Bruins went 30–3 and cruised through Pac-10 play in 1982, sweeping both matches against USC again, then claimed the national title.

The next season, the Trojans defeated UCLA twice during the regular season. Still, *The Times'* Ted Green wrote, "UCLA has the tradition, having won all those titles while sending a slew of prodigies into the pros, including Arthur Ashe, Charlie Pasarell, Jimmy Connors, Peter Fleming, Billy Martin, Brian Teacher and Eliot Teltscher."

The Trojans, deeper than UCLA, weren't as deep as Stanford, which beat USC three times, including the NCAA semifinals.

The Bruins followed their 1984 national championship with back-to-back Pac-10 championships in 1985 and '86. Over the two years, UCLA defeated USC four times, twice each year. But the Bruins failed to give Bassett another national title.

In 1987, with Rick Leach playing like the Pac-10's player of the year and Luke Jensen, John Carros and Scott Melville having premier seasons, USC steamrollered its competition from the first match of the season to the semifinals of the NCAA tournament.

The Trojans defeated UCLA, 5–2, at Westwood in a statement match at the ITCA Team Indoors Feb. 21. The easy win was impressive because the Bruins also had plenty of talent, finishing the season 23–8 and No. 2 in the nation.

When the teams came together for their first conference match, the Trojans again breezed to victory, defeating UCLA, 5–1, at USC. Then a month later, the Trojans made it three in row over the Bruins, winning, 8–1, at Westwood.

In the third match, USC's Luke Jensen crashed to the court and caught his right pinky between his racket handle and the court, and scraped his leg. Jensen needed four stitches but

kept playing against UCLA's Bud Furrow and completed a three-set comeback victory.

The Times' Lisa Dillman wrote, "They put the bloodstained clothes in the trophy case at USC's Marks Stadium as a reminder to future Trojans: To slay a Bruin, one must shed blood. But no one will ever have to remind Luke Jensen, the proud owner of the shorts, shirt and towel....

"'He brought [the clothes] in afterward and hung them up,' said Leach. 'I thought they should stay there as a reminder to show what it takes to beat UCLA.'"

It was a different story for the Trojans in the NCAA playoffs, where they came up short against Georgia, losing 5–4 in the semifinals to finish the season 32–1.

USC extended its winning streak over UCLA to five by winning both matches in 1988. The Trojans won, 6–2, at UCLA in April and followed a month later with a 5–4 victory at USC.

In 1989, the Bruins were solid again with Fritz Buehning winning the Pac-10 singles title and Brian Garrow being named the conference player of the year. In three matches against the Trojans, UCLA won easily with USC's toughest effort coming at the ITCA Team Indoor championships in February.

SWIMMING

Although USC's swimming team went 10–0 in dual meets in 1980, the Trojans struggled in the postseason, finishing fourth in the Pac-10 and sixth in the NCAA championship meets.

Part of USC's decline can be credited to the rise of Coach Ron Ballatore's UCLA program. At the start of the decade, the Bruins were finally starting to gain national respect after years of competing in the shadows of Peter Daland's dominant USC program.

The Bruins were consistently challenging the top teams in the country, and with a boost from Brian Goodell's three first places and UCLA's fourth-place finish at the 1980 NCAA championships, they began to win more recruiting battles for top athletes.

After Goodell graduated, the Bruins finished second at the NCAA championships and continued to produce individual national champions in 1981, with Rafael Escalas winning the 1,650-yard freestyle and William Barrett taking home the 200-yard individual medley title.

In 1982, Ballatore reached his goal in turning the Bruins into national champions. With USC struggling to a seventh-place finish at the NCAA championships, UCLA did almost everything right in taking home its first NCAA title.

Robin Leamy was Ballatore's main weapon, winning the 50- and 100-yard freestyles and swimming a leg on the Bruins' championship 400-yard freestyle relay team. Barrett also won his third consecutive 200-yard individual medley title for UCLA, which outdistanced Texas, 219 to 210, to win the school's first championship.

In 1983 and 1984, UCLA again had strong teams that finished in the top six at the NCAA championships. But the story of the Bruins' program was Tom Jager.

Known as the fastest swimmer in the world in his prime, Jager gave the Trojans fits with his consistency as he went on to become a five-time NCAA champion.

For Daland and the Trojans, watching the Bruins' climb was painful.

USC still had great athletes, such as NCAA individual champions James Fowler and Jeff Float, but Daland's teams did not have the same overall depth. Then in 1984, USC's McDonald's Swim Stadium opened, and the Trojans started to recover.

■ USC swimmer Mike O'Brien shows off the gold medal he won in the 1984 Olympics.

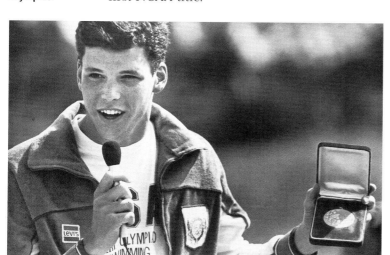

In 1985, the Bruins managed to take a one-point victory over the Trojans, winning for the fifth year in a row.

Then in 1986, the Trojans were determined to beat UCLA at McDonald's Swim Stadium, and the Bruins knew it. Ballatore told The Times, "Last year we won by one point and USC has gotten a lot better."

The Trojans won eight of 11 individual races to beat the Bruins, 60–53. Mike O'Brien won the 1,000-yard and 500-yard freestyle races, and Thomas Fahrner won the 200-yard breaststroke for the Trojans, who clinched the meet when Steve Bentley and John Clark fin-

MEETS WON
The 1980s

SWIMMING

USC 6 = UCLA 5

MEETS WON
The 1980s

WOMEN'S SWIMMING

UCLA 3 = USC 0
(1987–1989)

ished 1–2 in the 200-yard breaststroke in the next-to-last-event.

The Trojans finished the 1986 season 12–2, behind the Bruins at the NCAA championships. UCLA placed fifth with USC in seventh.

Over the next two seasons, USC continued to improve, finishing second in back-to-back NCAA championships, to Stanford and Texas.

■ **UCLA's Corey Pavin was a member of the U.S. Walker Cup Team.**

■ **Opposite: members of the 1987 Trojan swim team.**

WATER POLO

Throughout the 1980s, the Bruins fielded strong teams, but they continued to fall short at the end of the season.

From 1980 to 1989, UCLA finished No. 2 in the nation once, No. 3 three times, No. 4 once and No. 5 twice. During that same span, USC also had several hard-luck teams. The Trojans finished in the top five nationally seven times over the decade with their best seasons coming in 1983 and 1987, when they lost to California in NCAA championship matches.

The most dramatic match between USC and UCLA over the decade came in 1987 in an NCAA semifinal. Keith Leggett scored two goals in overtime to give USC a 12–11 victory.

Goaltender Kevin Stringer made 14 saves, including a penalty shot, for the Trojans, who rallied in overtime after blowing a late 9–7 lead in regulation. The victory was USC's fourth in four tries against UCLA during the season.

GOLF

Throughout the 1980s, UCLA and USC each produced more than their share of outstanding golfers. The Trojans won a share of their 13th Pac-10 team title in 1980 behind Craig Steinberg, who tied for first in the conference individual battle.

In 1981, USC's Ron Commans did one better when he won the NCAA individual championship and was named Pac-10 co-player of the year with Arizona State's Dan Forsman.

In 1982, the Bruins' Corey Pavin became the man as he won the Pac-10 individual title. UCLA, however, had a team that was more than Pavin. Jay Delsing and Mickey Yokoi along with Jeff Johnson were also important in leading the Bruins to their first team conference title.

The Bruins repeated as conference champions the next year, with Steve Pate replacing Pavin in the lineup and winning the Pac-10 individual title along with being named conference player of the year.

In 1984, it was the Trojans' turn, and they did so with Sam Randolph, who went on to win the Haskins Award for college golf's best player in 1986.

UCLA, which had won three of the last four conference championships, had a chance to win its fourth Pac-10, but the Trojans won to end the Bruins' run. The Bruins won the NCAA championship in 1988

BASKETBALL

Cynthia Cooper	1988		Gold
Pam McGee	1984		Gold
Cheryl Miller	1984		Gold

DIVING

Wendy Wyland	1984	Platform	Bronze

SWIMMING

Chris Cavanaugh	1984	400m Free Relay	Gold
Thomas Fahrner (Germany)	1984	200m Freestyle	Bronze
		800m Free Relay	Silver
		800m Free Relay	Bronze
Jeff Float	1984	800m Free Relay	Gold
Michelle Ford (Australia)	1980	800m Freestyle	Gold
		200m Butterfly	Bronze
Dan Jorgensen	1988	800m Free Relay	Gold
Mike O'Brien	1984	1500m Freestyle	Gold
Anne Ottenbrite (Canada)	1984	100m Breaststroke	Silver
		200m Breaststroke	Gold
		400m Medley Relay	Bronze
Dave Wharton	1988	400m Individual Medley	Silver
Cynthia Woodhead	1984	200m Freestyle	Silver

TRACK AND FIELD

Arto Bryggare (Finland)	1984	110m Hurdles	Bronze
Tonie Campbell	1988	110m Hurdles	Bronze
Don Quarrie (Jamaica)	1980	200 meters	Bronze
	1984	4x100m Relay	Silver

VOLLEYBALL

Carolyn Becker	1984		Silver
Dusty Dvorak	1984		Gold
Debbie Vargas Green	1984		Silver
Pat Powers	1984		Gold
Kim Ruddins	1984		Silver
Steve Timmons	1984		Gold
	1988		Gold
Paula Weishoff	1984		Silver
Sue Woodstra	1984		Silver

YACHTING

John Shadden	1988	470	Bronze

WOMEN'S VOLLEYBALL

Two of the best women's volleyball teams in the country at the start of the decade were the Trojans and Bruins. Coach Chuck Erbe's 1980 USC squad was loaded with talent but did not have one senior in the lineup. The Trojans, who won back-to-back AIAW national titles in 1975 and 1976, were led by conference MVP Cathy Stukel.

USC played UCLA seven times during the season and handed the Bruins six of their 11 defeats. One of the victories was played in front of a school-record crowd of 5,103 at the Sports Arena, with the Trojans winning a competitive four-game match.

The lone Bruin victory came on Oct. 31 at the UCLA Invitational. The Trojans then won 13 of their final 14 matches in winning their third national title since 1975.

The next season, with the NCAA taking over for the AIAW, UCLA Coach Andy Banachowski's team got off

**MATCHES WON
The 1980s
WOMEN'S
VOLLEYBALL
UCLA 18 ▪ USC 15**

■ USC's Tracy Clark shows her "killer" form.

faced the Trojans in the finals in the fourth meeting of the season between the teams.

USC picked the right time to win, defeating the Bruins in five games for its second consecutive national championship.

Erbe was ready for three in a row in 1982. The Trojans, however, did not have the same firepower of previous years and fell short, losing to Hawaii in the NCAA championship match. But USC did register two victories over UCLA, which finished fifth in the conference.

Finally, in 1983, Banachowski's team dominated its conference rivals, including USC. The Bruins, led by Patty Orozco, defeated the Trojans three times during the season and won their first conference title since 1978.

For USC, the season was a disappointment. Sophomore Tracy Clark along with Leslie Devereaux had strong seasons, but the Trojans finished 24–10.

The Trojans tried to regroup in 1984 with All-American setter Kim Ruddins back after leading the U.S. Olympic team to a silver medal at the Los Angeles Olympics. But despite a second All-American season from Clark, who had three 30-kill matches during the season, USC lost to Stanford in the West Regional final.

For Banachowski, 1984 was special. The Bruins split four games against USC and used their win over the Trojans at the close of the regular season to propel them to an NCAA title.

A key player for UCLA was Katie McGarrey, who played as a freshman on USC's 1981 championship team before transferring to UCLA, where she said the emphasis on sports wasn't so intense that it could negatively affect her studies.

With Liz Masakayan as the Bruins' dominant force, leading the team in kills, digs and aces, UCLA romped through the 1984 play-

to a great start, winning 13 consecutive matches. Then the Bruins lost three of their next eight before sweeping the Trojans in three games.

UCLA continued to have the upper hand over USC the next two meetings, beating the Trojans in back-to-back matches heading into the NCAA playoffs. As expected, the Bruins

Tracy Clark USC
An All-American "killer"

USC's first three-time All-American in women's volleyball was Tracy Clark, who led the Trojans in kills from 1982 through 1985.

Over that span, the Trojans failed to win an NCAA championship, but they finished runner-up in 1982 and third in 1985. Clark finished her career as the Trojans' all-time leader in kills, with 1,680, including a record-setting (since eclipsed) 36 against UCLA on Nov. 20, 1985.

After losing to UCLA, the defending national champions, in a grueling five-game match earlier in the season, Clark led USC to a 15–11, 15–10, 10–15, 5–15, 15–10 victory at the Sports Arena.

"That match was special because it was my 21st birthday," Clark said. "We normally played our matches at USC's North Gym, but that night we faced UCLA at the Sports Arena, which gave the rivalry a different feel.

"The match was close from the start. We jumped out to win the first two games, but then they came back and tied it up, forcing a fifth game. Every point in that game had drama because both teams wanted to win so badly."

The Times' Julie Cart wrote: "The football game is not until Saturday afternoon, but nothing, it seems, stands in the way of the USC–UCLA rivalry. The schools got a head start on their fussing and feuding [when] USC beat UCLA in a slight upset.

"'I felt that if we had any chance to win the national championship, we had to win this match,' USC Coach Chuck Erbe said. 'We had to beat a team that is as good as UCLA.'"

The final time Clark faced the Bruins also was her final collegiate match. It was in the consolation match of the 1985 NCAA Final Four, and Clark put on a show, leading the Trojans to a five-game victory, 15–7, 15–12, 8–15, 11–15, 15–3 at Kalamazoo, Mich.

"That last match was also special because all of my family from the Detroit area was there," Clark said. "Although I knew it was my final match, the importance of beating UCLA took over. We may not have won the national title that year, but we did beat the Bruins, which is almost just as good."

---

offs and then came from behind to defeat Stanford in the championship match.

Masakayan was named UCLA's first winner of the Honda Award, given nationally to the outstanding collegiate athlete in her sport.

The Bruins opened the next season with nine straight wins and were 14–3 when they beat the Trojans in five games in mid-October.

But when the teams faced off again, the Trojans rode the power hitting of Clark and Yvonne Lewis to a grueling five-game victory at the Sports Arena.

At the NCAA championships, the Bruins reached the semifinals, where they lost to Pacific. In the consolation game, UCLA faced USC, which had lost to Stanford.

In the third five-game match of the season between the teams, the Trojans outlasted UCLA to finish No. 3 in the nation.

The next season was Erbe's worst at USC. With Lewis suffering a season-ending knee injury, USC finished 2–32 overall, including three defeats to the conference-champion Bruins.

In 1987, UCLA beat the Trojans early in the season, then lost two matches later. And the next year, UCLA put together a great team but lost to Texas in the NCAA semifinal match.

After UCLA's second victory over USC that season, The Times' Maryann Hudson wrote, "For about 20 minutes, and a few other brief moments, the top-ranked UCLA women's volleyball team had as tough a workout as it has had all season…. But when the match was over … UCLA remained the only undefeated team in the country."

Before the start of the 1989 season, Erbe stepped down at USC and was replaced by Lisa Love. Love got the Trojans off to a strong start, winning 14 of their first 18 matches, but then USC lost nine of its last 14 and lost to Stanford in the first round of the NCAA playoffs.

UCLA handed the Trojans two of their defeats en route to completing its second undefeated Pac-10 season. With Elaine Youngs and Daiva Tomkus providing great leadership and freshman Natalie Williams stepping into the lineup, the Bruins went 18–0 in the conference and 30–3 overall, losing to Nebraska in the NCAA semifinals.

WOMEN'S BASKETBALL

Even after beginning to award women's basketball scholarships in 1976–77, USC continued to go through some growing pains against the Bruins.

UCLA won 13 of 14 games heading into the second meeting between the teams in the 1979–80 season. The Bruins, who would finish the season 18–12, two years removed from their first national championship, had owned the Trojans, but USC pulled out a 99–81 victory at Pauley Pavilion.

In 1980–81, UCLA again had a strong team, led by senior Denise Curry. UCLA defeated the Trojans twice in 1981 but gave up 102 points in a loss to USC on March 13.

The landscape of Southern California women's basketball changed in 1981–82, when twins Pam and Paula McGee enrolled at USC. With the sisters dominating inside and freshman Cynthia Cooper

providing solid play on the perimeter, the Trojans went 23–4 overall and 9–3 in the conference.

USC won two close games against UCLA to extend its winning streak in the rivalry to three games. USC lost to Tennessee in a Midwest Regional Final. The next season, the Trojans were even better with the addition of Cheryl Miller and point guard Rhonda Windham.

With Anne Dean and Jackie Joyner being Coach Billie Moore's key players, UCLA finished 18–11 with two late-season defeats by the Trojans.

GAMES WON
The 1980s
WOMEN'S BASKETBALL
USC 14 - UCLA 7

■ The magazine cover that the Trojans could only dream of featured their stars of the 1980s.

USC crushed the Bruins, 82–62, in their second meeting, their fifth win in a row over UCLA and part of the Trojan's 18-game winning streak to close the season. In the NCAA playoffs, Windham set a Final Four record with 16 assists in the semifinals, and Miller scored a game-high 27 points in the championship victory over Louisiana Tech.

The next season, USC thumped UCLA twice by a total of 40 points, led by Miller, who would win the first of her three consecutive Naismith Awards as the nation's top female basketball player. USC won its second consecutive NCAA title.

In 1984–85, UCLA brought USC back down to earth. The Bruins finished 20–10 overall and 10–4 in the conference, and swept two games from USC.

UCLA defeated USC, 77–73, at Pauley Pavilion, then beat the Trojans, 57–56, in the final regular-season game, becoming the first team to sweep a pair of games from a Cheryl Miller-led Trojan squad.

In 1985–86, Miller suffered a concussion and a neck injury, in an 89–67 victory, when she drove the lane and attempted what USC Coach Linda Sharp called "an NBA move." She tried to split two players, collided with one and fell.

When the teams faced each other again, the rematch was over early. With Miller getting 29 points and 15 rebounds, USC won easily, 89–57.

1980s UCLA Olympic Medalists

BASKETBALL			
Denise Curry	1984		Gold

GYMNASTICS			
Pam Bileck	1984	Team	Silver
Tim Daggett	1984	Team	Gold
		Pommel Horse	Bronze
Mitch Gaylord	1984	Team	Gold
		Vault	Silver
		Rings	Bronze
		Parallel Bars	Bronze
Julianne McNamara	1984	Uneven Bars	Gold
		Team	Silver
		Floor Exercise	Silver
Tracee Talavera	1984	Team	Silver
Peter Vidmar	1984	Team	Gold
		Pommel Horse	Gold
		All-Around	Silver

ROWING			
Carol Bower	1984	Eights with Cox	Gold
Kevin Still	1984	Pairs with Cox	Bronze

SWIMMING			
Bruce Hayes	1984	4x200m Freestyle Relay	Gold
Tom Jager	1988	4x100m Freestyle Relay	Gold
	1988	4x100m Medley Relay	Gold
	1988	50m Freestyle	Silver
Craig Oppel	1988	4x200m Freestyle Relay	Gold
Mark Stockwell (Australia)	1984	100m Freestyle	Silver
		4x100m Freestyle Relay	Silver
		4x100m Medley Relay	Bronze

WATER POLO			
Joe Vargas	1984		Silver

UCLA Olympic Medalists

TRACK AND FIELD

Evelyn Ashford	1984	100 meters	Gold
		4x100m Relay	Gold
	1988	4x100m Relay	Gold
	1988	100 meters	Silver
Jeanette Bolden	1984	4x100m Relay	Gold
Danny Everett	1988	4x400m Relay	Gold
		400 meters	Bronze
Greg Foster	1984	110m High Hurdles	Silver
Dave Laut	1984	Shot Put	Bronze
Sherri Howard	1984	4x400m Relay	Gold
Florence Griffith Joyner	1984	200 meters	Silver
	1988	100 meters	Gold
		200 meters	Gold
		4x100m Relay	Gold
		4x400m Relay	Silver
Jackie Joyner-Kersee	1984	Heptathalon	Silver
	1988	Heptathalon	Gold
		Long Jump	Gold
Steve Lewis	1988	400 meters	Gold
		4x400m Relay	Gold
Andre Phillips	1988	400m Intermediate Hurdles	Gold
Mike Powell	1988	Long Jump	Silver
Mike Tully	1984	Pole Vault	Silver

VOLLEYBALL

Jeanette Beauprey	1984	Silver
Karch Kiraly	1984	Gold
	1988	Gold
Ricci Luyties	1988	Gold
Doug Partie	1988	Gold
Steve Salmons	1984	Gold
Dave Saunders	1984	Gold
	1988	Gold

WRESTLING

Dave Schultz	1984	Freestyle, Welterweight	Gold
Mark Schultz	1984	Freestyle, Middleweight	Gold

The Trojans swept UCLA in 1986–87, with Windham as the catalyst. In the first meeting, she made several key plays down the stretch in the Trojans' 76–72 victory at UCLA.

In the rematch, Windham led USC with her shooting, making 12 of 17 field goals and scoring 24 points in an 81–75 victory at the Sports Arena.

USC extended its winning streak to six games over UCLA with a two-game sweep in 1987–88. Cherie Nelson destroyed the Bruins' defense in the second game with a career-high 38 points and 12 rebounds in an 86–63 victory at the Sports Arena.

The Bruins ended the streak the first time the teams faced each other the next season. UCLA took advantage of several USC defensive breakdowns in a 76–62 win in the Sports Arena. UCLA's Althea Ford had a big game, and the Bruins' backcourt took care of the ball enough to run the Trojans off their own home court.

USC used that loss as motivation for the rematch. With UCLA committing 20 turnovers and getting outrebounded, 49–38, the Trojans won, 90–75, at Pauley. Nelson dominated the game with 33 points and 11 rebounds in her last game in Westwood.

■ WOMEN'S TRACK AND FIELD

Although USC and UCLA both had women's track programs dating to the mid-1970s, the schools did not start competing in official dual meets until 1984. The Bruins had a long history of outstanding track athletes, from Evelyn Ashford, Francie Larrieu and Kate Schmidt to Florence Griffith, Jeanette Bolden and Sherri Howard, and had won NCAA championships in 1982 and 1983 before the rivalry's inaugural meet.

USC also had its share of great performers before 1984. Patty Van Wolvelaere was an Olympic hurdler in the late 1960s, and Sherry Calvert was a world-class competitor in the javelin in the 1970s.

But the Trojans lacked the rich history of the Bruins when the teams first met at Drake Stadium. That's why no one was too surprised when UCLA won the first meet, although the 76–74 score was much closer than expected.

The second time the teams squared off, in 1985, it wasn't that close. Behind a dominating effort from Jackie Joyner and Gail Devers, the Bruins ran off to an 89–43 victory at USC.

The next year, USC finally defeated the Bruins, thanks to an extraordinary effort from Leslie Maxie.

Her anchor leg in the 1,600 relay, the meet's final event, lifted USC over UCLA, 69–67. Maxie, a freshman, had already won the 400-meter hurdles in a school-record 56.72 seconds and had run the first leg of the winning 400 relay. She was supposed to run the third leg in the 1,600 until Coach Fred LaPlante changed the order because Gervaise McCraw,

■ Opposite: Bruin star Gail Devers.

JACKIE JOYNER

POLLY PLUMER

the scheduled anchor, had a hamstring injury and had asked for the switch.

Maxie, despite a pulled muscle, kept a slim lead on Devers, who was competing in her seventh event of the day, and pulled away to give the Trojans the victory.

Devers won the 100 and 200 meters, long jump and 100-meter hurdles. But it wasn't enough to beat the Trojans, who received a big effort from Wendy Brown, who won the high jump at 5–7 and the triple jump at 43–4 and finished second in the long jump at 20–10 3/4.

In 1987, the teams hooked up again in a classic, with Devers and Brown both expected to compete in multiple events.

The 1987 meet ended with the same score, USC winning 69–67, but it did not have to come down to the final event. With Brown establishing an American record in the triple jump at 44 feet, 11 3/4 inches, the Trojans had the meet won after the 200 meters.

Devers again had a big meet. She won four events, ran an electrifying leg on the sprint relay team, making up about an 8-meter deficit on the anchor leg, and placed third in the triple jump. In three dual meets against USC,

Devers competed in 19 events and won 13.

At the Pac-10 meet, USC and UCLA bumped heads when LaPlante filed a protest after Devers won the long jump, claiming she went out of turn on her last jump.

LaPlante's protest was upheld until UCLA Coach Bob Kersee got things sorted out with the meet's jury of appeals and Devers kept her first-place finish. The Bruins won the meet by outscoring the second-place Trojans, 121–107.

In 1988, UCLA defeated the Trojans, 89–54, at the Coliseum and then followed that victory the next season with a 101.5–28.5 trouncing at Drake Stadium. The Bruins ended the decade with a 4–2 record against USC.

MEETS WON
The 1980s
WOMEN'S TRACK & FIELD
UCLA 4 - USC 2
(1984–1989)

■ ■ ■ ■ ■ ■ ■ ■ ■ ■ ■ ■ ■

WOMEN'S TENNIS

After winning three consecutive national women's team tennis championships in the 1970s, USC began the decade looking for more victories.

Anne White, Sheila McInerney, Trey Lewis, Nina Voydat, Anna Lucia Fernandez and Anna Maria Fernandez played solid tennis all season, and the Trojans went 30–0 to win their fourth national title. USC swept three matches from UCLA during the season.

USC looked to extend its championship streak in 1981 and defeated UCLA twice during the regular season but lost to Florida at the AIAW nationals. With USC out of the way, UCLA won its first team national title behind

GAMES WON
The 1980s
WOMEN'S TENNIS
USC 19 - UCLA 3

All-Americans Kathrin Keil, Ann Hendricksson and Shelly Solomon.

In 1982, UCLA defeated USC three out of four matches, including a 5–4 victory in a semifinal match of the NCAA championships. But the Bruins failed to win their second title in a row.

The next season, USC Coach Dave Borelli had another strong team, and the Trojans finished 31–0, winning their sixth national championship. USC defeated UCLA in both matches.

USC reached the finals again in 1984 but lost to Stanford, finishing the season at 26–7, which included another two-match sweep over the Bruins.

In 1985, USC extended its winning streak to six over UCLA and won its second national championship in three years. Although the Trojans did not win a national title in 1986, they reached the finals again before losing to Stanford.

The Bruins finally beat the Trojans again in 1987. UCLA won the first match between the teams, 6–3, at USC behind a clutch singles victory from Maria LaFranchi.

In 1988, USC started on another winning streak with two victories over the Bruins, but it was the Bruins who came on strong at the end of the season, finishing third in the NCAAs behind doubles champions Allyson Cooper and Stella Sampras.

The next season, UCLA was runner-up to Stanford for the NCAA title. On their way to the second-place national finish, the Bruins got past USC in the tournament, 5–4. ■■

■ Opposite: Bruin track standout Florence Griffith at the 1984 Olympics, where she won a silver medal.

CHAPTER SIX

The 1990s

Westwood Takes Charge

for UCLA softball, a women's sport not offered at USC.

Probably the most spectacular achievement of the decade was the Bruins' 1995 NCAA basketball championship. Coached by Jim Harrick, a team led by Ed and Charles O'Bannon, Tyus Edney and Toby Bailey gave UCLA its first men's hoop title since John Wooden's final season 20 years earlier.

But there were sports casualties as well, as Title IX requirements of parity in spending for men's and women's sports forced UCLA to drop its men's swimming and men's gymnastics programs in 1994 to equalize budgets.

The 1990s will always be remembered as the one—or at least the first—decade in which UCLA owned USC in football. Coach Terry Donahue started the Bruins' run of eight consecutive victories with a 24–21 win in 1991, and Bob Toledo completed the string with wins from 1996 through 1998.

FOOTBALL

At the start of the 1990 season, few could have imagined that UCLA was poised to dominate USC for eight of the next 10 years. The Bruins were coming off a 3–7–1 season and had abruptly switched quarterbacks—from Jim Bonds to 19-year-old Tommy Maddox— at halftime of the second game of the decade's opening season.

Maddox didn't let his sudden introduction impede his downfield march. He showed real promise from the start and was leading the Pac-10 in total offense in his first season in the slot. Although the team record was just 5–5–1 by the time of the USC game, UCLA was probably a stronger team than its standing indicated.

The Trojans also had an effective young quarterback in sophomore Todd Mari-

■ **Bruin Coach Terry Donahue has good reason to cheer. UCLA beat the Trojans for eight straight years in the 1990s.**

Bruin dominance flowed over into other sports early in the decade. Although UCLA did not win as many national championships in the 1990s (16) as during the 1980s (21), the Bruins held a clear edge over the Trojans in volleyball, tennis and track and field, where UCLA won every regular-season meet with USC in the decade.

But after Heisman Trophy winner Mike Garrett replaced Mike McGee as USC athletic director in 1993, the Trojans began rebuilding their varsity programs with noticeable and notable success.

Overall, UCLA and USC combined for 22 national titles during the decade, including four for the UCLA men's volleyball team and three for the USC men's tennis team, and three

**GAMES WON
The 1990s**

FOOTBALL

UCLA 8 ▪ USC 2

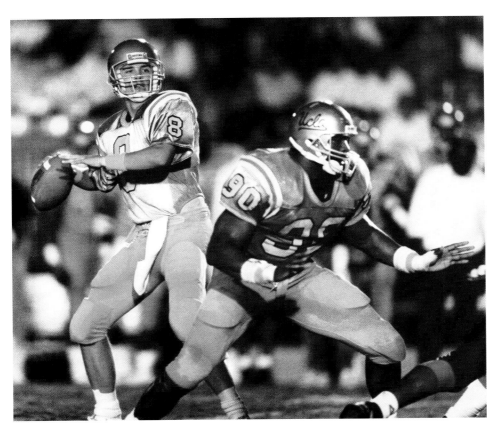

novich, who led the team to a 7–2–1 mark heading into UCLA week.

Maddox was a concern for the Trojans, who were vulnerable against the pass, and the young Bruin quarterback took advantage. He passed for a school-record 409 yards and three touchdowns, but his effort wasn't enough. Marinovich threw a 23-yard touchdown pass to redshirt freshman Johnnie Morton with 16 seconds remaining to give the Trojans a dramatic 45–42 victory at the Rose Bowl.

Marinovich finished with 16 completions in 25 attempts for 215 yards and two touch-

■ Top: Bruin quarterback Tommy Maddox prepares to throw behind the protection of Corwin Anthony.

■ Bottom: USC's Johnnie Morton snags a touchdown pass in front of UCLA's Dion Lambert in 1990. Later in the fourth quarter, Morton grabbed his second—and game-winning—touchdown pass.

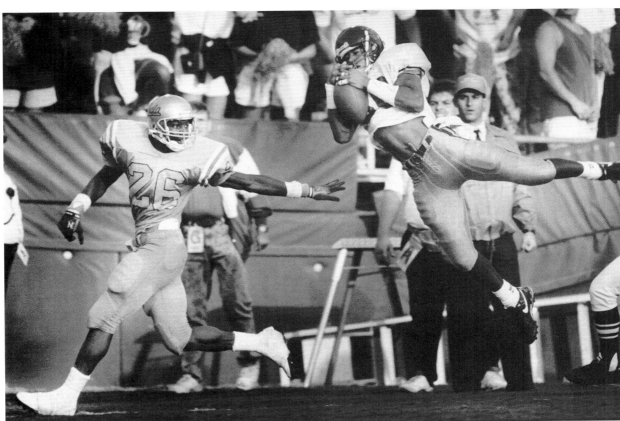

downs. The Trojans' Mazio Royster also had a big game with 157 yards and a touchdown in 31 carries.

In defeat, Maddox was a hero to many. The *Los Angeles Times*' Jim Murray wrote: "Move over Bob Waterfield. Make way for Tommy Maddox... the most dangerous guy with the football in the land.... What a quarterback he's going to be when he grows up. What a quarterback he is now!"

In 1991, the Bruins won seven of their first 10 games with Maddox again putting up impressive numbers. USC, with Marinovich having turned pro early, lost seven of its first 10 games, including five in a row leading up to the UCLA game.

At the Coliseum, the Trojans played one of their best games of the season, but UCLA, behind big plays from Arnold Ale and Mike Chalenski, won 24–21. It was the Bruins' first win against the Trojans since 1986.

UCLA benefited from a controversial call late in the second quarter, when Brian Allen's touchdown gave the Bruins a 17–0 lead. Fullback Maury Toy fumbled at the one-foot line, and it was several minutes before officials ruled that the Bruins had recovered and scored. It was 30 more minutes before reporters were notified that Allen

was credited with the touchdown, not Toy.

The Times' Bill Dwyre wrote at the time, "As confusing things go, this one ranks right up there with Pentagon doublespeak and any day on the stock market."

■ Trojan quarterback Todd Marinovich

Not many expected the Bruins to make it two in a row in 1992. USC had bounced back with Rob Johnson at quarterback and was 6–2–1 heading into the UCLA game.

Johnson, the brother of former UCLA quarterback Bret, who transferred to Michigan State after leading the Bruins to a 3–7–1 record in 1989, told *The Times*, "I dislike UCLA a little more than the rest because it's a big-time rivalry. Throwing in Bret's situation just adds to it."

The Bruins were 5–5 and going nowhere with senior quarterback John Barnes, a fourth-string walk-on who had started only two other games.

But against the Trojans, Barnes played like a Heisman Trophy winner and led the Bruins to a 38–37 victory. He passed for 204 of his 385 yards in the fourth quarter and brought the Bruins back from a 35–17 deficit, though the victory wasn't secure until USC failed on a two-point conversion with 41 seconds to play.

The key play was Barnes' 90-yard touchdown pass to J.J. Stokes that gave UCLA a 38–31 lead with 3:08 remaining. On the Trojans' final drive, Johnson drove the ball 69 yards in 11 plays for a touchdown, but his conversion pass intended for tight end Yonnie Jackson was knocked away by UCLA's Nkosi Littleton.

Before the start of the 1993 season, John Robinson was named to replace Larry Smith, whose losses in the final three games of the 1992 season, including a

disappointing defeat to Fresno State in the Freedom Bowl, had cost him the coaching job.

Robinson led USC to a 7–4 record heading into its game against UCLA at the Coliseum. The Trojans were led by the passing combination of Johnson to Morton and were one victory away from returning to the Rose Bowl for the first time since 1990.

But the Bruins also had a chance to go to the Rose Bowl if they could defeat USC.

It was another close game. With 50 second to play, UCLA safety Marvin Goodwin intercepted Johnson's pass to Tyler Cashman in the end zone to ensure UCLA's 27–21 victory.

The win ended UCLA's 10-game losing streak to USC when a trip to the Rose Bowl was on the line for both teams. The Bruins would not have won without tailback Ricky Davis, who rushed for 153 yards.

In 1994, USC was on a five-game winning

■ **UCLA quarterback Cade McNown fends off Trojan tackle Darrell Russell in 1996 game.**

streak and UCLA had lost six of eight as their matchup approached. All bets were on USC to come out on top.

But the Trojans couldn't do it, and it wasn't even close. USC failed to stop quarterback Wayne Cook, who completed 15 of 23 passes for two touchdowns in UCLA's 31–19 victory at the Rose Bowl.

UCLA's Sharmon Shah, later known as Karim Abdul-Jabbar, ran for 135 yards in 25 carries, including the go-ahead touchdown with a five-yard run in the third quarter. It was Shah's aggressive running that helped turn the game around for the Bruins, who trailed 12–3 at halftime.

After defeating Texas Tech in the Cotton Bowl and finishing the 1994 season with an 8–3–1 record, the Trojans opened the 1995 season ranked No. 7 in the nation. With Keyshawn Johnson being the main target for quarterback Brad Otton on offense and linebacker Scott Fields and Sammy Knight spearheading a solid defense, the Trojans dominated the Pac-10.

By the time USC faced UCLA at the Coliseum, the Trojans had a Rose Bowl berth wrapped up. For the 6–4 Bruins, beating USC would send them to the Aloha Bowl and put a positive spin on a disappointing campaign that featured rumors that Donahue was going to leave after the season.

Abdul-Jabbar was sidelined with an injury, but 18-year-old quarterback Cade McNown stepped up and passed the Bruins to a

24–20 victory.

On two big plays, McNown passed 59 yards to Jim McElroy to set up UCLA's first touchdown and hooked up with Kevin Jordan for a 35-yard pass play for the Bruins second touchdown. He also sealed the victory with a 21-yard scramble on third-and-13 in the game's final minute.

Donahue did step down after the season, and the Bruins turned to Bob Toledo. UCLA struggled in Toledo's first season, taking a 4–6 record into its game against USC.

Fortunately for Toledo, Robinson wasn't doing much better. USC had problems with consistency all season and had a 5–5 record, 2–4 in the six games leading up to UCLA.

The result was another UCLA victory in an exciting come-from-behind 48–41 double-overtime game at the Rose Bowl.

UCLA trailed by 17 points with five minutes to go, kicked a field goal and added a

■ Bruin receiver Danny Farmer hauls in 52-yard touchdown pass in front of USC defender Daylon McCutcheon in 1996 game.

Terry Donahue UCLA

His Trojan War lasted 28 seasons

Not many people have a better understanding of just what's at stake in the USC–UCLA rivalry than Terry Donahue. The former Bruin football coach was involved in 28 games against the Trojans as a player, assistant and head coach.

"'Winners talk and losers walk' is a statement that is never more true than when UCLA and USC face each other," said Donahue, now the general manager of the San Francisco 49ers. "You live with whatever happens in that game for 364 days, until you play again."

Donahue's first game against USC was in 1964, but as a walk-on defensive tackle for the Bruins, he didn't play in the Trojans' 34–13 victory.

"I really didn't get a taste of the rivalry then," Donahue said, "because I was on the bench eating oranges, watching the game."

He played a bigger role the next two seasons. As a starter on the defensive line who had earned a scholarship, Donahue helped the Bruins to narrow victories in 1965 and 1966.

After four years as an assistant at Kansas, he returned to UCLA after the 1970 season as an assistant coach, then became head coach in 1976 when Dick Vermeil left for the NFL. Donahue would keep that position for 20 years, building a 151–74–8 record, going 8–4–1 in bowl games.

But he had an inauspicious head coaching start against USC, which beat UCLA the first four times they played under Donahue's watch. Those losses almost cost him his job, but in 1980, the Bruins finally broke the string. Jay Schroeder's late touchdown pass to Freeman McNeil gave UCLA a 20–17 victory.

"Every game in the rivalry left an indelible mark in my head, but that game was key," Donahue said. "Because without that one, there might not have been any other experiences for me in the rivalry."

Donahue's record against the Trojans began and ended with streaks—he lost the first four, then won his last five to finish his head coaching career with a 10–9–1 record over the crosstown rivals. No other Bruin football coach has won five in a row over USC.

"One of the things that I am most proud of is having a winning record against SC," Donahue said. "To know that we beat those guys more than they beat us when I was coach is very special to me."

Donahue's final victory was in 1995, a 24–20 upset of John Robinson's 11th-ranked Trojans, a victory that gave him his winning mark against USC.

"This rivalry is just so hard to explain to somebody outside who has never experienced it," Donahue said. "The pageantry is one of [a] kind.... I don't know if I would call it hatred, but it is certainly intense. You know that you were competing against the best, and you didn't like the other guys very much when you played. That's what the rivalry is all about."

touchdown by Keith Brown before failing on an on-side kick that gave the Trojans the ball and a seven-point lead with 1:37 to play. After forcing a turnover, the Bruins triggered an overtime when Skip Hicks ran for an 11-yard touchdown with 39 seconds left in regulation. His 25-yard scoring run in the second overtime was the game winner. Freshman Danny Farmer made five receptions during the game, including a 52-yard touchdown catch early in the second half that sparked the Bruin offense's catch-up performance.

UCLA overcame Trojan freshman wideout R. Jay Soward's single-game record of 260 yards receiving to extend the rivalry unbeaten streak to six. McNown finished with 356 yards passing and Skip Hicks rushed for a game-high 116 yards and the two touchdowns.

UCLA senior defensive back Abdul McCullough told *The Times*: "If you had told me when I came here that I would never lose to USC and I would be the second straight UCLA

■ **Opposite: Bruin Coach Terry Donahue, left, and Trojan Coach John Robinson on the field before the 1993 game.**

John Robinson USC

Coach redux, but not victorious

John Robinson led USC to a national championship and four Rose Bowl victories in two stints as the Trojans' football coach. But while he won his first four games against UCLA, he finished his career 5–7 against the Bruins.

"The thing about the rivalry [is] that both teams were so powerful," said Robinson, who coached at USC from 1976 to 1982 and again from 1993 to 1997. "They were both ranked in the top 10 nearly every year and the winner of the game always seemed to go to the Rose Bowl."

Robinson replaced John McKay, who left USC to be the first coach of the Tampa Bay Buccaneers. In his first season, Robinson led USC to an 11–1 record and a Rose Bowl victory over Michigan. In reaching Pasadena, the Trojans defeated the Bruins, 24–14, at the Coliseum.

"That first game against UCLA was very special," said Robinson, now the coach and former athletic director at the University of Nevada Las Vegas.

Robinson held an edge over UCLA early, going 5–2 against the Bruins through 1982, when he resigned to take an administrative job at USC. Within months, however, Robinson jumped to the NFL, where he directed the Los Angeles Rams from 1983 to 1991.

By the time Robinson returned to USC, replacing Larry Smith before the 1993 season, the Bruins had beaten USC two years in a row.

Robinson couldn't break that streak. He lost to the Bruins every year from 1993 to 1997, three times to Terry Donahue and twice to Bob Toledo. "The games were extremely close and competitive, just like they were the first time around," Robinson said. "The only difference was that we didn't win as many."

Robinson finished his USC career with a 104–35–4 record, 67–14–2 in his first stretch, including one national title and three Rose Bowl victories. During his first tenure USC was hit by sanctions from the Pacific-10 and NCAA that prohibited the team from competing in bowl games in 1980, 1982 and 1983. His second stretch with the Trojans produced a 37–21–2 record and the 0–5 mark against the Bruins.

Despite his record against UCLA, the game remains special to him.

"The SC-UCLA rivalry has always been different than other rivalries," he said. "Because people have always been ... in the same community, the rivalry doesn't have the hate that some other rivalries have.... You know how you hear stories of how a Michigan guy would not go through Columbus, Ohio? I don't think that the SC-UCLA rivalry has that element to it."

graduating class to say that, I would have never believed it…. It couldn't have been written any better by a screenwriter."

The next season, the Bruins added to the script with another win. In a make-or-break season for Robinson, the Trojans knew they had to beat UCLA. They also knew that a victory could possibly save Robinson's job after the Trojans went 6–4 over the first 10 games.

But the Bruins wouldn't cooperate. UCLA was 8–2, on an eight-game winning streak and ranked seventh in the country when they met the Trojans at the Coliseum.

With the UCLA band chanting "Six more years," McNown passed for three touchdowns and Hicks ran for 117 yards and a touchdown in the Bruins' 31–24 victory.

There were moments in the game when USC appeared ready to end the streak. Soward and quarterback John Fox hooked up for an 80-yard touchdown pass play on USC's first offensive play and Chad Morton scored on a 49-yard touchdown run to give the Trojans a 21–14 second-quarter lead.

But in the end, USC fell short again. Trojan seniors had never experienced a win over UCLA. The defeat ended Robinson's second tour of duty with the Trojans, with an 0–5 mark against UCLA.

Paul Hackett replaced Robinson but had no better luck against the Bruins in 1998. The Trojans entered with a 7–3 record but were playing the best UCLA team in over four decades.

The Bruins had crushed opponents all season, winning nine consecutive games to move to No. 3 in the nation. The week of the USC game, UCLA fans were not only discussing the Bruins' unbeaten streak over the Trojans but also a national championship.

Freshman running back DeShaun Foster scored four touchdowns and led the Bruins to

■ Jonathan Himebauch laments the Trojans' 1997 loss.

a 34–17 victory at the Rose Bowl.

By 1999, the Bruins were struggling. They had a 4–6 record going into the game against the Trojans at the Coliseum and were playing with former fourth-string quarterback Ryan McCann because starter Cory Paus had broken his collarbone the previous week.

Across town, the Trojans were also struggling and also had a 4–6 record going into game against UCLA.

This year, though, for the first time since 1990, belonged to the Trojans, who defeated the Bruins 17–7.

For USC, ending an eight-year winless streak against the Bruins salvaged a disappointing season. Chad Morton, who had guaranteed a USC victory over UCLA in August, was carried off the field by fans.

Morton, who rushed for 143 yards, told *The Times*, "Being carried off the field, there's no greater feeling. You wouldn't believe the amount of pressure that's been placed on me since I made that guarantee. I haven't slept all week. I've been pacing, and haven't been able to eat. The team was so fired up, and they backed me up."

BASKETBALL

In 1989, at the start of his second season as UCLA basketball coach, Jim Harrick put together an offense that took better advantage of sophomore forward Don MacLean's shooting.

By giving MacLean more opportunities to touch the ball, Harrick opened things up for the rest of the Bruins because opposing defenses were forced to concentrate on slowing the high-scoring forward.

And slowing MacLean wasn't easy, as the Trojans learned in the first meeting between the teams in the 1989–90 season. MacLean made 13 of 17 shots and scored 35 points to lead UCLA to an 89–72 victory at Pauley Pavilion.

Fellow forward Trevor Wilson benefited from the Trojans' ill-fated focus on MacLean, scoring 27 points with 13 rebounds.

The defeat dropped USC Coach George Raveling to 0–7 against the Bruins.

■ Trojan Coach George Raveling confers with Claude Green, left, and Avondre Jones. Below: USC's Harold Miner sets up a shot over UCLA's Mitchell Butler in his big 1992 game.

USC's freshman guard, Harold Miner, made the difference in the rematch, scoring 27 points, including a clutch free throw with 30 seconds left, to give USC a 76–75 upset victory. This time, the Trojans did contain MacLean, holding him to 12 points.

The Trojans also got a break on an official's call in which Miner was credited with a three-point basket on a shot that videotape showed should have counted only for two.

The next season, the Trojans improved significantly on their 12–16 record but still lost to UCLA in the opening game. They couldn't control MacLean, Gerald Madkins played tough defense on Miner and Bruin forward Tracy Murray scored 29 points in a 98–81 win at Pauley.

As in the previous season, the second game was a different story. Miner scored eight of USC's final 12 points in a 76–74 victory at the Sports

GAMES WON
The 1990s
BASKETBALL
UCLA 14 – USC 6

Arena. USC would finish the season 19–10, UCLA at 23–9.

But it was only Raveling's second victory in 10 tries against UCLA.

For the 1991–92 season, Murray and MacLean led UCLA to the nation's top 10 list, but in Los Angeles, the Bruins were No. 2. The Trojans swept both games against them.

Duane Cooper and Yamen Sanders combined for 43 points as USC won, 86–82, at Pauley in the first meeting. Sanders had 10 rebounds to go with his career-high 20 points, and Miner added 22 points.

MacLean, who had 21 points, was upset with his Bruin teammates. "To lose to a team like this, in our own gym, is a joke," MacLean told reporters. "… On their best day, they shouldn't be able to beat us."

Before the rematch, Raveling taped a copy of MacLean's comments on the door of the USC basketball office. And the Trojans made sure the words would come back to haunt their rivals.

With Miner scoring 29 points and grabbing 13 rebounds, USC beat the Bruins again, 83–79, at the Sports Arena. It was the Trojans'

first sweep of UCLA since 1985 and moved them into a first-place tie in the Pac-10 with the Bruins.

Still, the Bruins wound up winning the Pac-10 title and finishing 28–5; the Trojans finished an excellent 24–6, but a loss to Washington State ended the conference title hopes.

When the teams met for the first time in 1992–93, the Bruins were determined to end a three-game losing streak to USC. UCLA ran the

■ Bruin forward Tracy Murray has company on his journey to the basket.

Trojans ragged with a 90–80 victory as big men Richard Petruska and Rodney Zimmerman dominated inside.

But USC bounced back in the second game, with senior guard Rodney Chatman scoring 30 points in the Trojans' 72–62 win at Pauley.

Again in 1993–94, UCLA was all business in the first matchup. Ed O'Bannon scored 24 points in a 101–72 victory at Pauley. It was the most lopsided win in the

■ UCLA's O'Bannon brothers: Charles, above, and Ed, left, shooting over USC's Lorenzo Orr.

series in 20 years.

The Times' Thomas Bonk wrote: "George Raveling was asked when he felt the game slipping away. 'At the tip,' he said."

Undeterred by the first-game humiliation, USC rebounded in the rematch and won, 85–79, at the Sports Arena.

With point guard Tyus Edney sidelined much of the game because of foul trouble, the Bruin offense never got on track. Mark Boyd led USC with 17 points and six rebounds and became the first USC four-year starter to finish his career with a winning record against the Bruins at 5–3.

In 1994–95, UCLA had a season to remember. Not only did the Bruins win their first NCAA championship since 1975, they enjoyed their first sweep of the Trojans since 1989 to boot.

USC was without Raveling, who had been seriously injured in a car accident and replaced by Charlie Parker. And in the first matchup, UCLA was without ailing point guard Edney. That left the door open for backup Cameron Dollar, whose critical five assists in the second half sparked the Bruins to a 73–69 victory at the Sports Arena.

In the second game, freshman guard Toby Bailey took over with a 24-point game in the Bruins' 85–66 victory at Pauley.

The victories over USC were important that season, to be sure, but the lasting image of UCLA's 1994–95 campaign was of Edney's game-saving, full-court drive at the buzzer to

Baron Davis UCLA

He made a point of winning

From the 1994–95 season through the 1998–99 season, the UCLA basketball team enjoyed a 10-game winning streak over USC.

A key player for the Bruins during part of the stretch was point guard Baron Davis, a Los Angeles native who led the Bruins to a 4–0 record against the Trojans in the 1997–98 and 1998–99 seasons.

"I never lost to SC, and I'm proud of that fact," said Davis, who has gone on to become one of the best point guards in the NBA with the New Orleans Hornets.

"I remember this one game we had against them at Pauley Pavilion. They really thought they were going to beat us. They really did. They were up late in the game and started talking trash, but we came back and beat them. We always knew we would."

Davis was referring to his final game against USC, a 68–63 victory at Pauley Pavilion on Feb. 17, 1999.

After having lost to UCLA by 18 points a month earlier, USC stayed close this time and was tied with the Bruins, 61–61, with less than four minutes to go. But UCLA turned on its full-court press and shut down the Trojans.

A clutch shot by Davis helped put the game away. Playing with the flu and sore knees, Davis beat USC's Quincy Wilder off the dribble from the top of the three-point circle. He pulled up for a fall-away 15–footer with 36 seconds left that gave UCLA a 67–63 lead. Davis finished with a team-high 17 points and seven assists.

Davis left college for the NBA after his sophomore season, having never reached the Final Four but having defeated the crosstown rivals each time he had faced them. "And," he said, "that's always a good thing."

State, and though he started, he played very little in the final, an 89–78 victory over Arkansas.

UCLA couldn't repeat its success in 1995–96, but Charles O'Bannon almost single-handedly made sure that USC suffered for another season.

In the first meeting, O'Bannon had a career-high 27 points and added 13 rebounds and seven assists in the Bruins' 99–72 victory at Pauley Pavilion. O'Bannon made 11 of his 14 shots, leading UCLA to a school-record 73.1% shooting night.

O'Bannon did it again in the rematch at the Sports Arena. On his 21st birthday, O'Bannon's 12-foot jump shot with four-tenths of a

defeat Missouri in the second round of the NCAA tournament. Edney was injured in UCLA's semifinal victory against Oklahoma

■ **Toby Bailey cuts through the USC defense on his way in for the basket in 1997 game. Below: UCLA Coach Jim Harrick celebrates a victory by cutting the net.**

Lavin's first game against USC was a success, a 96–87 victory at the Sports Arena. And the rematch was even easier as the Bruins cruised to an 82–60 victory, with Toby Bailey getting a game-high 24 points and seven rebounds in the Bruins' sixth consecutive victory over USC.

The next season, the Bruins maintained their edge over the Trojans with two easy victories. Senior forward Kris Johnson scored a game-high 20 points and added five assists in a 101–84 victory at Pauley.

A month later, UCLA extended the streak to eight games with a sloppy 82–75 overtime victory at the Sports Arena. Bailey scored UCLA's last six points in regulation and made four more points, plus two assists and a rebound, in the overtime period.

UCLA closed out the '90s with two more victories, extending the streak over USC to 10 games. The Bruins won the first game, 98–80, at the Sports Arena, handing USC its worst home loss in 25 years.

The Trojans were struggling by the time of the rematch at Pauley, and the Bruins added to their misery. USC stayed within five points through the second half but couldn't deal with UCLA's full-court press at the end and lost, 68–63.

second remaining gave the Bruins a 61–59 victory. He said afterward, "I haven't had a birthday this good in a while."

Not surprisingly, USC was in turmoil. Parker was fired as coach and replaced full time by assistant Henry Bibby, the former UCLA All-American. Bibby had actually served as USC's interim coach for the last nine games of the 1995–96 season, including that 61–59 loss to UCLA.

But under Bibby that season, the Trojans finished at 13–17.

UCLA was upset by Princeton in the first round of the NCAA tournament and then had its own management shuffle. Harrick was fired before the start of the 1996–97 season for lying about a recruiting violation and was replaced by former assistant Steve Lavin.

Kings Again UCLA

The amazing 1994–95 Bruin season

They were 4.8 seconds that seemed to last forever, and when those seconds had finally ticked off the clock, UCLA was on its way to exorcising the demons that seemed to be haunting the Bruin basketball program.

Under Jim Harrick, UCLA had won at least 20 games for six seasons in a row heading into the 1994–95 campaign, but many of those seasons had ended more quickly than anticipated. The unfulfilled promises had reached a peak in 1994, when the Bruins were unceremoniously ushered out of the NCAA tournament by Tulsa, the second time in four years they had been upset in the first round.

Harrick's job wasn't quite on the line, but there were certainly rumblings that his teams weren't reaching the heights they should.

Many around Westwood, including Harrick, thought the 1994–95 season might be different. Ed O'Bannon was one of the premier forwards in the game, Tyus Edney was an exceptional point guard, George Zidek a bruising center. The team was deep and versatile.

"I do believe we are bigger and stronger, more physical than we've ever been since I've been here," Harrick said before the season. There was even talk of a run to the Final Four, talk that intensified as the team began the NCAA tournament on a 13-game winning streak, then ran the streak to 14 with a throttling of Florida International.

Then, alarmingly, history appeared to be repeating itself. In the second round against eighth-seeded Missouri, top-seeded UCLA suddenly found itself trailing by a point with 4.8 seconds remaining.

Edney took an in-bounds pass and began a frantic run down the left side of the court, dribbling behind his back to avoid one defender, then pulling up in the lane to launch a shot with less than a second to play, the ball and UCLA's season suspended in midair long enough for all the memories of failed finishes to flash through the Bruins' minds.

"Boy, it was like an eternity watching that ball," Edney's father, Hank, said afterward. "I was standing, my heart was racing."

Toby Bailey, a Bruin guard, had a similar thought at the time: "I was right under the basket. I could see it perfectly. It was like in slow motion. It hit off the glass and headed toward the rim."

Then the ball slid through the net as the buzzer sounded, the Bruins taking a 75–74 victory that sent them to the Sweet 16 ... and perhaps with the feeling that this just might be one of those special teams destined for greatness.

"I remember Christian Laettner hitting two buzzer-beaters in Elite Eight games to take Duke to the Final Four," Harrick said afterward. "I believe in my heart that sometimes along the way your team has to face some of this and overcome adversity in this manner."

From that point on, UCLA cruised, finally dispatching Arkansas, 89–78, for the Bruins' first national championship since John Wooden's last season, in 1974–75.

For Edney and the rest of the Bruins, that was the pinnacle of their basketball careers. Harrick was fired by UCLA less than two years later after lying to administrators about a recruiting incident, and none of the players went on to successful professional careers.

Edney's simple comment afterward said it all: "It's just the biggest shot of my life so far."

BASEBALL

The 1990 season ended for UCLA and USC in separate NCAA Regional finals. But during the regular season, the Trojans held a 4–2 edge in games.

After USC won two of three games in early March, UCLA junior catcher Paul Ellis got hot at the plate. With Ellis hitting home runs at a regular pace, the Bruins stayed in the hunt for a postseason berth heading into their final three games against the Trojans.

Ellis, who had hit a total of five home runs in his first two seasons, hit 23 in 48 games before the USC series. He added two more against the Trojans, the only Pac-10 team he hadn't homered against to that point, to lead the nation with 25. But still, USC won the rubber game of the series at Dedeaux Field, thanks to Mike Robertson, who went four for four with two homers in a 7–5 Trojan win.

UCLA lost to eventual national champion Georgia Southern in the Midwest Regional final, though Ellis wound up with 29 homers, then a Bruin record, and 83 runs batted in. USC lost to Louisiana State in the South Regional final.

In 1991, the Trojans' Jackie Nickell was named conference pitcher of the year and USC won its first Pac-10 title since 1978. USC narrowly beat UCLA in their first four games by a cumulative score of 26–17, but the Bru-

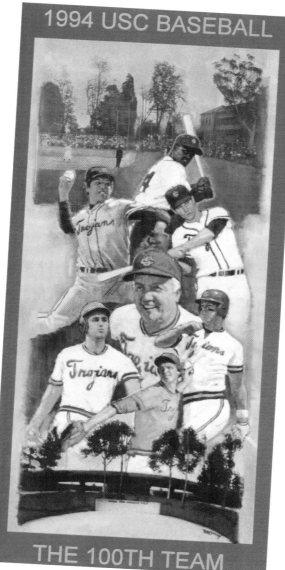

1994 USC BASEBALL

THE 100TH TEAM

ins, behind speedy outfielder Joel Wolfe, who stole 35 bases that season, won the final two games. Still, UCLA finished 10 games behind USC.

The next season, UCLA split six games with USC, including a victory on the next to last day of the regular season that sent the Bruins to the Mideast Regional of the NCAA playoffs, and the Trojans home.

Freshman All-American Mike Mitchell and Ryan McGuire along with Michael Moore carried UCLA's offense, which established a school record with 128 stolen bases. Pete Janicki was named Pac-10 pitcher of the year for the Bruins, who couldn't advance beyond the first round in the tournament.

The schools split six games again in 1993, with the Bruins winning two of three late in the season to finish two games ahead of the Trojans in conference play. All-American McGuire, who hit .376 with 26 home runs and 91 runs batted in, led UCLA to its third NCAA playoff appearance in four years. McGuire was named conference co-player of the year.

In the final game between the teams, the Bruins again needed a victory to finish ahead of the Trojans in the Pac-10 standings. They got it, an 8–7 squeaker, on David Ravits' two-out, bases-loaded single in the bottom of the 10th inning.

In postseason play, neither team advanced

beyond the regional.

The next season, USC finished 41–20, including four victories in six games over the Bruins, who struggled to a 22–36 record.

Heading into their first three-game set against UCLA, USC Coach Mike Gillespie warned his team about the Bruins, who were 6–17 overall and 2–4 in conference: "They're definitely going to win some big games and ruin someone's season."

That's exactly what UCLA did at Jackie Robinson Stadium. Pitcher Brian Stephenson blanked the hot-hitting Trojans, 6–0, quieting a lineup with such solid hitters as Aaron Boone and Walter Dawkins.

USC won the next two games, but when the teams met again, UCLA spoiled USC's conference hopes with a 4–3 victory.

USC finished the regular season third in the Pac-10 and was knocked out of the NCAA playoffs by LSU in the South Regional.

In 1995, the Trojans put everything together and won the conference title outright. USC finished 49–21, including a 21–9 record in league play with victories in five of six games against UCLA.

In the NCAA tournament, USC reached the College World Series but lost in the final to Cal State Fullerton.

The next season, the Trojans dominated the Pac-10, winning their second consecutive league title. Along the way, USC won four of six games against the Bruins, who finished third in the league.

The NCAA playoffs proved difficult and unfruitful for both schools as both teams lost in the regional round.

■ **UCLA's Troy Glaus at the plate.**

■ Trojan pitcher Seth Etherton after a game-winning strike-out in 1998.

In 1997, the Bruins started the season as the team to beat in the Pac-10.

With a lineup led by Eric Byrnes, Troy Glaus and Eric Valent, and pitchers Jim Parque and Tom Jacquez, the Bruins opened the season, 20–3–1. When they faced the Trojans for the first time, UCLA kept on winning, taking two of three from USC.

But the Trojans returned the favor the first two games of the rematch. The Bruins needed a victory in the final game to stay ahead of USC in the conference race, and they played their best game of the season against the Trojans, winning 14–4 at Jackie Robinson Stadium.

Unfortunately for the Bruins, their NCAA run ended at the College World Series, where they were making their first appearance since 1969. UCLA was eliminated by Mississippi State.

What UCLA came close to

GAMES WON
The 1990s
BASEBALL
USC 36 ▪ UCLA 24

accomplishing in 1997, the Trojans did in 1998. With a pitching staff highlighted by big-game performers Seth Etherton and Mike Penney, USC bounced back after finishing second in the Pac-10 to win its first NCAA championship since 1978, beating Arizona State in the highest-scoring NCAA title game, 21–14.

The Trojans won four of six games against the Bruins as UCLA, which opened the season with 13 freshmen on the 25-player roster, finished 10 games behind the Trojans in league play.

The intense rivalry peaked in the final meeting between the teams. A day after UCLA defeated the Trojans, 18–17, at Dedeaux Field, USC rallied back from a four-run seventh-inning deficit to win, 17–12.

In 1999, the Bruins finished behind the Trojans in the Pac-10 but defeated USC four of six times.

■ ■ ■ ■ ■ ■
TENNIS

UCLA's tennis team began the 1990 season with high hopes. Coach Glenn Bassett had one of his top teams with Bill Barber, Jason Sher and Jason Netter as the key singles players, along with doubles specialists Mark Knowles and Fritz Bissell.

The team did not disappoint. Barber won 19 singles matches, Sher won 18 and Netter won the Pac-10 individual title. The Bruins won the league title for the second consecutive year, giving Bassett his 13th Pac-10 championship. The highlight of UCLA's season was a two-match sweep over the Trojans, who also had a strong team.

UCLA defeated USC, led by All-Americans Byron Black and Kent Seton, 5–4, then romped 5–1 in Westwood in the second match to clinch the conference title.

The first time UCLA faced USC in 1991, it was at the ITCA Team Indoors at Louisville, Ky., and the Bruins won easily, 5–2. By the time the teams met for the first time in league play, UCLA was ranked No. 1, USC No. 2. But not for long.

With a 53-match home winning streak on the line, the Bruins lost to the Trojans, 5–2, at the Los Angeles Tennis Center on April 3. Key singles victories by USC freshman Brian MacPhie over Knowles and Black over Netter set the tone.

The next time the Bruins faced USC, it wasn't even close. The Trojans swept UCLA, 6–0, at USC. The victory was a springboard to the NCAA championships, where USC won its first national title in 15 years, defeating Georgia in the finals.

In 1992, both L.A. teams were loaded again and split their matches during the regular season. Both were good enough to reach the NCAA semifinals, but neither could make it to the championship match.

Before the start of the 1993 season, the Bruins counted on Fritz Bissell and Sher to be their team leaders, and they stepped up with great seasons. Sher went 25–2 in dual singles play, and Bissell won the Pac-10 singles championship.

As a team, UCLA started just as well, beat-ing the Trojans at the team indoors and in a regular-season match before slumping later in the season. USC won the third time they played.

That was the final season for Bassett at UCLA. Athletic Director Peter Dalis told *The Times*, "I would say since

MATCHES WON
The 1990s
TENNIS
UCLA 17 – USC 6

Bruin tennis aces Jason Sher and Bill Barber, opposite.

1984 [when Bassett won his last NCAA championship], we have not had the preeminence in tennis that we had previously, and I did have some concern about our recruiting."

Still, Bassett's record had been a strong one. He never had a losing season, and his winning percentage was best among active NCAA Division I coaches. "It's going to be hard," Bassett told *The Times* about his forced retirement. "I've been here since 1948 … so it will be a big adjustment."

USC went on to win its second national title in three years by defeating Georgia in the 1993 finals.

UCLA did not look far for Bassett's replacement. The Bruins hired former player Billy Martin, an assistant under Bassett for 10

years, to take over in 1994. Unfortunately for Martin, the Trojans had the dominant team in college tennis and trounced the Bruins, 6–1, in their first match. With the Trojans riding the play of Wayne Black and Jon Leach, they maintained their No. 1 ranking for much of the season.

But USC encountered problems. The Trojans had to default their second match against the Bruins because Brett Hansen, Lukas Hovorka, Leach and Black were declared ineligible for accepting expense money beyond that allowed by the NCAA while competing in summer professional tournaments.

Although UCLA had two players, Robert Janecek and Sebastien LeBlanc, also declared ineligible, the Bruins had enough players to

the history of the series.

The key match for the Bruins came when UCLA's Justin Gimelstob faced Adam Peterson, who had defeated the Bruin in three tough sets early in the season. They split the first two sets, and with a boisterous crowd watching intently, Gimelstob took the third set to spark the Bruins to a 5–2 victory.

In 1996, the Bruins extended their winning streak over the Trojans to five by sweeping two matches, 5–2 and 7–0.

The Bruin domination continued in 1997 behind Alex Decret and Eric Taino. UCLA swept the Trojans, 4–3 and 6–1, to extend its winning streak to seven.

In 1998, Coach Dick Leach's Trojans won their first six matches and were set to end their three-year losing streak to the Bruins, who were ranked second nationally. With George Bastl leading the way at No. 1 singles, USC defeated UCLA, 4–3, to stop the losing streak at seven.

In the featured match, Bastl and Jean-Noel Grinda played a three-set thriller, with Bastl winning, 6–1, 3–6, 7–6.

In 1999, the Bruins picked up another sweep behind Pac-10 doubles champions Jong-Min Lee and Grinda. The Bruins won the first match, 5–2, and the second, 6–1, the ninth time in 11 matches to close the decade.

compete and accepted the default.

USC ended up winning its second consecutive NCAA title and third in four years after the four suspended players successfully petitioned the NCAA for reinstatement. The Trojans defeated Stanford in the championship match.

In 1995, the Bruins finally turned the tables on the Trojans. After defeating USC, 4–3, at Westwood early in the season, UCLA won at USC, 5–2, to give the Bruins a 74–73 lead in

Glenn Bassett UCLA

Never a losing season

When Glenn Bassett replaced J.D. Morgan as head coach of UCLA's men's tennis program in 1967, USC was the top program in town, having beaten the Bruins in the NCAA championship match the year before.

USC won again in 1967 and by 1969 had won four titles in a row, twice with UCLA as runner-up.

But in 1970, the Bruins under Bassett finally turned things around, winning the national championship with standout players like Haroon Rahim and Jeff Borowiak, the 1970 national singles champion.

By the time Bassett stepped down as UCLA's coach in 1993, the Bruins had won at least a share of seven NCAA titles while putting together a 614–99–2 record. His UCLA teams never had a losing season and featured 46 All-American players, including Jimmy Connors.

Bassett, inducted into the Collegiate Tennis Hall of Fame in 1993, insisted on his players' hitting a lot of balls during practices, something that occasionally wore thin with the players until they realized the benefits of the hard work.

"He likes to have you hitting lots of balls. And when you do get into matches, you don't have to think about it. You just reel off the shot," Billy Martin said while he was still a player for Bassett. Martin succeeded Bassett as coach in 1994.

"He pushes you to attain heights that you wouldn't have reached on your own. He is somewhat demanding, but it's easier to do it for somebody when you realize he is putting in 100% too."

After leaving UCLA, Bassett served as a volunteer coach with Pepperdine in 1994 and 1995 and then took over as the Waves' head coach in 1996. He retired after coaching Pepperdine to a 22–7 record in 1996.

■ Glenn Bassett, UCLA '51, is the only person in NCAA history to win an NCAA tennis title as a player, assistant coach and head coach.

VOLLEYBALL

Jim McLaughlin couldn't have had a better start as the USC men's volleyball coach in 1990. The Trojans defeated the defending national champion Bruins twice, and then moved on to win their fourth national championship.

The victories over the Bruins gave them a chance to reach the postseason. In the first match at Pauley Pavilion, USC lost the first game, then won the next three. In the rematch at the UCLA Classic, the Bruins were on top of their game and were ranked No. 1.

But UCLA couldn't contain college player of the year Bryan Ivie, and the Trojans pulled out another four-set victory. In the Western Intercollegiate Volleyball Association tournament, USC and UCLA both lost to Long Beach State, UCLA in the championship game. The Trojans and Bruins were both 23–5, and USC, in part because of its sweep of the Bruins, was given the at-large bid to the NCAA championships, even though UCLA had advanced to the WIVA title game.

UCLA, out of the Final Four for only the sixth time in 21 years, was shocked.

Once in the Final Four, the Trojans made the most out of the opportunity and got their revenge against Long Beach State, defeating the 49ers in the championship match.

The next season, USC didn't have to slip in the back door to reach the NCAA championship round. The Trojans beat the Bruins twice in their first three matches in 1991, with USC defeating UCLA in the UC Santa Barbara tourney and at Pauley Pavilion in a league match, then losing to the Bruins in the UCLA Classic a month later.

With All-American Mike Sealy leading the way, UCLA reached the finals of the WIVA tournament, where the Bruins faced—who else?—the Trojans.

Before the match, USC Coach Jim McLaughlin was confident. "I think we have the best team," he told *The Times*.

McLaughlin and the Trojans' confidence did not sit well with the Bruins, who were still smarting from the prior year's perceived insult.

But McLaughlin's confidence was well-founded. Ivie got a match-high 41 kills in leading the Trojans to a 13–15, 15–5, 15–6, 9–15, 15–10 victory at UC Irvine's Bren Center.

USC reached the NCAA championships, but the title went to Long Beach State.

In 1992, UCLA took care of the Trojans by sweeping all three matches, with Sealy being named college player of the year.

After a three-year national championship drought, the Bruins were back in business in 1993. Coach Al Scates still had two of the best players in college volleyball in Sealy and Jeff Nygaard. UCLA also had solid role players in senior Dan Landry and sophomore Kevin Wong.

In three matches against USC, the Bruins lost only one game, and they breezed through the NCAA tournament as well, sweeping Ohio State and Cal State Northridge to give Scates his 14th title.

The next season, UCLA's six-match winning streak over the Trojans ended in their first meeting. The Bruins were swept by USC in two games at the UC Santa Barbara Invitational, but then UCLA took off, sweeping through the rest of the season, defeating the Trojans twice at Pauley Pavilion.

The Bruins' attempt to repeat as national champions fell short in the NCAA final in a loss to Penn State.

MATCHES WON
The 1990s
VOLLEYBALL
UCLA 17 - USC 6

swept USC along the way.

UCLA began the 1997 season on a seven-match winning streak over USC, and the Trojans began with a new coach, Pat Powers, who replaced McLaughlin.

The Bruins got No. 8 in a row early in 1997, followed by a four-game victory that was the 900th win of Scates' remarkable career.

"We came out fired up," senior captain Paul Nihipali told the Daily Bruin. "We always get up for USC, and we especially wanted the win tonight for Al."

UCLA reached the 1997 NCAA championship match, but Stanford kept the Bruins from their third title in a row.

Over the final two years of the decade, the Bruins stretched their streak over USC to 11 matches with one

■ **Clockwise from upper right: UCLA's Brandon Talia-ferro and Danny Farmer play USC's Omar Rawi and Eli Fairfield in 1998.**

In 1995, the Bruins didn't lose a game to the Trojans. The key player for Scates was Stein Metzger, a junior setter.

In the second sweep of the Trojans, who were ranked No. 2 behind the top-ranked Bruins, Metzger dished out 65 assists to go along with eight kills, seven digs, three blocks and an ace.

With Metzger setting up Nygaard to per-fection, the Bruins completed a 34–1 season, which included their third consecutive 19–0 league record. This time they beat Penn State in the NCAA championship match.

In 1996, the Bruins repeated as national champions, defeating Hawaii for the title, and

victory each season. In 1998, they reclaimed the national championship with a victory over Pepperdine.

In 1999, Powers spiced up the rivalry when he told reporters: "The rivalry always makes you want to win, but I think my play-ers feel the same playing UCLA as they do playing Stanford."

Scates and the Bruins used his remarks as inspiration, and they crushed the Trojans in three games at USC.

"It's all the more pleasant to win in this little gym, where the band's drummer plays while our team is serving," Scates told the Daily Bruin.

TRACK AND FIELD

By the 1990s, UCLA's track and field program had left USC at the starting blocks. The Bruins dominated the Trojans throughout the decade in the regular season, winning every head-to-head matchup to run their streak to 21 consecutive victories.

USC made a couple of coaching changes to resurrect its program, with some measure of success, but the Trojans could never entirely close the gap. In a sport that no longer generated the spirited, widespread interest that it had a decade or two before, USC's program had slipped even further off the front pages.

UCLA and Coach Bob Larsen began the decade with a powerful, deep team led by Olympic 400-meter gold medalist Steve Lewis, and even though USC had a few standouts, such as quarter-miler Quincy Watts and intermediate hurdler George Porter, the Bruins won easily at the Coliseum, 94–68. That was the 12th consecutive victory over USC, and it gave the Bruins a 46–0–1 overall dual-meet record.

Neither USC nor UCLA did well at the Pac-10 or NCAA championship meets, but the Trojans' failure to make an impact in 1990 cost Coach Ernie Bullard his job.

To turn things around, Athletic Director Mike McGee turned to former UCLA Coach Jim Bush, who told *The Times*, "The last few years, I've been helping over here, and people said, 'How can you do that, Coach, you're a Bruin?' And I said. 'No, I'm a Trojan now.' …

"We're going to bring USC back…. We're going to win."

Well, not right away. UCLA rolled again in 1991, defeating USC, 114–32, in a triangular meet, the largest margin of victory ever between the schools.

USC had a few winners, such as Watts in the 400, but UCLA dominated behind hurdler Marty Beck, pole vaulter Jay Borick and javelin thrower Eric Smith.

Little changed the next year, a 123–30 Bruin win in another three-way meet including Cal State Northridge.

UCLA sprinter Tony Miller won the 100 and 200 meters and anchored the winning 400-meter relay team to highlight the romp.

UCLA went on to win its fourth Pac-10 title in six years, but the Trojans got some measure of revenge by finishing third in the NCAA championship to the Bruins' eighth-place finish.

But the regular-season routs continued, a 103.5–57.5 score in 1993, 97–61 in 1994, years in which the Bruins won their second and third consecutive Pac-10 titles. Sprinter Marcus

Reed won the 100 and 200 against the Trojans in '93 and John Godina won the shot put and discus.

After the 1994 season, there was more change in store for the USC program. Athletic Director Mike Garrett decided to combine the men's and women's programs under one coaching staff again (it had also done so under Bush in 1990 and 1991). Ron Allice, a former Long Beach City College coach, was picked to head the program.

Heading into the 1995 dual-meet against UCLA, Allice tried to add some pizazz to the rivalry, one that in the golden days had packed the Bruins' 12,100-seat Drake Stadium and often put 30,000 fans in the Coliseum. But often in the early and mid-1990s, crowds had dropped well below 2,000.

Allice promoted the meet heavily and brought back Olympic champions Jackie Joyner Kersee, Gail Devers, Quincy Watts and Kevin Young for an invitational meet. He also moved the USC–UCLA meet to the USC cam-

pus. His strategy worked as far as generating interest, as 3,115 people attended. But on the track, the outcome was the same. UCLA won, 90–71, with sprinter Ato Boldon and Godina double winners.

UCLA then won its fourth consecutive Pac-10 title and nearly won its first NCAA title since 1988, finishing second behind Arkansas.

With a 109–52 thumping in 1996, UCLA extended its streak over USC to 18. Boldon again swept the 100 and 200 meters and ran the opening leg on the Bruins' winning 400-meter relay team.

UCLA won its fifth conference title in a row and finished third at the NCAA championships.

By 1997, the Trojans began to turn the corner under Allice. Although USC lost to UCLA again, 88–75, the Trojans made the meet interesting behind quarter-miler Jerome Davis. And at the Pac-10 championships, UCLA's five-year dominance came to an end with USC taking home the team title.

With Jerome Davis winning the 400 meters and running a leg on the Trojans' win-

Left to right: Sultan McCullough, Bryan Harrison and Darrell Rideaux.

ning 400- and 1,600-meter relay teams, USC outscored UCLA, 135–130, to win its first league title since 1978.

UCLA made it 20 in a row in the regular season over USC in 1998, but in 1999, the Trojans came as close as possible without winning. Only a remarkable finish in the last four events gave UCLA an 82–81 victory.

Before a standing-room-only crowd at Cromwell Field, the Bruins outscored USC, 24–8, in the final four events.

UCLA sophomore Steve Michels pulled an upset in the pole vault with a personal best, the Bruins finished 1–2–3 in the discus and 1–2–3–4 in the 5,000 to ensure the victory before USC won the final event, the 1,600 relay.

That gave the Bruins a 10–0 record in the '90s in regular-season meets with USC, and 21 in a row.

■ ■ ■ ■ ■ ■ ■ ■ ■ ■

WATER POLO

The 1990s began with UCLA dominating USC in water polo, winning 15 consecutive matches until the Trojans finally broke through in 1995. But then the Bruins reestablished themselves as the kings of the sport with their third national championship of the decade in 1999.

In 1990, UCLA under Bob Horn was considered one of the best programs in the country. The Bruins were loaded with talented young players, such as All-American Dan Hackett, and finished the season 24–8 with a third-place finish in the NCAA tournament.

That season marked the end of an era at UCLA. Horn retired after 28 seasons with the Bruins. In that time, his teams won three NCAA titles, finished second four times and third seven times. And they won 13 conference championships.

But the Bruins remained a power with Guy Baker as coach. UCLA reached the NCAA finals in 1991, losing to California. It was the sixth time in seven years that the Bruins reached the Final Four but failed to win a national title.

In 1992, USC Coach John Williams, along with assistant Jovan Vavic, began to attract players from outside the United States. The Trojans finished third in the NCAA tournament that year and were runners-up to Stanford in 1993 and 1994.

By 1995, the rivalry between USC and UCLA was at an all-time high, and finally, at the end of the regular season, the Trojans' 8–7 victory over the Bruins ended the

■ **Bruin Dan Hackett**

MATCHES WON
The 1990s

WATER POLO

USC 20 ■ UCLA 13

BASEBALL			
Jacque Jones	1996		Bronze

BASKETBALL			
Cynthia Cooper	1992		Bronze
Lisa Leslie	1996		Gold

SWIMMING			
Brad Bridgewater	1996	200m Backstroke	Gold
Dan Jorgensen	1992	800m Free Relay	Bronze
Kristine Quance	1996	400m Medley Relay	Gold
Bjorn Zikarsky (Germany)	1996	400m Free Relay	Bronze

TRACK AND FIELD			
Mark Crear	1996	110m Hurdles	Silver
Balazs Kiss (Hungary)	1996	Hammer	Gold
Inger Miller	1996	400m Relay	Gold
Quincy Watts	1996	400 meters	Gold
		4x400m Relay	Gold

VOLLEYBALL			
Nick Becker	1992		Bronze
Dan Greenbaum	1992		Bronze
Bryan Ivie	1992		Bronze
Steve Timmons	1992		Bronze
Paula Weishoff	1992		Bronze

**MEETS WON
The 1990s

SWIMMING

USC 4 - UCLA 0

UCLA ENDED
SPORT IN 1994**

keep the Bruins ranked No. 1.

The next three times USC faced the Bruins, the Trojans won. The fifth time they met that season was the big one: the NCAA final. Behind goalkeeper Matt Swanson, the Bruins defeated the Trojans, 8–7, to win their second consecutive national title.

Randy Wright scored a two-point goal and Braxton-Brown and Matt Armato scored key goals for the Bruins, who kept USC winless in five NCAA championship matches.

In 1997, the Trojans wouldn't be denied and swept the Bruins in three matches. Marko Pintaric's five points highlighted a 12–7 victory, Allen Basso scored four in a 10–9 win in the NorCal tournament, and goalkeeper Richard McEvoy stopped the final shot and a UCLA comeback effort for an 8–7 victory in the MPSF first round.

USC reached the championship game of the NCAA tournament again, only to lose to Pepperdine.

In 1998, USC finally broke through. After stretching their winning streak to five over the Bruins, the Trojans lost to UCLA late in the season, but that game was of little consequence. What did matter was USC's run in the NCAA tournament, which ended with the school's first national championship after a victory over Stanford in the final. Pintaric was named national player of the year, and co-coaches John Williams and Jovan Vavic were

string of UCLA victories in head-to-head matches at 15.

But in the Mountain Pacific Sports Federation semifinals, UCLA bounced back for a 9–7 win that was a springboard for the Bruins' first national championship since 1972.

In 1996, the Bruins set the tone early against the Trojans when they beat USC, 8–7, in an intense overtime game in the championship of the SoCal tournament. Jeremy Braxton-Brown scored a goal and tapped away USC's last possession in overtime to named coaches of the year.

The next season, USC and UCLA took turns as the nation's No. 1 team during the regular season. UCLA lost to USC in the final of the NorCal tournament on Ivan Babic's two pointer, but the Bruins bounced back later with a 7–5 victory, thanks to two goals each from Armato and Wright. And in the final regular-season matchup, third-ranked USC upset top-ranked UCLA, 10–7.

But ultimately, it was all UCLA in the postseason. The Bruins defeated Stanford in the final of the MPSF tournament, then beat the Cardinal again to win their sixth national championship.

■ For Lisa Leslie, right, and Natalie Williams, it was a rivalry within the rivalry.

■ ■ ■ ■ ■ ■ ■
WOMEN'S BASKETBALL

Before the start of the 1989–90 season, Marianne Stanley succeeded Linda Sharp as women's basketball coach at USC and lost both games to UCLA in her first season. But it was the next season that the rivalry picked up steam.

USC's Lisa Leslie, who has since become one of the stars of the WNBA with the Los Angeles Sparks, and UCLA's Natalie Williams, who would become a two-year All-American, landed on the college scene.

The teams split a couple of four-point games.

In the first game, Leslie, a 6-foot-5 freshman, was held to two points in the first half while saddled with foul trouble,

but she led the way in the second and finished with a game-high 18 points in a 73–69 victory at Pauley Pavilion.

UCLA returned the favor with an 83–79 victory in the regular season finale, and in 1991–92, things got even tighter. USC swept two game this time by a total of four points.

Leslie had 21 points and 15 rebounds in the second game, but a basket from Joni Easterly, with eight seconds remaining, was the difference in USC's 73–71 victory.

Lisa Leslie USC and Natalie Williams UCLA

The matchup that brought out the best in each

Lisa Leslie, a three-time All-American basketball player at USC, the 1994 Naismith Award winner as the nation's top player and a member of two Olympic gold-medal winning teams, has become one of the WNBA's most successful star players with the Los Angeles Sparks.

And in eight games against UCLA, Leslie was the primary reason the Trojans won seven times.

"It was always big time whenever we played the Bruins," said Leslie, who averaged 20.1 points and 10.1 rebounds in her four seasons, 1990–91 through 1993–94. "The games were easy to get up for because, I mean, you're talking about pride there—more than anything."

In her final game against UCLA, Leslie had one of her best efforts in a Trojan uniform. In 26 minutes, she had 24 points, 15 rebounds and five blocked shots in an 83–66 victory at Pauley Pavilion.

Leslie's main rival was UCLA's Natalie Williams, a two-sport standout whose career rebound average of 12.8 is a women's Pac-10 record. For four seasons, the Leslie vs. Williams matchup seemed to be the key in the rivalry.

"We were very competitive against each other during that time," Leslie said. "She would come over from playing on UCLA's volleyball team and we would go at it. I think we brought out the best in each other whenever we played."

From 1989 to 1994, few athletes stamped their names on UCLA athletics more forcefully than Natalie Williams.

Williams was a four-time All-American in volleyball from 1989 to 1992, leading the Bruins to NCAA titles in 1990 and 1991. She played basketball from the 1990–91 season through 1993–94, leading the Bruins in scoring and rebounding for three consecutive seasons.

And when it came to the Trojans, Williams was often at her best. Unfortunately for the Bruins, USC's program had greater depth at the time and enjoyed more success.

Williams was a dominant force on both ends of the court, finishing with a game-high 28 points and career-high 23 rebounds in an 85–70 loss as a senior.

UCLA basketball coach Billie Moore compared Williams, the daughter of NBA player Nate Williams, to former Bruin All-Americans Ann Meyers and Denise Curry. "They, at various times, have dominated the game, but I don't think that I've ever seen a more dominating performance than Natalie's," Moore said after the game. "It was as awesome a performance as I've ever seen."

Williams' teams had greater success on the volleyball court, where she also could dominate. She was named MVP in consecutive Final Fours in 1990 and 1991 and became the first UCLA athlete to compete in two sports on the same day.

In November 1992, Williams played four minutes in a basketball game, then as her teammates were playing the second half of the early-season game, she got ready to play a volleyball match against USC. She led the Bruins to an important volleyball victory.

Williams acknowledged afterward that it was basically a stunt, but still it was something no UCLA player had done before.

Williams went on to play professional basketball in the ABL and WNBA.

In 1992–93, USC swept two more from UCLA, with Leslie and Easterly again the main scorers in a 22–7 season. But after the season, both USC and UCLA hired new coaches.

Former USC All-American Cheryl Miller took over for Stanley, whose contract was not renewed because she wanted pay parity with men's Coach George Raveling. She filed suit against USC, charging gender discrimination, but lost. Over at UCLA, Kathy Olivier, a Bruin assistant coach, replaced Billie Moore, who retired after 19 seasons.

The Trojans won the first match of the 1993–94 season, 85–70, but it took a real team effort to offset Williams' performance. The Bruin All-American had a game-high 28 points and career-high 23 rebounds.

The Trojans completed the season sweep a month later when Leslie scored 24 points, grabbed 15 rebounds and blocked five shots in an 83–66 victory at Pauley Pavilion. Williams sat out the game because of a knee injury.

In 1994–95, USC ran its streak over UCLA to eight games with two more wins.

Cheryl Miller resigned before the start of the 1995–96 season to take a basketball broadcasting position and was replaced by associate coach Fred Williams. Tina Thompson was Williams' go-to player and had another big season for the Trojans, leading the team in almost every offensive category.

In the first game against UCLA, she was at her peak. She scored a career-high 49 points and pulled down 15 rebounds in a 96–77 victory.

Then in the rematch, thanks to Nicky Hilbert's 33 points and Erica Gomez's 18 points, 11 rebounds and 10 assists, the Bruins finally ended the Trojans' win streak at nine with an 80–64 victory at Pauley Pavilion.

USC established control again in 1996–97, winning 60–56 at Pauley and 87–74 in the Sports Arena on the way to the NCAA tournament, where the Trojans lost in the second round. That was Williams' last game as coach. He was replaced before the start of the 1997–98 season by Chris Gobrecht, whose first two seasons against UCLA didn't go as she might have hoped.

The Bruins swept USC

1990s UCLA Olympic Medalists

BASEBALL			
Troy Glaus	1996		Bronze
Jim Parque	1996		Bronze
BASKETBALL			
Reggie Miller	1996		Gold
GYMNASTICS			
Kerri Strug	1996	Team	Gold
SOCCER			
Joy Fawcett	1996		Gold
SOFTBALL			
Joanne Brown (Australia)	1996		Bronze
Kerry Dienelt (Australia)	1996		Bronze
Sheila Cornell Douty	1996		Gold
Lisa Fernandez	1996		Gold
Tanya Harding (Australia)	1996		Bronze
Dot Richardson	1996		Gold
Christa Williams	1996		Gold
SWIMMING			
Tom Jager	1992	50m Freestyle	Bronze
		4x100m Freestyle Relay	Gold
Annette Salmeen	1996	800m Freestyle Relay	Gold

GAMES WON The 1990s

WOMEN'S BASKETBALL

USC 13 · UCLA 7

1990s UCLA Olympic Medalists

TRACK AND FIELD

Evelyn Ashford	1992	4x100m Relay	Gold
Ato Boldon (Trinidad)	1996	100 meters	Bronze
		200 meters	Bronze
Gail Devers	1992	100 meters	Gold
	1996	100 meters	Gold
		4x100m Relay	Gold
John Godina	1996	Shot Put	Silver
Jackie Joyner-Kersee	1992	Heptathlon	Gold
	1992	Long Jump	Bronze
	1996	Long Jump	Bronze
Steve Lewis	1992	400 meters	Silver
		4x400m Relay	Gold
Mike Marsh	1992	200 meter	Gold
		4x100m Relay	Gold
	1996	4x100m Relay	Silver
Mike Powell	1992	Long Jump	Silver
Janeene Vickers	1992	400m Intermediate Hurdles	Bronze
Kevin Young	1992	400m Intermediate Hurdles	Gold

VOLLEYBALL

Karch Kiraly	1996	Beach	Gold
Doug Partie	1992		Bronze
Kent Steffes	1996	Beach	Gold

WOMEN'S VOLLEYBALL

UCLA began the '90s as the premier program in women's volleyball, led by two-sport star Natalie Williams and Holly McPeak. The Bruins swept the Trojans on their way to the 1990 NCAA championship, and in 1991 the team was even better.

With Williams and Elaine Youngs, UCLA dominated opponents at the net, swept two more matches from the Trojans and repeated as national champs.

USC was on an 11–game winning streak when it played UCLA the first time that season and took one game from the Bruins, the first since 1988, but lost that match, then a second later in the season.

Nevertheless, Bruin Coach Andy Banachowski was concerned that his team lacked the fire it had shown in winning the title a year earlier. His public comments that the team didn't seem as strong as the previous one, that it wasn't as quick, might have fired up the squad, because the Bruins repeated as champions with a victory over Long Beach State in the NCAA final.

The 1992 Bruins were again loaded. UCLA lost only eight games all season and won 33 matches in a row, extending an overall streak to 43. The Bruins also beat up on the Trojans two more times to extend their streak in the

for the first time since 1990 in Gobrecht's first season, then in 1998–99 they did it again. In the first of those games, UCLA trounced a depleted USC team, 94–53, in front of a record regular-season crowd of 9,530 at UCLA.

The Bruins finished the '90s with their fourth victory in a row over the Trojans, 82–64, at USC. Maylana Martin, who would be named an All-American and Pac-10 player of the year after the season, took charge in the second half and finished with 38 points and 18 rebounds.

rivalry to 10. But their quest for a third consecutive national championship fell short against Stanford in the NCAA title game.

The next three seasons, UCLA continued to win but failed to win another NCAA title, losing to Stanford again in the championship match in 1994. The Bruins extended their streak over the Trojans to 14, though some of those victories were difficult to come by.

UCLA's biggest test against the Trojans was their final meeting in 1994. With senior Annett Buckner and junior Jenny Johnson dominating at the net, the Bruins had to come from behind to pull out a five-game victory at USC.

Finally, in 1995, USC broke the seven-year winless string against UCLA in a five-game thriller led by senior outside hitter Kelly Kuebler.

"This is just fabulous," she told *The Times.* "To this day, last year's loss was the worst day of my life. Coming in

here and beating them in the same gym is really special."

The Bruins avenged the defeat with two hard-fought victories over Trojans at USC's North Gym. UCLA won in five games the second time the teams played in 1995, and the Bruins won again in 1996.

But after that first match in 1996, the tide began to turn.

MATCHES WON
The 1990s

WOMEN'S
VOLLEYBALL

UCLA 14 - USC 6

■ Holly McPeak, left, and Natalie Williams.

USC won the rematch in three games at Pauley Pavilion and reached the NCAA playoffs for the fifth season in a row, losing to Stanford in the Pacific Regional semifinals.

In 1997, USC defeated the Bruins twice for its first season sweep since 1982.

Junior middle blocker Alaina Kipps was the story of the match, recording six kills and a match-high 11 of USC's 15 blocks against the Bruins. Kipps posted a combined 23 blocks in two matches against UCLA in 1997.

The next season, USC stretched the streak to five with two more victories, but in 1999, UCLA stopped the slide and won both matches.

■ Bruin high jumper Amy Acuff won the NCAA outdoor championship twice.

■ ■ ■ ■ ■ ■ ■ ■ ■ ■ ■

WOMEN'S TRACK AND FIELD

As it did in men's track and field, UCLA held a sizable edge over USC at the start of the decade in women's track. Bruin Coach Bob Kersee told *The Times*: "This is the deepest team I've been associated with since, perhaps, the 1982–83 teams."

The Bruins ran away with a 90–40 victory at the Coliseum over the overmatched Trojans. UCLA's Tonya Sedwick won the 400 meters, the long jump and ran a leg on the Bruins' winning 400-meter relay team.

USC's Ashley Selman, who won the javelin, told *The Times*, "We're so outnumbered. We have 15 people. They have 15 distance runners."

UCLA won its fourth consecutive Pac-10 title that year and finished second at the NCAA championships, behind Louisiana State.

Before the start of the 1991 season, former UCLA men's coach Jim Bush took over as the head men's and women's track and field coach at USC. But USC still trailed the Bruins on the track.

With freshman Dawn Dumble providing solid points in the shot put and discus, and Janeene Vickers back as one of the nation's top quarter-milers, the Bruins rolled over the Trojans, 95–40, at Drake Stadium.

At the Pac-10 championships, the Bruins finished second behind Oregon, ending UCLA's four-year title run. But in 1992, USC finally caught up with its rival.

Anchored by sprinter Inger Miller and intermediate hurdler Michelle DeCoux, the Trojans expected to end UCLA's four-year dual-meet winning streak over them.

And they did.

The Trojans trounced the injury-depleted Bruins, 80–30, to give USC its first victory in the series since 1987. Miller won the 100 and 200 meters and Amy Goodwin won the 800 and 1,500 meters.

In 1993, the Bruins won the Pac-10 title and finished third in the NCAAs. Jeanette Bolden took over for Kersee in 1994 and duplicated those results.

In 1995, Dumble set meet records in the shot put and discus in an 84–52 thumping of the Trojans. UCLA won its third consecutive conference title and finished second behind LSU at the NCAA championships.

In 1996, the Trojans and Bruins competed in a thriller at Drake Stadium. UCLA needed a victory in the 1,600-meter relay, the meet's final event, to beat the Trojans, 74–70.

Mame Twumasi, Camille Noel, Andrea Anderson and Darlene Malco finished the race in a season-best time of 3:36.56, beating the Trojans by almost six seconds.

But the Trojans avenged that loss at the Pac-10 championships, where they won the conference title for the first time in school history, thanks in part to victories in the 100 and 200 meters by freshman Torri Edwards.

In 1997, UCLA won its fifth in a row in the regular season over USC, 82–63, and returned as conference champion, then finished third in the NCAA championships.

The next season, the Bruins crushed the Trojans, 104–50, with freshman sprinter Shakedia Jones winning the 100 and 200 meters and running a leg on the winning 400-meter relay team.

Joanna Hayes and Anderson also had big days in helping the Bruins to their sixth consecutive victory over the Trojans. Hayes won the 100-meter high hurdles and the 400 lows and ran legs on both the 400- and 1,600-meter relay teams. Anderson won the 400 and placed third in the 200, and also ran legs on both relays.

MEETS WON
The 1990s
WOMEN'S TRACK & FIELD
UCLA 9 – USC 1

■ Angela Williams after winning the 100-meter dash at the NCAA outdoor championships in 1999.

MEETS WON The 1990s
WOMEN'S SWIMMING
USC 6 - UCLA 4

MATCHES WON The 1990s
WOMEN'S WATER POLO
UCLA 9 - USC 1 (1995-1999)

GAMES WON The 1990s
WOMEN'S SOCCER
UCLA 7 - USC 2 (1993-1999)

■ Keri Phebus was a standout for the Bruins.

After winning their second Pac-10 title in a row and finishing second in the 1998 NCAA meet, the Bruins were strong again in 1999. Seilala Sua, the two-time defending NCAA champion in the discus, was the Bruins' top point-scorer.

Against the Trojans, Sua added the shot put and javelin to her resume, and UCLA romped, 91–63, at USC's Cromwell Field.

The victory gave UCLA a 9–1 head-to-head record against USC in the 1990s, and the Bruins capped off the decade with their third consecutive Pac-10 title and top-three finish at the NCAA championships, ending up second to Texas.

WOMEN'S TENNIS

At the start of the 1990s, USC's tennis program was solid under Coach Cheryl Woods, but the Trojans had trouble finishing. USC split with UCLA during the season and finished tied for third with the Bruins in the Pac-10. But UCLA finished third nationally with a 23–7 record, while the Trojans ended with a 19–8 mark, which included defeats in six of their final eight matches.

In 1991, UCLA swept both matches from the Trojans and fin-

MATCHES WON The 1990s
WOMEN'S TENNIS
UCLA 14 - USC 6

ished second in the nation with a 23–5 record.

Then in 1992, the Trojans won, 5–3, at USC to end a three-match losing streak to UCLA. The Bruins won the rematch, 5–2, at Westwood.

The schools continued to split their two-match season series until 1996, when the Bruins began a six-match winning steak over the Trojans. With Keri Phebus, the NCAA singles and doubles champion in 1995, leading Coach Bill Zaima's team, UCLA swept the Trojans in 1996, 1997 and 1998.

In 1999, USC ended a three-year losing streak with a 6–3 victory in the first meeting between the teams. UCLA won the rematch to finish the decade with a 14–6 record against the Trojans. ■

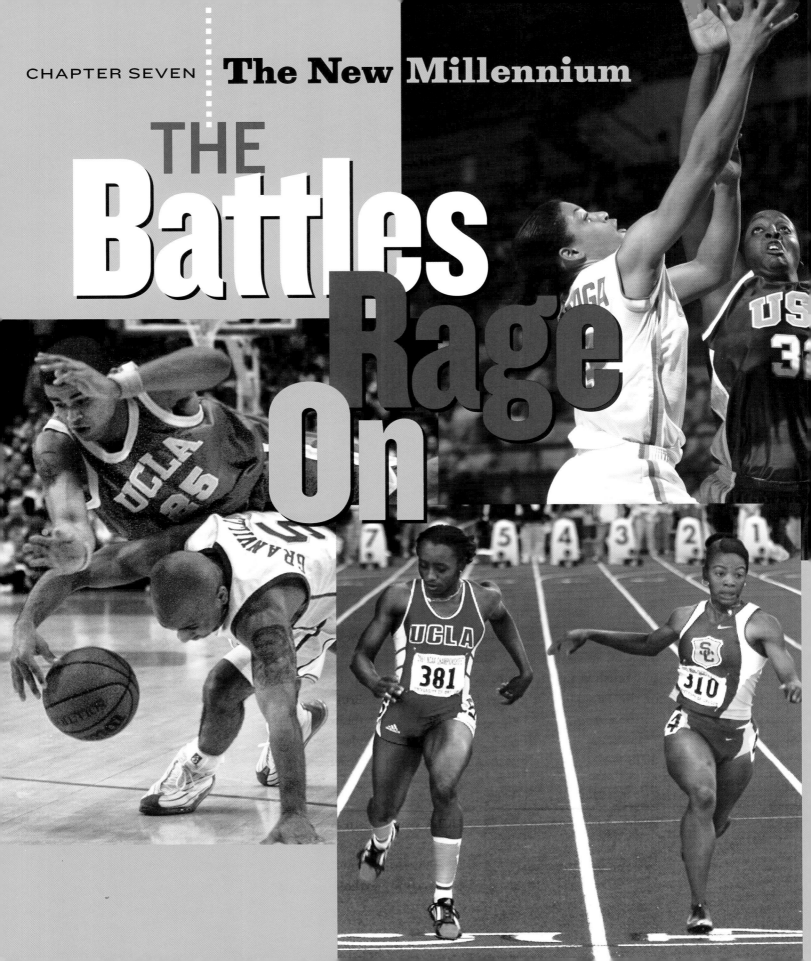

CHAPTER SEVEN

The New Millennium

THE Battles Rage On

At the start of the new millennium, USC's athletic programs began once again to enjoy some success at the expense of their crosstown rivals. Under Athletic Director Mike Garrett, the Trojans ended lengthy losing stretches in football and basketball that had begun in the 1990s, wiping away images of their teams as doormats to the Bruins in these high-profile sports.

Opposite, clockwise from top: UCLA's Gennifer Arranaga and USC's Ebony Hoffman; USC's Angela Williams edges out UCLA's Shakedia Jones in 2001; Earl Watson tumbles over Brandon Granville.

In 2001, the USC women's track and field team won an NCAA outdoor championship, and in 2002, the Trojans won national titles in men's tennis and women's volleyball. The next year, USC pulled off a fall sweep with national championships in football, men's water polo and women's volleyball, followed by a women's water polo crown in the spring.

Across town, the Bruins were making some noise of their own, winning national titles in men's volleyball and water polo in 2000 and women's championships in water polo in 2000, 2001 and 2003. In addition, the women's soccer team enjoyed considerable success as the decade progressed, ending up the nation's second-ranked team in 2003.

In all, the ongoing national success of both schools proves again that the rivalry between the Bruins and Trojans over the better part of eight decades continued to be played out at the very highest level of collegiate sports.

FOOTBALL

Both USC and UCLA got off to fast starts in 2000, with each team winning its first three games. Then things turned sour for both.

USC lost five in a row and was 4–6 by the time of the UCLA game; UCLA lost three of four and was 6–4 when they ran on to the Rose Bowl field to play the Trojans.

USC, for only the first time since 1960-61, was on its way to its second consecutive losing season, and Coach Paul Hackett's job was in jeopardy.

In an attempt to motivate his players, Hackett had video machines in USC's Heritage Hall replay great moments in rivalry history over and over during the week leading up to the UCLA game.

Hackett's motivational ploy apparently worked. The Trojans defeated UCLA, 38–35, on a field goal from backup kicker David Bell, who had missed his three previous attempts during the season.

The winning 36-yarder might not have made it if it had been kicked from a few yards farther. "It was the ugliest best kick I ever had in my life," said Bell, who got a chance to kick only because John Wall, who had replaced the ineffective David Newbury, was injured.

The game was an offensive showdown. Even in losing, UCLA gained 557 yards and held the lead four times during the game. But each time, the Trojans, led by quarterback Carson Palmer, came roaring back. Palmer drove USC 47 yards in less than a minute for the final kick and finished with 26 completions in 37 attempts for 350 yards and four touchdowns.

"This was our bowl game, and we needed to win this game," Palmer told reporters. "This win will help get some people off our backs."

UCLA players were stunned that they hadn't held on against a team that was tied for last in the Pac-10. Wide receiver Brian Poli-Dixon told

The Times, "We lost to the worst team in the Pac-10.... We basically gave them the game."

The victory, however, didn't spare Hackett. He was fired after the Trojans closed the season with a home loss to Notre Dame. His

■ Coaches had short stays in the early years of the deacde. UCLA's Bob Toledo, left, and USC's Paul Hackett.

■ Opposite: Carson Palmer, USC's fifth Heisman Trophy winner, greets fans after 2002 win over Bruins. Below: Troy Polamalu exults after a big team win in 2002.

■ UCLA running back DeShaun Foster

replacement was Pete Carroll, a former NFL head coach with the New York Jets and New England Patriots.

The Bruins' season didn't end well, either. They finished with three consecutive losses, including one to Wisconsin in the Sun Bowl.

But the Bruins seemed to have turned things around by 2001. They opened the season with six consecutive victories, including four over ranked teams.

In his first season with the Trojans, Carroll had gotten off to a shaky start, losing four of his first five games. But then USC got hot behind Palmer.

The Trojans won four of five games, with their only defeat coming against Notre Dame. Carroll's Trojans had fought back to .500 for

their game against UCLA.

The Bruins were less than full strength at kickoff because running back DeShaun Foster, the team's top rusher, was declared ineligible for the rest of the season for accepting free use of an automobile, a violation of the NCAA's "extra benefit" rules.

Without Foster, UCLA was no match for the Trojans, losing 27–0. Bruin quarterback Cory Paus was sacked five times and completed only seven of 15 passes for 45 yards with two interceptions before being replaced in the fourth quarter. UCLA gained only 28 yards on the ground and never drove inside the USC 20-yard line.

USC cornerback Antuan Simmons returned an interception for one touchdown. Safety Troy Polamalu blocked a punt to set up a field goal and had an interception to set up a touchdown.

Palmer completed 14 of 23 passes for 180 yards, including a four-yard scoring pass to Keary Colbert, in USC's third consecutive victory over UCLA.

After the game, Carroll stood on the band director's stand in front of the Trojans' student section, smiling and waving. "We've got to be the best 6–5 team in the nation," Carroll told reporters.

In 2002, the Trojans took their program to a higher level behind Palmer, who excelled in offensive coordinator Norm Chow's system. After losing two of their first five games, the

Pete Carroll USC

Off to a winning start on his rivalry march

USC's Pete Carroll thought he knew all about the rivalry against UCLA even before he coached his first football game against the Bruins in 2001.

More than three decades earlier, Carroll, who grew up in the Bay Area, went with a high school friend to a USC–UCLA game at the Coliseum. It left an indelible mark.

USC and UCLA were both 8-0-1 heading into the 1969 game, with the Pacific-10 title up for grabs. The Bruins took a 12-7 lead with five minutes to play, but three minutes later Sam Dickerson caught a 32-yard scoring pass in the corner of the end zone to give USC a 14-12 victory, sending the crowd of more than 90,000 into a frenzy.

"That was such a classic game to watch, and I knew then that this was as good as it gets," Carroll recalled.

Carroll's first game coaching against the Bruins was a 27-0 victory for USC. In the locker room afterward, he told reporters that it was great to beat the Bru-

ins but said it meant more to him that the win put the Trojans above .500, at 6-5.

It wasn't until a few months later that Carroll's view of the rivalry's meaning deepened, and it took a former UCLA coach, Terry Donahue, to show him.

Carroll ran into Donahue and his wife on the USC campus. The Donahues were there to watch their daughter play tennis.

"We talked for a while and then I invited him to take a walk through Heritage Hall," Carroll said. "Well, they finally decided to go in, and it was so fun to watch them. They were like little kids looking at all of the trophies and talking about different games and players. Terry had grown up with the rivalry, played in it and coached in it.

"But what I remember most is that Donahue told me that he had lost the first four games in the rivalry. I know he won a lot at the end and ended up with a winning lifetime record against USC. But the intensity that he carried about the matchup and how it worked on him for

years, I will never forget. I felt very fortunate because it gave me a chance to see what to expect if I lost."

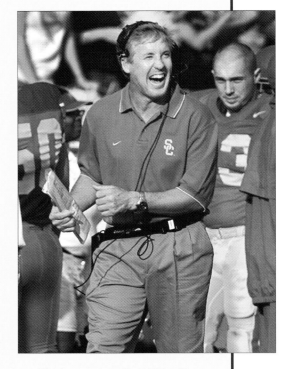

That's something Carroll hasn't experienced in his first three seasons at USC. The Trojans beat the Bruins 52-21 in 2002 and 47-22 in 2003.

Trojans won five in a row heading into the UCLA game at the Rose Bowl.

UCLA had won three straight to improve its record to 7-3 but turned out to be no match for USC. The Bruins were completely dominated in a 52-21 trouncing that started poorly for UCLA—Tab Perry fumbled on the opening kickoff, USC recovered and Palmer hit Kareem Kelly with a 34-yard touchdown

pass 16 seconds into the game—and only got worse as the game progressed.

Palmer completed 19 of 32 passes for 254 yards and four touchdowns, and the Trojan defense limited the Bruins to 40 yards rushing.

The 52 points were the most scored by either team in the series since USC defeated UCLA, 52-0, in 1930, the second meeting between the teams.

Karl Dorrell UCLA

Trojan test tougher as a post-grad

Well before he was named the Bruins' head football coach in 2002, Karl Dorrell had made his mark on the rivalry with the Trojans. A Bruin receiver in the mid-1980s, Dorrell scored on an intentionally tipped go-for-broke pass thrown by Matt Stevens just before halftime in UCLA's 45–25 victory in 1986.

"We practiced the same play every week, but never had it work in a game until that day," Dorrell said. "USC had the best coverage called, and the play worked perfectly, with Flipper Anderson tipping the ball just like he did in practice, and it went right to me. All I had to do was catch it."

Dorrell's catch helped UCLA knock off USC, which had been ranked 10th in the nation.

"It doesn't matter what the records are," said Dorrell, who was a senior in the 1986 season. "The UCLA–SC game is about pride.... We didn't have a great season, but from our standpoint, we felt that we had a better team than how we played. We were just inconsistent all season, but we put it all together against USC that day."

Growing up in San Diego, Dorrell admired the Trojans' O.J. Simpson, Anthony Davis, Ricky Bell, Charles White and Marcus Allen and tried to pattern himself after those great runners.

But after deciding to enroll in Westwood, Dorrell had to switch plans and re-fashion himself into a wide receiver.

After a brief stint with the Dallas Cowboys, Dorrell began his coaching career as a graduate assistant at UCLA, then spent 12 years on the collegiate level before moving to the staff of the Denver Broncos as wide receivers coach before taking the UCLA job in December 2002.

The next time Dorrell faced USC, he walked the UCLA sideline as coach. Dorrell had replaced Bob Toledo.

In Dorrell's first game coaching against USC, the Bruins never had a chance in a 47–22 loss at the Coliseum. USC had a 33–2 lead by halftime, at which point the Bruins had more yards in penalties, 50, than they had in offense, 36. USC finished the 2003 season as co-national champion; UCLA wound up a disappointing 6–7.

"The pressure is really the same as it was when I was a player," Dorrell said. "Because it's such a big rivalry in Los Angeles, you have all the elements. The city is split and everyone is aware of the game. If you don't win, you'll feel the pain because it's such a big issue year in and year out."

USC finished the regular season 10–2 and as Pac-10 champions, and Palmer became the school's fifth Heisman Trophy winner. After defeating Iowa in the Orange Bowl, the Trojans finished as the No. 4 ranked team in the nation.

The 2002 regular season ended Bob Tole-do's seven-year career as UCLA coach. The Bruins lost decisively to Washington State, 48–27, after the USC debacle, and Athletic Director Dan Guerrero fired the coach before the Bruins played in the Las Vegas Bowl. With Assistant Athletic Director Ed Kezirian taking over as acting coach, UCLA wound up the season with

■ USC's Matt Leinart stepped into some big shoes in 2003—and they fit well.

With the defeat, UCLA seniors finished their careers without a victory over USC, the lingering memory after the game the chants from Trojan faithful as they walked off the Coliseum field, "Five more years! Five more years!"

Dorrell's first season ended at 6–7 after the Bruins' fifth consecutive defeat, a 17–9 loss to Fresno State in the Silicon Valley Bowl. USC's season was as successful as UCLA's was disappointing: The Trojans completed their season with a 28–14 victory over Michigan in the Rose Bowl and a share of their first national championship in 25 years.

a 27–13 bowl win over New Mexico. Eventually, UCLA selected former Bruin wide receiver Karl Dorrell as the new head coach.

Despite the loss of Palmer, the Trojans were even better in 2003 than they were in 2002. With Matt Leinart stepping in at quarterback, USC lost only once during the regular season.

In their matchup against the 6–4 Bruins, the Trojans extended their winning streak in the rivalry to five with a 47–22 victory at the Coliseum.

Leinart completed 23 of 32 passes for 289 yards and two touchdowns in about three quarters of work. USC wide receiver Mike Williams had 11 catches for 181 yards and two touchdowns.

BASKETBALL

UCLA Coach Steve Lavin's team had plenty to prove after finishing third in the Pac-10 in 1999 and being bounced out of the NCAA tournament in the first round by Detroit Mercy.

But the Bruins still began the 1999–2000 season with a 10-game winning streak over the Trojans, who hadn't defeated UCLA since 1994. USC Coach Henry Bibby, who had played for John Wooden and the Bruins, was 0–6 against his alma mater.

With a lineup that featured high-scoring

freshman Jason Kapono, UCLA was 9–3 heading into the first USC game, at the Sports Arena. The Trojans were riding a four-game winning streak, had won six of seven and were in first place early in the Pac-10 season.

They stayed there. Behind Jeff Trepangier's career-high 26 points and David Bluthenthal's 12 points and 12 rebounds, USC won, 91–79. Five Trojans scored in double figures and USC out-rebounded UCLA, 45–35.

USC's Sam Clancy told *The Times,* "We sent a big message here…. Coach told us before the

■ UCLA's Jason Kapono, right, and USC's Sam Clancy, below.

game that UCLA is no different than we are. Just because it says 'UCLA' on their jerseys doesn't mean they are any better than we are."

UCLA's night did not get off to a good start when its team bus broke down en route to the arena, and the Bruins had to walk and jog a mile to arrive after 7 p.m. for a 7:30 tipoff. Lavin told reporters: "It was probably a Trojan bus driver."

A month later, things were different for the rematch. At Pauley, UCLA shot 68% in the second half in an 83–78 victory.

Kapono made nine of 10 shots in the second half and finished with a season-high 27 points, 25 after halftime. UCLA guard Earl Watson, who played the entire game without a turnover, added 22 points and had seven assists.

In the 2000–01 season, USC assumed the rare role as favorite in the rivalry. By the time

Henry Bibby USC

He's a convert, not a turncoat

Perhaps no individual has played more significant roles on both sides of the rivalry than Henry Bibby, an All-American guard under John Wooden at UCLA and the current coach of the USC men's basketball team.

Bibby arrived in Westwood from Franklinton, N.C., in the summer of 1968, while UCLA was winning national titles annually. And the summer before his sophomore year, his first on the varsity, he discovered the intensity of the rivalry with USC.

It was only a summer pickup game, but Bibby watched as teammate Sidney Wicks tried to choke USC's Mack Calvin.

"When I first came to Los Angeles, I didn't know much about USC, or UCLA for that matter," Bibby said. "I was really uncomfortable doing many things, except when I was on the basketball court.

"I started playing with Sidney and those guys at the park. We'd just go find basketball courts and play. This one day, Sidney got into it with Calvin. He tried to kill him. I knew about the rivalry then."

As a player, Bibby lost the first time he played USC, in 1970. The Trojans handed John Wooden his last defeat at Pauley Pavilion, 87–86. That would be the final time Bibby would lose to USC.

With Bibby directing Wooden's offense, UCLA won five in a row over USC and three consecutive NCAA championships from 1970 to 1972.

Bibby's loyalties changed when he was named USC coach, replacing Charlie Parker with nine games to play in the 1995–96 season. In his first four seasons, Bibby went 0–7 against his alma mater.

Then finally, on Jan. 12, 2000, the Trojans defeated the Bruins, 91–79, ending a 10-game losing streak to UCLA.

"This was a big win," Bibby said after the game. "We plan on changing things around here and this is a good start."

Bibby was right. Over the next four seasons, his teams were 5–4 against the Bruins, including a four-game winning streak through the 2003–2004 season.

"UCLA will always be the program to beat," Bibby said. "I will always have my special memories of playing for Coach Wooden, but I'm a Trojan now. What happened when I played for the Bruins happened a long time ago."

of the first UCLA game, the 19th-ranked Trojans had been in the top 25 for 10 consecutive weeks.

Lavin's struggling team was not ranked, and the game marked the first time since 1962 that a ranked Trojan team played an unranked Bruin team in basketball.

The teams switched roles at tipoff, however, with UCLA building a 19-point lead in the second half before holding on for an 80–75 victory at Pauley Pavilion.

UCLA set the tone early with physical play as Dan Gadzuric knocked USC's Desmon Farmer to the floor on a drive in the lane and Watson drove Bluthenthal into the scorer's table.

USC rallied behind Clancy's 31 points and 13 rebounds to make the game close, cutting the lead to three, 76–73, after holding UCLA to one field goal in a 10-minute stretch. But USC failed to make plays down the stretch, dropping Bibby's record to 1–8 against UCLA.

For the rematch at the Sports Arena, both teams needed a victory to stay in the conference race. Only UCLA got it, as the Trojans hurt themselves with three consecutive turnovers late in the game.

Kapono scored 20 points, including a key three-point basket, in the Bruins' 85–76 victory. The win completed a season series sweep for UCLA, which had defeated USC in 13 of 14 games, including three in a row.

Both USC and UCLA made it to the NCAA tournament and both reached the Sweet 16 before losing.

In 2001–02, both the Bruins and Trojans entered their initial matchup of the season perfect in the Pac-10 at 4–0.

Despite his lack of success against the Bruins, Bibby was getting his players to believe in themselves, and the Trojans defeated the Bruins, 81–77, despite a career-high 34 points from the Bruins' Matt Barnes. The victory was USC's ninth in a row, the school's longest streak since 1992, and it ended UCLA's nine-game winning streak.

Bluthenthal finished with 16 points and 18 rebounds, and Errick Craven had 13 points, five rebounds, two assists and two steals in 28 minutes.

The pressure leading up to the rematch was intense. Barnes had emerged as the

■ Bruin coach Steve Lavin, surrounded by his team in 2002, struggled against the Trojans and was replaced in 2003 by Ben Howland, below.

Bruins' leader, and UCLA trailed USC by a game in the Pac-10 race when the teams met again at Pauley Pavilion.

In a tight game that featured plenty of mistakes but all-out effort, UCLA emerged with a 67–65 victory on a three-point basket at the buzzer by Billy Knight. Knight had plenty of incentive against the Trojans. He had planned to attend USC but said he was told that his scholarship had been given to Jeff Trepagnier before he could make the decision. So, with the clock running down and USC ahead 65–64, Gadzuric grabbed an offensive rebound and passed to Knight, who made that winning shot.

Lavin again did well in postseason play, guiding the Bruins to the Sweet 16, where they lost to Missouri. USC finished the season with a 22–10 record after losing to North Carolina Wilmington in overtime in the first round of the NCAA tournament.

The next season, both teams had to rely on inexperienced players. Lavin no longer had Gadzuric, Rico Hines or Barnes, while Bibby couldn't count on Clancy, Brandon Granville or Bluthenthal.

USC won the first meeting, 80–75, behind 25 points from Farmer and 24 from Errick Craven, the Trojans' first win in West-

wood since 1993. Kapono was held to 10 points, only three in the second half, by tough Trojan defense.

By the time the teams met again, Lavin's job status was up in the air. Despite having a 10–3 record against USC and twice as many NCAA tournament appearances as Bibby, the Bruins' 4–13 record heading into the rematch was not a great endorsement.

USC made it 4–14 with an 86–85 victory. In the final seconds, Errick Craven was fouled by sophomore Ryan Walcott. With 4.4 seconds remaining, Craven's two free throws won the game for the Trojans.

Farmer led USC with 28 points and nine rebounds, and Craven had 19 points, eight rebounds, five assists and two steals.

The victory gave USC its first season sweep over UCLA since 1992 and extended the Bruins' losing streak to nine games.

The loss dropped Lavin's record to 1–3 in his last four games against the Trojans, and after the season ended, he was fired and later replaced by Ben Howland.

A month before the two teams played for the first time in the 2003–04 season, UCLA had a dedication ceremony of Nell and John Wooden Court at Pauley Pavilion. One of the 100 former Bruin players to attend was Bibby.

"I have a lot of respect for UCLA. I'm not there anymore, but Coach Wooden is my guy. He's a guy that I respect, that I love, that I'd go anywhere for," Bibby told *The Times*.

Both teams struggled leading into the first matchup, the Trojans losing nine of 17 games, the Bruins at 9–6.

With Farmer scoring 28 points, 14 in each half, USC won at Pauley Pavilion, 76–69. The Trojans led by as many as 19 points in the second half, but UCLA rallied behind center Ryan Hollins' career-high 21 points.

USC completed its second consecutive sea-

■ **Dan Gadzuric is poised to slam one home.**

▨ **Right: Trojan Desmon Farmer collides with UCLA's Cedric Bozeman.**

son sweep over UCLA at the Sports Arena. In his final home game as a Trojan, Farmer scored nine points in a row in overtime to give the Trojans a 78–77 victory for their fourth consecutive win in the rivalry, USC's longest streak against UCLA in 61 years.

Farmer finished with 28 points, including 11 of USC's 13 points in overtime, and Jeff McMillan had 19 points and a career-high 18 rebounds. UCLA had a chance to send the game into a second overtime, but Dijon Thompson missed his first of two free throws with half a second left.

Neither USC nor UCLA finished above .500 in 2004, and both failed to play in a postseason tournament.

■■■■■■■■ BASEBALL

USC essentially owned UCLA in the first four years of the decade on the baseball field, winning 19 of 24 games and in one stretch winning 11 in a row. The Bruins struggled overall, and at the end of the 2003 season Gary Adams announced that 2004—his 30th season—would be his last as coach.

■ Trojan pitching ace Rik Currier

The Trojans won two games from the Bruins in their first meeting in 2000, a nonconference series in which one game was postponed because of rain. USC sophomore pitcher Mark Prior figured prominently in both of those victories—not only with his arm but with his bat as well.

In the first game, a 10–7 victory, Prior gave up four hits and struck out 13 in 7 2/3 innings. With Brian Barre going five for five with four singles and a double, the Trojans scored more than enough runs for Prior, who retired 18 consecutive batters.

The second game was tied, 3–3, in the bottom of the ninth inning when USC Coach Mike Gillespie called on Prior to pinch-hit with one out and runners on first and second.

Prior, who had struck out in his two previous at-bats, singled in the winning run for a 4–3 victory.

When the teams met in April for the first time in conference play, UCLA was 20–12 and USC was 22–11. Both teams were 5–1 in the Pac-10.

Rik Currier, starting in place of Prior, who was ill, pitched a five-hitter and struck out 12 in a 5–1 victory by USC in the first game. UCLA bounced back with a 15–5 win against freshman Anthony Reyes in the second and then beat Prior, 8–5, in the third at Jackie Robinson Stadium.

UCLA finished as Pac-10 co-champion with Stanford and Arizona, and the Trojans and Bruins advanced to postseason play, USC losing to LSU and Florida State in the College World Series and the Bruins falling to Louisiana State in an NCAA super regional.

With Prior and Currier back in 2001, the Trojans opened the season regarded as one of the nation's best teams and were No. 1 heading into a nonconference series at UCLA.

The Bruins' Josh Karp and Prior went head to head in the first game. Prior outpitched Karp, leaving with a 3–1 lead after seven, but UCLA won, 4–3, on Adam Berry's three-run homer in the bottom of the ninth.

USC won the next two games, 6–0 behind Currier's two-hit pitching over eight innings and 5–4 on Mike Morales' single in the 11th inning.

**GAMES WON
Through 5/04
BASEBALL
USC 22 - UCLA 8**

In late April, the Trojans swept three games at Dedeaux Field. Prior struck out 14 in a 2–0 shutout. USC held on for a 7–6 win in Game 2, then swept the series with a 7–1 win on Reyes' one-hit pitching over eight innings.

Gillespie's Trojans won the Pac-10 title and advanced to the College World Series, where they were eliminated by Tennessee.

Although the Bruins did not qualify for postseason play, Brian Baron finished with a .443 batting average, breaking Don Slaught's school record of .428 set in 1979.

In 2002, USC started slowly and lost five of its first seven games, but the Trojans finished strong, swept UCLA for the first time since 1984 and won the Pac-10 title.

In the opening game of the first series against UCLA, Matt Chico pitched the Trojans to a 1–0 victory, outdueling Chris Cordeiro. Brian Barre's home run on the second pitch of the game was the difference.

There was no effective Bruin pitching in the second game as the Trojans got 26 hits in a 26–4 victory. USC completed the sweep with a 6–3 win.

The opener of the second series went 12 innings before Bill Peavey's single gave the Trojans a 5–4 win. USC hit four homers in a 16–10 victory in the second game and completed the sweep with a 13–3 thumping in the third game, a victory that clinched the conference title.

In the NCAA playoffs, the Trojans were eliminated by Stanford in the Super Regionals.

After finishing 26–35 in 2002 and failing to reach postseason play, Adams began to feel heat from Athletic Director Guerrero, who had already gotten rid of the football and basketball coaches and was not pleased with the baseball

program's direction, which included consecutive seventh-place finishes in the Pac-10.

In their first meeting with the Trojans in 2003, the Bruins took it to USC, breaking a streak of 11 losses with a 7–4 victory at Jackie Robinson Stadium.

And after a 9–6 USC win in the second game, UCLA took a series from the Trojans for the first time in three years with a 17–5 trouncing. The Bruins scored 10 runs in the first inning to make the game a laugher from the start.

Things didn't go so well for the Bruins in the rematch at Dedeaux Field. USC swept, 7–6, 7–4 and 8–5, sending UCLA toward a 28–31 final record.

In 2004, the teams split their six games, with each winning three. The Bruins fared poorly in the first game of the opening series of 2004, as the Trojans came out swinging and tallied six runs in the first. USC added another five runs in the eighth to win 11–4.

The following day, freshman Trojan pitch-

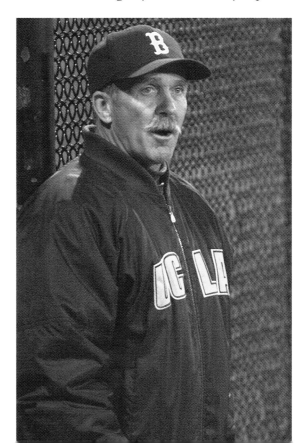

■ Gary Adams retired in 2004 after 30 seasons as the Bruins' baseball coach.

Dan Guerrero UCLA

Need to beat Troy never lets up

Dan Guerrero was named UCLA athletic director in 2002, and in his first year on the job, the Bruins won four team NCAA championships—in soccer, women's gymnastics, women's water polo and softball.

Guerrero, who graduated in 1974 from UCLA, was a career .343 hitter on the UCLA baseball team in his three years as starting second baseman. In those years the Bruins suffered mightily at the hands of the Trojans, so now Guerrero takes special delight in beating his crosstown curse.

"I had the dubious distinction of playing baseball at UCLA for four years with USC winning the national championship every year that I played," said Guerrero. "To this day, one of the few at-bats that I can still vividly remember was the first time that I came to the plate to face the Trojans' Steve Busby.

"He's the best pitcher that I ever faced. Everyone on our team kept talking about how hard he threw, and I certainly witnessed that firsthand. But it wasn't a fastball that caught my attention. He happened to throw me the best curveball that I ever saw for a called third strike. It was a pitch that I definitely was not expecting."

Although the Bruins struggled against the Trojans, Guerrero did have his moments.

"I personally had some success against them, in terms of my at-bats," Guerrero said. "One of my best hits came at [USC's] old Bovard Field when I doubled off the wall to help us win one of our few against them."

Guerrero never made it as a professional baseball player, but he has been a successful administrator. After earning a master's degree in public administration, Guerrero went on to become athletic director at Cal State Dominguez Hills and then UC Irvine before taking over at UCLA.

Beating USC was one of Guerrero's priorities after returning to Westwood.

"Being from Southern California, the dynasty is ingrained in you even before you have an opportunity to be a part of it," said Guerrero, a standout athlete at Banning High in Wilmington. "Once you become a part of it, it never lets go. It always remains with you."

---

er Ian Kennedy blanked the Bruins for 7 1/3 innings and struck out eight as USC beat UCLA, 5–0.

The Bruins avoided a sweep with a 13–7 win in the third game of the series. Matt Thayer's two-run triple in the third inning gave the Bruins the go-ahead runs in what was the final game at Dedeaux Field for Bruin Coach Adams, who retired at the end of the season.

When the teams met again a month later at Jackie Robinson Stadium, freshman Trojan Cyle Hankerd broke a 4–4 tie in the eighth inning with a two-out double, and USC beat the Bruins, 6–4.

The Bruins bounced back the next day with a 12–6 victory. Preston Griffin and Brett McMillan had three hits each for the Bruins.

The Trojans were seemingly headed for a clear victory in the third and final game of the season between the two schools until Bruin Chris Denove's single in the bottom of the ninth inning capped a six-run rally and drove in the winning run for a 13–12 Bruin win.

The Trojans had a 9–4 lead going into the bottom of the eighth inning, but the Bruins cut the lead by scoring three runs in their second to last at-bat thanks in part to Bruin second baseman Mike Svetlic, who went 4-for-6 with three RBIs during the game and hit a two-run single in the inning.

In the top of the ninth, the Trojans added three more runs as Baron Frost led off with a home run and freshman Hankerd hit a two-run single.

As the bottom of the ninth inning opened, the score was 12–7 in the Trojans' favor, but the USC pitchers couldn't hold on to the lead. The first two Bruin batters walked. Then relief pitcher Jon Williams allowed four singles and walked two, loading the bases for Denove, who hit a single off freshman reliever Paul Koss for the game-winning run.

The Bruins finished the season by making the NCAA regionals for the first time since 2000, ending Adams' 30-year UCLA coaching career on a high note. Adams was named the Pacific-10 Conference's coach of the year for 2004, the third time he had won the honor.

TENNIS

In 2000 and 2001, UCLA, coached by Billy Martin, had one of the nation's top tennis teams but failed to win even a conference championship until 2002, its first since 1996. Meanwhile, USC, struggled until midway through the 2002 season and then broke through for something much bigger than a conference title: a national championship.

The Bruins spent part of the 2000 season ranked No. 1 and played like it in two matches against the Trojans: 5–2 and 4–3 victories.

The next year, UCLA spent most of the season atop the rankings and swept a struggling USC team again; the second victory was the 13th in 14 matches over the Trojans.

But UCLA wasn't strong enough to get through the NCAA tournament. The second-seeded Bruins lost to No. 7 Southern Methodist in the quarterfinals.

In 2002, the Bruins defeated the Trojans in their first meeting, extending their winning streak in the rivalry to seven. Their second meeting was a match in the quarterfinals of the National

2000s	UCLA Olympic Medalists		
BASKETBALL			
Natalie Williams	2000		Gold
SOCCER			
Joy Fawcett	2000		Silver
SOFTBALL			
Christie Ambrosi	2000		Gold
Joanne Brown (Australia)	2000		Bronze
Jennifer Brundage	2000		Gold
Kerry Dienelt (Australia)	2000		Bronze
Sheila Cornell Douty	2000		Gold
Lisa Fernandez	2000		Gold
Tanya Harding (Australia)	2000		Bronze
Stacey Nuveman	2000		Gold
Dot Richardson	2000		Gold
TRACK AND FIELD			
Andrea Anderson	2000	4x400m Relay	Gold
Ato Boldon (Trinidad)	2000	100 meters	Silver
		200 meters	Bronze
John Godina	2000	Shot Put	Bronze
SWIMMING			
Malin Suahnstrom (Sweden)	2000	4x200m Freestyle Relay	Bronze
WATER POLO			
Robin Beauregard	2000		Silver
Nicolle Payne	2000		Silver
Coralie Simmons	2000		Silver

MATCHES WON Through 5/04

TENNIS

UCLA 8 • USC 5

Indoors. The Bruins entered the competition ranked among the top three teams in the nation, but the 12th-ranked Trojans pulled off an upset.

The next time the schools met was a classic matchup at USC, with everything coming down to the final singles match between UCLA's Lassi Ketola and Daniel Langre. Ketola's victory gave UCLA a 4–3 win and sent the Bruins on their way to the Pac-10 title.

But USC's victory in the indoor tournament had helped spark the team, which improved as the season wore on. In the NCAA championships, USC worked its way through to the final against Georgia and defeated the Bulldogs for its 16th national title. UCLA finished third.

In 2003, UCLA, led by Tobias Clemens, swept USC in the regular season by 6–1 and 7–0 scores, then met the Trojans again in the second round of the NCAA tournament. The Bruins didn't lose a match to eliminate the Trojans but were defeated by Vanderbilt in the NCAA semifinals.

The schools, each with strong nationally ranked teams, split their two matchups in 2004. When the schools met for the first time, the Bruins, ranked sixth in the nation to the Trojans' No. 19 spot, held on to a close 4–3 victory.

By the time the teams met again, the Trojans were ranked seventh in the nation and the Bruins had slipped to the No. 10 spot. This time Trojan senior Adriano Biasella upset Tobias

Clemens to give USC the match-clinching point for a 4–3 win.

The Trojans ended the season as the Pac-10 Conference champions and the No. 6 team in the nation. The team advanced to the semifinal round of the NCAA tournament, where it lost to Baylor.

The Bruins, meanwhile, met Baylor in the NCAA final round, where they too lost, coming up short on the chance to win their 16th national tennis championship. They ended the year ranked third in the country.

VOLLEYBALL

UCLA's dominance over USC continued with only one interruption in the early 2000s.

Al Scates' team, led by senior setter Brandon Taliaferro, began the 2000 season with a 11-match winning streak over USC, a streak the Trojans finally brought to an end in the 23rd annual Kilgour Cup at UCLA.

Behind Donald Suxho, USC upset top-ranked UCLA in five games for its first victory over the Bruins at Pauley Pavilion since 1990 and its first victory after seven losses to UCLA in the Kilgour Cup.

That proved to be only a bump on the road for the Bruins, who went on to win their 18th NCAA title by defeating Ohio State in the championship match.

■ Trojan tennis coach Dick Leach retired at the end of the 2002 season after his team won the NCAA championship. Below: Ryan Moore was one of the Trojans' strongest players.

In 2001, UCLA easily defeated the Trojans three times to give the Bruins 14 victories in the last 15 matches against the Trojans. UCLA fell just short, though, of repeating its national championship, falling to Brigham Young in the title match.

It was more of the same in 2002, UCLA winning the three times the schools met behind Jonathan Acosta's and Matt Komer's strong play at the net, and in 2003 the Bruins stretched their winning streak over the Trojans to nine with three more victories. And in 2004, the Bruins beat the Trojans three more times, and their string of wins stretched to 12. The Bruins ended the season ranked third in the nation.

TRACK AND FIELD

UCLA began the 2000 season with a new coach, Art Venegas in place of Bob Larsen, who had retired, and, at least in dual meets, the Bruins continued their mastery of the Trojans.

USC, though, had something extra to offer in postseason competition — and soon would end the string that had so long tied up the program.

UCLA extended its 21-year, dual-meet string over USC with an 88–75 victory that was propelled by the Bruin distance runners.

The 1–2–3 finish by Paul Muite, Dan Brecht and Bryan Green in the 5,000 meters gave UCLA the victory in a meet that had a distaste-

ful ending. The Trojans won the final event, but their 1,600-meter relay team was disqualified for excessive showboating during the race.

But at the Pac-10 championships a week later, the Trojans ran away from the field to win their second conference title in a row, with UCLA finishing a distant fourth.

In 2001, the Trojans finally ended their losing streak with an 82–81 victory behind Djeke Mambo and Ryan Wilson. Mambo scored a meet-high 13 points, winning the long and triple jumps and finishing second in the high hurdles; Wilson won the 110-meter high hurdles and 400-meter intermediate hurdles.

Trojan Coach Ron Allice told *The Times*, "It is truly a great feeling. Because these guys will forever be known as the jinx busters and remember this for the rest of their lives."

The "jinx" was back in 2002 as UCLA routed USC, 121–81 at Drake Stadium. UCLA won 14 of 19 events.

Then in 2003, UCLA edged USC, 82–81, overcoming the performance of USC sprinter Wes Felix, who won the 100 and 200 and ran legs on two winning relays.

■ The Bruin men's volleyball program has won 18 NCAA championships since 1962 under Coach Al Scates.

In 2004, UCLA dominated the dual meet with a 111–52 pounding of the Trojans. The Bruins won 12 events, sweeping five of them. Senior Dan Ames swept the throwing events, and Chad Galbreath won the long distance races. The Bruin victory margin was the largest since 1982.

■ Trojan Ryan Wilson, 2001 All-American in the 110m high hurdles.

Adam Wright scored three goals in a 6–5 win in the third, and UCLA continued winning all the way through the NCAA tournament, defeating UC San Diego in the title game for the Bruins' seventh national championship.

In 2001, UCLA rode the play of freshman Brett Ormsby to sweep three matches against

■ ■ ■ ■ ■ ■ ■ ■ ■

WATER POLO

UCLA was the nation's No. 1–ranked water polo team at the start of the decade, though the team had lost two of three matches against USC dating back to 1998. And USC won again in their first match of 2000, 5–4 in the SoCal tournament.

But that was about all the success the Trojans would have for a while against the Bruins.

Sean Kern scored four goals to give UCLA a 7–5 win in the second meeting of 2000.

the Trojans. Ormsby scored three goals in each of the first two matches and scored the game-winner in the third.

The next season, UCLA extended its streak to six with a 9–7 victory over USC in the fifth-place match at the SoCal tournament.

Then USC rebounded in a Mountain Pacific Sports Federation match, riding a goal from Jeff Larson with 1:05 remaining in the second overtime period to a 10–8 victory.

The Bruins won the third match, 6–3, in the championship match of the NorCal tourna-

MATCHES WON Through 5/04

WATER POLO

UCLA 10 - USC 6

2000s	USC Olympic Medalists		
BASKETBALL			
Lisa Leslie	2000		Gold
SWIMMING			
Lindsay Benko	2000	800m Free Relay	Gold
Kim Black	2000	800m Free Relay	Gold
Klete Keller	2000	400m Freestyle	Bronze
		800m Free Relay	Silver
Lenny Krayzelburg	2000	100m Backstroke	Gold
		200m Backstroke	Gold
		400m Medley Relay	Gold
Kaitlin Sandeno	2000	800m Freestyle	Bronze
Erik Vendt	2000	400m Individual Relay	Silver
DIVING			
Dorte Lindner (Germany)	2000	Springboard	Bronze
WATER POLO			
Sofia Konoukh (Russia)	2000		Bronze
Bernice Orwig	2000		Silver
TRACK AND FIELD			
Mark Crear	2000	110m Hurdles	Bronze
Torri Edwards	2000	400 Relay	Bronze

ment, with Brandon Brooks recording 16 saves, then added another victory to close the regular season 12–10.

"We never get sick of playing SC, especially when we are beating them," Brooks told the *Daily Bruin*.

The teams met again in a thriller in the MPSF tournament. UCLA was two seconds away from a first-round defeat but rallied for a 7–6 "sudden-victory" overtime win. It happened this way: Ormsby scored late in the second overtime to send the match into "sudden-victory" overtime, and then senior Dan Yeilding ended the match with a game-winning goal 29 seconds into the period.

The teams met only twice in 2003. UCLA upset No. 1 USC, 6–5, in overtime in front of a packed house at Sunset Canyon Recreation Center, but in the rematch, USC's Predrag Damanjov scored in the final minute of the second overtime for a 7–6 Trojan victory.

Damanjov, a 6-foot-5, 280-pound senior from Belgrade, had more dramatic touches for the Trojans. He scored three goals, including the insurance goal in overtime, to give USC a 9–7 victory over Stanford in the NCAA championship match.

WOMEN'S BASKETBALL

Neither team seemed capable of taking command in the rivalry in the early 2000s, and how well a team was doing when it faced its rival didn't always make a difference in a series that got very physical at times.

In the first meeting of the 1999–2000 season, at Pauley Pavilion, UCLA dominated from the start in an 82–62 victory. Maylana Martin and Janae Hubbard dictated play inside; Martin finished with 20 points and 10 rebounds, and Hubbard had 19 and nine.

Both teams were struggling by the time of the rematch; USC was on a three-game losing streak and UCLA had lost five of six. USC had what it took to end its troubles, coming back from an 11-point deficit in the first half to win, 73–69. Tiffany Elmore scored 20 points, including a jump shot with 51 seconds left that gave the Trojans a 69–67 lead.

The 2000–01 season started horribly for

GAMES WON
Through 5/04
WOMEN'S BASKETBALL
USC 7 - UCLA 3

UCLA, which was 1–12 and on a six-game losing streak before the USC matchup at Pauley. The Trojans weren't faring much better, at 5–7 with a five-game losing streak.

The Bruins used a 16–1 run and a game-high 23 points from Michelle Greco to defeat USC, 65–53. Natalie Nakase, one of the shortest players in college basketball (she was listed as 5–2 but was actually barely 5 feet) led the Bruins during their second-half run.

In the rematch, UCLA made only seven of 21 free throws and the Trojans made key plays late in the second half in a 61–56 victory at the Sports Arena.

UCLA had another weak team in 2001–02, and USC swept two games but again had to work for each victory.

In a physical game at Pauley, USC was the team left standing in a 67–57 victory.

From *The Times*' report on the game: "It isn't only the men's teams that take the USC–UCLA basketball rivalry seriously.

"The Trojan women's team defeated the Bruins … in a game that had all the bone-jarring basketball and cross-town rancor a fan could ask for. Bodies hit the hardwood again and again. Coaches on both sides howled over any perceived missed call."

In the rematch at the Sports Arena, Aisha Hollans scored 24 points and Jessica Cheeks 15 points to lead the Trojans to a 71–58 victory.

In 2002–03, the Bruins maintained their aggressive style and were 4–0 in conference play when they met USC, 1–3 in the conference, at Pauley Pavilion.

UCLA won, 72–64. Michelle Greco scored a game-high 28 points, including UCLA's final seven.

The second time the teams met, the game

■ UCLA's Janae Hubbard lays up a shot over USC defenders Tennille Grant, left, and Tiffany Washington.

featured 11 lead changes in the second half. Finally, USC held on for a 72–68 victory. Ebony Hoffman, who scored 21 points and had a career-best 21 rebounds, made a key play when she tipped in a missed free throw by Meghan Gnekow with 12 seconds left.

USC and UCLA played each other in the 2003–04 Pac-10 opener, and the Trojans ran away with a 64–51 victory behind seniors Cheeks and Hoffman at the Sports Arena.

In the rematch in Pauley Pavilion, UCLA rallied late in the second half to win, 68–64. The Bruins' full-court pressure defense contributed to 14 turnovers and helped UCLA outscore USC, 26–14, in the final 10 minutes. Nikki Blue led the Bruins with a game-high 26 points.

UCLA, at 17–12, got into the NCAA tournament but, despite 33 points from Blue, lost to Minnesota in the first round, 92–81.

WOMEN'S VOLLEYBALL

At the start of the decade, both USC and UCLA expected big things from their women's volleyball teams. But only one of the teams would manage to reach the pinnacle with an NCAA title, then improve on that with perfection.

With Jerritt Elliott as interim coach, filling in for U.S. Olympic coach Mick Haley, the Trojans won their first 14 matches in 2000, including a difficult four-game match over the Bruins.

The key to the Trojans' success was a freshman class that included Toni Anderson, April Ross, Kelli Lantz, Katie Olsovsky and Nicole Davis, regarded by many as the top recruiting class in the nation.

The Bruins, even in the defeat, did grab one measure

of success. By winning the third game, they ended USC's 38-game winning streak.

In the rematch, the Bruins took it to the Trojans, with a three-game sweep at Pauley Pavilion. With Kristee Porter leading the way with 20 kills and 19 digs, UCLA won convincingly, 15–9, 15–3, 15–13.

In postseason play, Wisconsin eliminated UCLA first, then defeated USC in the NCAA semifinals.

The next season, Haley arrived and USC pulled out two victories over UCLA. In the first match, at USC, freshman Alicia Robinson had an error-free performance, with 14 kills, in a three-game sweep. In the rematch, UCLA was without Porter, who had been ruled ineligible for violating the NCAA's "extra-benefit" rule. But UCLA still gave USC all it could handle, winning the first two games before losing in five, 25–30, 28–30, 30–21, 30–22, 15–11.

The victory was USC's first in Westwood since 1998.

After losing to Arizona in the 2001 NCAA playoffs, USC started the next season with 15 consecutive victo-

■ The Trojans' 2002 NCAA women's volleyball victory is celebrated by, from left, Katie Olsovsky, Keao Burdine and April Ross.

MATCHES WON Through 5/04

WOMEN'S VOLLEYBALL

USC 8 - UCLA 1

Andy Banachowski UCLA

The "one and only" of hundreds of women

UCLA's Andy Banachowski, one of the nation's pioneering coaches of women's volleyball, has been the leading force behind the Bruins' program since its inception in 1965. Banachowski began coaching the women's teams while still an All-American player on two Bruin national championship men's teams in 1965 and 1967, making him the women's team's "one and only" leader.

In his nearly 40-year career, Banachowski has coached Bruin women's volleyball teams to six national titles and more than their share of victories over USC, including 14 in a row from 1988 to 1994.

"It was a great run for us," Banachowski said of that stretch of wins. "We just were on a hot streak against them." Over that seven-season span, the Bruins won two national championships and twice finished as the nation's No. 2 team.

The 13th consecutive victory over the Trojans was one Banachowski remembers well, a five-game comeback at Pauley Pavilion.

USC appeared poised to end its seven years of frustration against UCLA by winning the first two games, 15–13 and 15–9. And in the third game, the Trojans had a 14–12 lead and were serving for the match.

But behind Annett Buckner's career-high 37 kills, UCLA refused to let the streak end that night. The Bruins won the last three games, 16–14, 15–13, 15–9.

"They really had us beat," said Banachowski, who, in 1997, was the first women's coach to be inducted into the U.S. Volleyball Association Hall of Fame. "Even some of their players started to celebrate because it looked like the string was over. But our kids came back."

Banachowski's memories of games against USC are not all rosy. After turning the Bruins' program into a powerhouse in the early 1970s, winning the Division of Girls' and Women's Sports national championship in 1972 and back-to-back Association for Intercollegiate Athletics for Women titles in 1974 and 1975, UCLA lost to USC in the AIAW championship match in 1976. The Bruins lost again in the first NCAA championship match played at Pauley Pavilion in 1981.

"It's unfortunate that I remember the painful matches so well," he said. "Losing to them in 1976 sticks out in my mind because they had one of their best teams with Debbie Green. We played them tough but came up short.

"In 1981, it was a thrilling match that I think did a lot for women's volleyball. But again, we ended up losing in a battle. But that's what the rivalry is all about."

ries. In their first match against the Bruins, the No. 1-ranked Trojans dominated in three games at USC to go to 16–0.

USC's blocking tandem of Olsovsky and Emily Adams either rejected or altered nearly every Bruin attack.

The rematch wasn't much of a contest either, with Adams, Ross and Keao Burdine leading the way in a three-game sweep at Pauley Pavilion.

In the NCAA playoffs, USC swept through its competition to win its first national championship since 1981.

In 2003, USC opened as the No. 1 team in the nation with a not-so-modest goal: a perfect season. The Trojans began with nine consecutive victories before facing the Bruins at Pauley Pavilion. With career-high efforts from Adams and Anderson, the Trojans won, 30–21, 22–30, 30–19, 30–22, in front of 2,003. The Bruins' only solace: their second-game victory that stopped USC's 30-game winning streak.

Adams led the Trojans with a personal-best 23 kills. Anderson posted a career-high 55 assists.

The second match was a mismatch, a three-game sweep at USC that led to a straightforward assessment of USC by UCLA Coach Andy Banachowski afterward: "They have the power to overwhelm you."

USC, after knocking off the Bruins in four games in the NCAA final, then accomplished what it had set out to do and completed the season 35–0 with a victory over Florida in the NCAA championship match. The Trojans became the first repeat champion to finish the season undefeated.

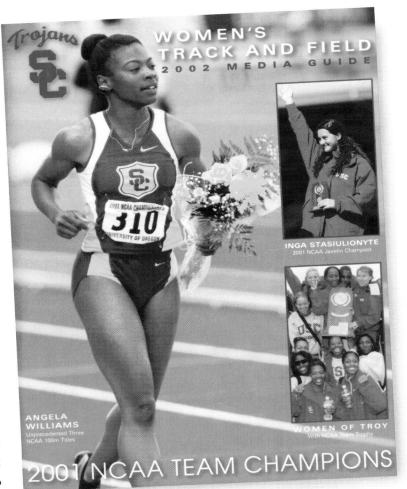

WOMEN'S TRACK AND FIELD

UCLA began the 2000 season having defeated USC seven years in a row in dual meets and continued that streak through 2003, winning four Pac-10 championships along the way. But in one meet during that span, the Trojans picked just the right time to peak: the 2001 NCAA championships.

In 2000, the Bruins defeated the Trojans, 86–68, in a dual meet at Drake Stadium. Seilala Sua won the javelin, shot put and discus as UCLA dominated the field events. The Bruins would go on to win the Pac-10 title, then finish third in the NCAA championship.

In 2001, the Trojans closed the gap and were narrowly defeated in the dual meet, 85–78, when Adia McKinnon, Sheena Johnson, Ysanne Williams and Michelle Perry gave the Bruins the victory in the final event, the 1,600-meter relay.

The Pac-10 meet that year looked like a repeat of the dual meet, going down to the final event. Again, the Bruins won, but this time there was a twist. On the third leg, USC's Kinshasa Davis was leading until she dropped the baton as she was being passed by McKinnon.

USC ended up fifth, when a second-place finish would have given them the championship. UCLA won the meet with 155 points, two more than USC.

Finally, though, the Trojans got redemption. Highlighted by Angela Williams' victory in the 100 meters, the Trojans won the NCAA title as they scored 64 points to beat second-place UCLA, which finished with 55 points.

UCLA's depth ensured a 111–92 victory in the 2002 dual meet, the Bruins' 10th in a row over the Trojans.

Then at the Pac-10 championships, the two schools did just what had been done so often: They fought each other closely, event for event, and came to the final event, the

MEETS WON
Through 5/04

WOMEN'S TRACK & FIELD

UCLA 5 · USC 0

Jeanette Bolden UCLA

The winning force behind Bruin women's track

When Jeanette Bolden replaced legendary Bob Kersee as coach of the UCLA women's track and field program after the 1993 season, she took over a program that had just won a Pacific-10 Conference title and had placed third at the NCAA championships.

And the program has continued its winning ways under Bolden, particularly against the school across town.

Since 1993, the Bruins are 11-0 against USC. And they have dominated the Pac-10 as thoroughly as John Wooden's teams ruled the nation in the Bruins' basketball heyday. Bolden's teams have won the Pac-10 championship in nine of her 11 seasons, USC winning the other time in 1996, and Bolden has been named conference coach of the year nine times. In 2004, the Bruins won their eighth consecutive Pac-10 title.

"I don't have to do anything to get the team ready because they know," Bolden said of facing the Trojans. "The rivalry builds up throughout the year from football and basketball to volleyball and water polo....

"It's always been about beating SC," added Bolden, a five-time All-American sprinter for UCLA in the early 1980s and a gold medalist in the 400-meter relay in the 1984 Olympics. "When I ran at UCLA, we did not compete against USC in dual meets. UCLA and USC women did not begin competing against each other until after I left."

Bolden's first close call as coach came in 1996. The Bruins trailed, 68–61, heading into the final two events at Drake Stadium. UCLA's Darlene Malco then ran a lifetime-best 23.57 to edge USC's Torri Edwards (23.81) in the 200 meters. And 15 minutes later, Malco anchored UCLA's winning 1,600-meter relay team for a 74–70 Bruin victory.

"The UCLA–SC meet brings out the best," Bolden said. "There's always going to be something in the meet that happens that is unexpected."

In 2001, the Bruins and Trojans locked up in another close meet.

With one event remaining, UCLA led by two points and needed a victory in the 1,600-meter relay to win the meet. In a dramatic final leg, UCLA's Michelle Perry held off Brigita Langerholc to give the Bruins an 85–78 victory at USC's Loker Stadium.

"That meet was incredible ... a close meet all the way to the end," Bolden said.

"But that's what you expect from a UCLA–SC meet. I always tell my team that you work hard for USC, the Pac-10 meet and the NCAA championships, and they are equal in importance.

"It's just that when you beat SC, you have bragging rights in the city for a year."

1,600 relay, with the championship hanging in the balance. UCLA's Sheena Johnson, who had won the 400-meter hurdles, took the lead on the third leg, and freshman Monique Henderson brought home the victory to give the Bruins a three-point win over the second-place Trojans.

At the 2002 NCAA championship meet, Angela Williams became the first person— male or female—to win four consecutive titles in the 100 meters, but it was not enough for the Trojans, who failed to repeat as nation- al champions, finishing third behind South Carolina and UCLA.

In 2003, the Bruins cruised to a 104–59 victory over the Trojans at USC's Loker Stadium. Henderson's victories in the 200 and 400 meters put the meet out of reach. From there, UCLA went on to win the Pac-10 championship, its seventh in a row.

In 2004, it was more of the same as the Bruins flew past the Trojans, 93–70, marking their 12th consecutive dual meet win over USC.

Monique Henderson ran in three winning UCLA races, including a world-leading mark of 51.20 seconds in the 400 meters. UCLA later won its third NCAA championship. The Bruins then won the NCAA team title

**MATCHES WON
Through 5/04
WOMEN'S
TENNIS
USC 7 - UCLA 4**

WOMEN'S TENNIS

UCLA and USC women took turns taking the upper hand on the tennis courts for the first five years of the 2000s.

The Bruins came from behind to win the last three matches in the first contest in 2000, at USC, then won easily in the rematch at Westwood. The key win for UCLA was at No. 4 singles, when senior Elizabeth Schmidt defeated Anita Loyola in three sets.

Led by freshman Sara Walker, the Pac-10 singles champion, UCLA reached the quarterfinals of the NCAA championships before losing to No. 1 Stanford.

The next season, USC turned things around and defeated the Bruins twice, 5–2 at UCLA and 6–1 at USC. The Trojans had similar luck in the NCAA tournament, losing in a quarterfinal match to Georgia.

The two teams split their matches during the regular season in 2002, but they met a third time in the third round of the NCAA championships. UCLA came away with a 4–1 victory by winning two doubles matches and three singles matches. USC's only point came when Jewel Peterson defeated Megan Bradley at No. 1 singles. Bradley and Sara Walker were both named singles and doubles All-Americans after the Bruins' quarterfinal loss to Georgia.

In 2003, USC again swept UCLA in the regular season. The Trojans won, 4–3, in Westwood in the first match, with Peterson and Tiffany Brymer picking up a key win in doubles over Laura Gordon and Walker.

In the rematch, UCLA won the doubles point but could not hold off USC in singles as the Trojans won five of six matches to win, 5–2, at USC.

The Trojans again won both matches in the 2004 regular season. The first match was a close one, with USC squeaking out a 4–3 victory when Luana Magnani and Carine Vermeulen upset the Bruins' Jackie Carleton and Lauren Fisher in a doubles match. In the teams' second match, UCLA won the doubles matchups but lost the singles games, and USC took home a 5–2 win. UCLA defeated USC in the NCAA meet and finished second in the tournament.

WOMEN'S SOCCER

Since the Bruin and Trojan women began competing in soccer in 1993, UCLA has dominated the matches, with a 12–2–1 record and a win streak dating to 1998.

Although the Bruin domination continued into the new decade, the Trojans at least got a tie in 2000 as the teams battled to a 1–1 score in overtime. The Bruins went on to the finals of the NCAA playoffs, where they lost in their first-ever appearance in the championship round.

By the next year, the Bruins were back in form against the Trojans, winning their match 2–1 on their way to the Pac-10 championship. In 2002, UCLA shut out USC in

**GAMES WON
Through 5/04
WOMEN'S
SOCCER
UCLA 5 - USC 0
(1 TIE)**

The Gauntlet
A knight's prize for rivalry winner

In 2004, the Gauntlet returned to Heritage Hall, thanks in a big way to USC's No. 1–ranked football team and its men's basketball and women's volleyball team sweeps over UCLA.

"Two legendary teams. One legendary challenge."

That's the motto the Lexus automobile dealerships of Southern California gave the competition they created in 2001 to promote the rivalry between USC and UCLA. The winner receives a 150-pound cast bronze trophy called the Lexus Gauntlet, modeled after the piece of armor knights would throw to the ground to spark a fight-to-the-death duel.

The competition pits the schools against each other in all 18 of the men's and women's sports in which the two schools meet throughout the academic year. Points are awarded to winners of each matchup, with at least 57.5 points needed to win the trophy. Ten points are awarded to the winners of the football, men's and women's basketball, and women's volleyball competitions. Five points are given to the winners in men's and women's water polo; men's and women's track and field; men's and women's tennis; men's and women's golf; women's swimming and diving, soccer, cross country and rowing; and men's baseball and volleyball.

USC won the trophy in the 2001–02 school year; UCLA won the following year. In both years, the schools were so evenly matched that the complicated scoring system took the computations into "tie-breaker" territory. In 2002, the Trojan baseball team's victory over the Bruins brought home the Gauntlet; in 2003, the UCLA men's tennis team provided the winning margin for the Bruins.

■ Lexus promoted its support of the **UCLA–USC Gauntlet** competition with a bit of humor.

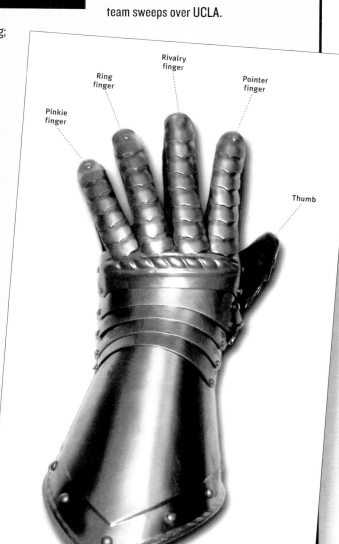

both of their matches, 2–0 and 1–0.

And in 2003, the Trojans were again shut out, 2–0. The Bruins went on to win the Pac-10 title and reach the Final Four of the NCAA playoffs, their seventh straight appearance in the tournament. ■

MATCHES WON Through 5/04
WOMEN'S WATER POLO
UCLA 8 - USC 3

MEETS WON Through 5/04
WOMEN'S SWIMMING
USC 4 - UCLA 1

Acknowledgments

Lonnie White

This book does not have enough pages to individually thank everyone who helped make this project a reality, but I have to give a special thanks to Carla Lazzareschi, The Times' book development general manager, who gave me the opportunity to showcase the greatest rivalry in collegiate sports.

Of course, the book would have never made it to press if not for the magnificent editing skills of Mike James. I would also like to thank Gary Rubin and Bobbi Olson, who both had the difficult task of fact checking and copy editing a book written by a novice author.

The sports information staffs at both USC and UCLA played a major role from start to finish with the project. I want to give special gratitude to Tim Tessalone and the Trojans' staff of Jason Pommier, Paul Goldberg, Vicky Hammond and Chris Huston. Particular thanks also go out to Marc Dellins and members of the Bruins' sports information staff: Bill Bennett, Steve Rourke, Rich Bertolucci, Liza David and Marisa Schwertfeger.

Kudos to UCLA Athletic Director Daniel Guerrero and USC Athletic Director Mike Garrett, along with USC's senior associate athletic directors Daryl Gross and Steve Lopes, who both coached me when I was in college.

Thank you Lori Shepler for taking my personal photo and Joe Jares, Valerie Gutierrez, Steve Pratt, Kristin Hayward, Assibi Abudu, Sahaiya Abudu, Hanaiya Abudu, Nasir Abudu and Saharra White for their research help.

I also can't forget my co-workers at the Los Angeles Times: Mike Terry, J.A. Adande, Bill Plaschke, Paul Netter, Claire Noland, Jason Reid, Tim Brown, Houston Mitchell, Pete Thomas, Helene Elliott, Gary Klein, Chris Foster, Jerry Crowe, Jay Christensen, T.J. Simers, Larry Stewart, Dave Morgan, Mike Kupper, Jennifer Preece, Kelly Burgess and sports editor Bill Dwyre.

On the personal front, I would like to thank those who helped support my first book, including my sister, Zeline Waller; uncles Ralph Benton, Alfred Morgan, Alvin Maxie and Gordon Johnson; aunts Delva Esdaile, Mary Maxie, Gladys Irvis and Connie Morgan; cousins Lise Esdaile, Arthur Morris, Sandra Terry and Marvin Morgan; nephews Katoni Waller, Timothy White and Jihad White; nieces Tunisia White, Alexandria White, Mekka White, Madinah White, Taahiarah White and Zuri White.

Thanks for the support from friends Derrick Taylor, Randy Tanner, Brad Turner, Randy Hill, Art Thompson, Rick Jaffe, Ron Brown, James Fisher, Dennis Thurman, Martin Chesley, Katoni Waller, Desmond Terry, Charles White, Ken Henry, Mark Armijo, Herb Johnson, Ian Jaquiss, Andre Hayes, James Kelly, Dexter Levy, Randy Franz, Rob Parker, Pete Benson, Al Ramirez, Andy Hill, Henry Bibby, Kraig Sanders, Tim Ware, Jeff Maree, Fred Williams, Kennedy Pola, Mike Altieri, Michael Roth, Eric Williams, George Conti, Steve Vanderpool, Guy Hunter, Kirk McCoy, Mike Sherrard, John Jackson, Joe Safety, Tara Davis, Elizabeth Morales, Amy Wilson, Constance Williams, Dejeune Champion-Tanner, Denise Garcia, Joyce Glass, Nadine Jackson, Marny Elliott, Nancy Pretto, Janis Carr, Dana Sims, Denelda Goolsby, Helisa Horton, Zeline Waller, Elliott Teaford and Randy Harvey.

Finally, I would be remiss not to thank my wife, Kimberly, who gave me the support and love needed to complete a project of this magnitude. Much love to my sister, Theresa White, who taught me how to read and helped give me confidence to take on the project; my brother, Tim White, who has always been there for me; my father-in-law, Fletcher Lynch, who has been a steady influence; and my mother-in-law, Faye Joiner, the true writer in the family.

Index

Numbers in **boldface** indicate photos

267

■ Overleaf: The basket-ball teams hold separate meetings during a January 2002 game at the Forum.

Overleaf: The basketball teams hold separate meetings during a January 2002 game at the Forum.